Bullies

From the Playground to the Boardroom

Strategies for *Survival*

Jane Middelton-Moz *and* Mary Lee Zawadski

Health Communications, Inc.
Deerfield Beach, Florida
www.hcibooks.com

**Library of Congress Cataloging-in-Publication Data
is available from the Library of Congress**

©2002, ©2014 Jane Middelton-Moz and Mary Lee Zawadski

ISBN-13: 978-0-7573-1807-8 (Paperback)
ISBN-10: 0-7573-1807-X (Paperback)
ISBN-13: 978-0-7573-1812-2 (e-Pub)
ISBN-10: 0-7573-1812-6 (e-Pub)

HCI, its Logos and Marks are trademarks of Health Communications, Inc.

Publisher: Health Communications, Inc.
       3201 S.W. 15th Street
       Deerfield Beach, FL 33442-8190

R-04-02

Cover design and inside book design by Lawna Patterson Oldfield

IN MEMORY OF
Judalon Jeffries—1957-2001
Dennis Allen Zawadski—1944-2008
Christina Grof—1941-2014

Who always found the sacred in the ordinary
and offered their gifts to so many.

And to the Miracles That Are Our Grandchildren:

Each child born is our reassurance
that the Creator still has faith in humankind.

Logan Alexander Middelton

Canaan Neil Middelton

Anastasia Sabine Mehengan Middelton

Della-Jane Van Avery

Mira Middelton

Luca Middelton

Jamie Sakohianiisaks Labelle Goodleaf

Sage Karakwinetha Labelle Goodleaf

Christopher Flannery

Ryan Flannery

Natalie Flannery

Emma Knight

Lily Knight

Dakota Thomas Ivanoff

Lauren Kristine Youmans

Tess Nadine Youmans

William Stuart Youmans

Kate Marie Youmans

Contents

Foreword

Who among us has not been the victim of a bully? Whether it be the kid in elementary school who terrorizes all the other six-year-olds on the playground, the mid-level manager whose temper tantrums keep her staff constantly on edge, or the belligerent driver behind you who tailgates until you get out of his way, bullies are all around us all the time.

In twenty years of producing television shows about families and relationships, I've come across every kind of bully you could think of. I've seen bullies who at three years old had already gained control of the household, and I've had teenagers appear on the show who were so angry and hostile that their own parents were afraid of them. I've visited with grown women who were reduced to terrified children by their bullying boyfriends or husbands, and men whose every move was controlled by their domineering wives or girlfriends.

The worst, of course, was when we produced several shows about Columbine, and the terrible tragedy that took place there. As a country we were shocked and outraged that children, let alone children from "good families," could have intentionally acted so violently. Years of torment had made something snap in these boys, who then took their misplaced aggression out on other children in the ultimate act of violence.

Sadly, Columbine is not the lone example of unchecked bullying behavior that has impacted our nation's young people. I have aired many tragic stories of attempted suicide and domestic violence, all caused by bullying. Along with our exploration of what went wrong in these real-life stories, we have produced dozens of other shows on "out of control" teenagers. These youths were so unmanageable that their parents had desperately reached out to us for help. In an attempt to "tame" their children to the point they could listen to reason, we established our own "Boot Camp," where the kids were exposed to ultra-strict discipline, intense exercise, prison-like accommodations and daily counseling sessions. We were attempting to find an answer and take steps toward solving this growing national problem.

We found, as did Jane Middelton-Moz and Mary Lee Zawadski, the authors of this important book, that at the core of many of our society's most disturbing issues—spousal abuse, drug and alcohol abuse, workplace harassment, uncontrollable teens and road rage—is the bully. He or she doesn't confine his actions to an occasional taunt or misplaced criticism. Instead, bullying is a cruel and deliberate act of intimidation with the intent to gain power or control over another person. It leaves its victims with intense feelings of vulnerability, fear, shame, and low self-esteem. Even worse, many ignore the bullying behavior and never take a stand. When allowed to continue on his or her destructive course, this person, so in pain and in need of counseling themselves, wreaks havoc on so many other lives.

We saw this, and looked for the answers that would fix the problem. We asked our viewers to call or e-mail us with their ideas. And call and write they did, but mostly with more heart-wrenching stories that confirmed for us that bullying was moving from a national problem to a national epidemic with tragic implications.

Statistics show the extent of the problem. The numbers are staggering:

- According to the U.S. Department of Justice, one out of every four children will be bullied by another youth in school this month.

- The American Association of School Psychologists reported that every day in America over 160,000 children miss school for fear of being bullied.
- The Centers for Disease Control estimates that 81 percent of students surveyed admitted to bullying their classmates.
- Studies indicate that two-thirds of the attackers in thirty-seven school shootings committed their crimes as revenge for constant persecution by their classmates.
- Teasing, bullying and rejection tops the list of triggers in contemplated suicides.

This isn't just a problem confined to school-age children. Many adults have faced the sting of the bully's bite:

- As many as 20 million Americans face workplace abuse on a daily basis.
- An estimated 90 percent of the workforce suffers abuse from bosses sometime in their careers.
- Domestic violence is the leading cause of injury to women between ages fifteen and forty-four in the United States.
- Thirty percent of Americans say they know a woman who has been physically abused by her husband or boyfriend in the past year.

But we're just a television show, and although Regis will tell us that you can usually get the right answer if you "ask the audience," we came up cold: lots of stories and shocking statistics but no solutions.

Then I had the opportunity to read the manuscript for *Bullies*, and I knew that there was hope. Jane Middelton-Moz and Mary Lee Zawadski have taken important steps in defining the problem and finding interventions and solutions that work. They even offer us insight from the bullies themselves. They teach us how to stop the cycle of victimization, how to stand up for ourselves, and give us a blueprint for making our schools safe havens instead of a maze of metal detectors.

Every teacher, every parent and every counselor should read this important book. It should be in the library of every CEO and mid-level manager. For the first time, I am hopeful that we can help our children by learning to be better parents in the early years, better teachers in the school years, and better employers in the adult years. If we all take the time to read this groundbreaking book I am confident that we can and will get this terrible problem under control.

Sally Jessy Raphael, 2002

Preface

Jackie Robinson, professional baseball's first African-American player was met by taunts and jeers as he walked out onto Cincinnati's Crosley Field in 1947. A teammate and one of baseball's icons of the day, "Pee Wee" Reese, was sickened by what he was hearing from the crowd. As recounted by his son, "My father walked from his shortstop position and draped his arm around his teammate. The simple gesture not only stopped the racial razzing that day, but sent a profound message throughout baseball and the nation" (Reese, 2001).

It's sad that Pee Wee's message didn't inspire someone who went to school with an East Indian boy who eventually committed suicide to escape the pain of continual bullying from his classmates or the thousands like him who endure the pain of brutal emotional abuse by peers in schools, significant others in relationships, coworkers or bosses in the workplace or by those that just don't like the way another looks, walks or even prays. One young man wrote in a suicide note: "Mom, after my death, go to the schools and talk with the kids. Tell them to stop bullying each other because it hurts deeply. I'm taking my life to show how much" (Moharib, 2000).

This book is written for bullies, their victims, and for those who may witness the bullying of others and feel too fearful or powerless to intervene.

Bullying is not merely, as many minimize, an occasional stinging comment made by a significant other at the breakfast table, a bad day with the boss, or children wrestling on the playground. Bullying is cruelty deliberately aimed at others with the intent of gaining power by inflicting psychological and/or physical pain.

Bullying behaviors are varied: name calling, humiliation, spreading rumors, gossiping, public ridicule, scapegoating and blaming, isolating, assigning poor work areas and job assignments or denying holiday and vacation time in the workplace, punching, hitting, kicking, taunting, ostracizing, sexualizing, or making ethnic or gender slurs.

Those who are the targets of bullying often feel intense vulnerability, fear and shame, and increasingly lower self-esteem that may increase their likelihood of continued victimization. Victims may become depressed and feel powerless. Many who have been bullied over a long period of time become suicidal. Others may retaliate in acts of violence or begin to bully others. Unfortunately many people who victims seek out for support dismiss their feelings by saying, "It has happened to all of us, just ignore it," or by thinking *He/she must deserve it.* For too many, bullying has become such a part of the fabric of everyday life that many look the other way and have become numb to its devastating effects. Others see bullying behavior, yet avoid intervening because they feel powerless to stop it.

Studies indicate that two-thirds of the attackers in thirty-seven school shootings felt persecuted due to long histories of being bullied by classmates, that being the target of bullying is a major factor in youth suicide, and that millions of Americans face workplace abuse on a daily basis.

Many bullies have been perfecting their skills of intimidation since early childhood. Without intervention, the feelings and beliefs of childhood bullies become strengthened and ingrained. Bullying on the playground is frequently only the beginning of a life pattern that culminates in domestic violence and/or bullying in the workplace. Bullies depend upon the confusion, fear or feelings of powerlessness in their intended victims, and the silence of those around them to continue their behavior.

We learned, through many interviews with those who had been lifelong bullies until someone had the courage to intervene, that bullies are temporarily empowered, and that both bullies and their victims are injured by the helplessness, apathy and silence of others. We need to create workplace, school, and community norms where aggression toward others is unacceptable, not because of strict laws or severe punishment but because we care about one another.

Courage does not mean that we are without fear; it means, as Pee Wee Reese demonstrated in 1947, that we don't let our fears stop us from taking action. "It is not death or pain or loss that robs us of power: It is the fear of death, the fear of pain, the fear of loss that turns the manipulated into victims and the manipulators into terrorists" (Abdullah, 1995, p. 56).

Many of us were forced to examine our responses to fear on September 11, 2001, when planes hijacked by terrorists hit the World Trade Center and Pentagon, while another, prevented from hitting its target due to the heroism of its passengers, crashed into a field in Pennsylvania. Bullies depend on our fear, powerlessness and silence to continue their behavior, and terrorism can never be effective unless we live in fear, powerlessness, and paralysis.

For some, the increased feelings of powerlessness engendered by the terrorist attacks on September 11 led to further isolation, disconnection, suspicion, intolerance, discrimination, and emotional and/or physical abuse directed at others. Newspapers reported incidents of violence and harassment aimed against Muslim-Americans or others mistakenly identified as "the enemy" throughout North America. One news correspondent asked a young Muslim-American if he had received any backlash since the terrorist attacks. "'Yesterday,' he replied, 'a white guy pulled up next to me in a Jeep and said, 'Where are you from?' I said, 'Iraq.' The guy said, 'I hate you,' and pulled out a gun. Fortunately for this young man, the gun was never fired but he conceded it was terrifying" (Muller, 2001).

For many others, however, September 11 was an awakening from a long sleep. Many who had learned to "mind their own business," and coexist with their neighbors soon found themselves seeking out others for comfort. They re-established connection with family, and made eye contact and conversation with others on the street rather than blindly walking on. Our heroes changed from rock stars, movie stars, and sports stars, to those members of our communities who, with little thought to their own safety, help, aid and protect others.

For millions of us, the visions of human beings carrying others down flights of stairs rather than thinking only of their own safety; firefighters and policeman running up stairs to rescue others while others walked down; construction workers lifting steel as they tried to save one more life; thousands offering clothes, financial support and blood; and neighbors standing shoulder to shoulder at candle-light vigils reinforced how much we need each other. These images increased our connectedness to one another and supported the belief that we truly have something to offer, and that we in the final analysis are not helpless and powerless after all.

Throughout this book you will learn about the beliefs, values and environments that support the development of bullies and share their stories. You will learn about step-by-step behaviors that will protect individuals against intimidation by significant others, peers, bosses, and coworkers who bully in person and in the cyber world. Successful interventions in the workplace, on the Internet, and on the playground will be presented as well the power of what has been the silent majority to eradicate bullying of all types, empowerment based on choice.

Jane Middelton-Moz

Acknowledgments

We would like to acknowledge the tremendous support of many individuals during the writing of *Bullies*. Without their love, support, patience, hugs, kindness, understanding, laughter, knowledge, time and energy, this book would not have been possible.

Jane would like to thank her husband, friend and life partner, John Fletcher and her family Shawn Middelton and Annie VanAvery, Damien and Lisa Middelton, Forrest Middelton, Jason Middelton and Damien Matsumoto, Suzy Goodleaf and Diane Labelle, Melinda and Michael Knight, Laura Fletcher, Michael Fletcher, Theresa McCabe, Catherine Flannery, Kate Howe, Alex and Bea Ward, Rose Fletcher, Jeannie Ferguson, Kathy Medici, Sarah Potter, and all of her grandchildren listed in the dedication for their caring, support, love, and humor. A special thank-you to Sarah Healy Middelton, for her love and support and for the valuable articles clipped from journals, newspapers and magazines. Mathew Ferguson for his technical help and Lisa Valyou for her healing touch. She would also like to thank Rebecca Martell, Leo Nadeau, Gerry Labelle, Tiffiny Hubbard, Ann and Terry Harrmann, John and Sharon Krueger, Cindy Edsall and Tom and Marla Housholder, for their enlightening conversations, friendship and continued support. A special "thank-you" to Mary Johnson, Elizabeth J. Lyon and Michael Johnson for their compassion and wisdom.

Mary Lee would like to thank her husband Denny, her son Tom for his support, unconditional love, and care since Denny died. Her daughter and son-in-law Kristine and Christopher Youmans for their support, patience, laughter, and love. She would also like to thank her Grandma Dina and parents William and Ruth Mihokanich, who taught her to believe in herself. A special thank you to the many people I have had the privilege to work with in their healing journey. You have all taught me so much.

We are grateful to the kind, courageous and generous people, bullies and victims, who shared the gift of their stories in order to offer hope to those who continue to suffer as bullies and victims. Without you, this book could never have been written.

We would like to thank Paul Von Esson for the day he offered us out of his busy schedule, and for his creativity, excitement, and belief in children, our communities, and the vision that we all can become culture carriers in a world without victims.

A special thank-you to Rod, Luke, and Sam Jeffries, and the late John and Jean Jeffries, for their wisdom, kindness, humor, tears, and courage.

Thank you to our friends, too numerous to mention, who sent e-mail, articles, and newspaper clippings, and to those we have met in our travels who have shared the gifts of their experiences with us.

A special thank-you to Diane Laut for her competence, beauty, caring, laughter, personal support, and for just being the beautiful person she is. Also a special thanks to John Fletcher, Shirley Ann Walker, Theresa McCabe, and Diane Labelle for hours of proofreading.

Thank you to Christine Belleris for her expert knowledge and editorial support as well as her compassion and caring, the continued support and caring of Peter Vegso, and the staff at Health Communications.

We appreciate the numerous authors whose works we've cited in *Bullies* and those who have been quoted in the text, for their continued work. Their clinical gifts have influenced our thoughts and challenged our minds.

Finally, a special acknowledgment to the countless compassionate, creative and courageous elders, adults and youth who we have met in our travels: our clients, interns, consultees and members of our workshops and seminars. In their courage to speak the truth, they continue to teach us the depth and strength of the human spirit.

Moving Out
of Denial

The small Hitlers are around us every day,
tormenting us with their promises, rejoicing in our
weaknesses, demanding our trust, our votes,
and our lives, while remaining totally indifferent
to everything except their thirst for power.

Jay Carter from Nasty People

t was June Grittman's job to keep traffic moving at
Portland International Airport. Just before 10:00 PM she approached
the driver of a sleek Mercedes-Benz coupe parked in a no-parking
zone. She asked the operator of the vehicle to move his car. According
to June, he ignored her for a time, then cursed her for telling him to
move, calling her every dirty name in the book, explaining that he
could "buy and sell" people like her. According to the March 12, 1997,
Oregonian, the incident escalated when June stepped in front of his car
to write him a ticket. "Witnesses said that the driver bragged that he
made $3 million a year and that if Grittman didn't get out of the way, he

would run over her." In a later court hearing, Grittman testified that the driver moved forward with his car and hit her knees. He then backed up a few inches and hit her harder, throwing her onto the car's hood and drove away. June said she suffered knee and lower-back injuries as well as emotional trauma from the incident (Smith, 1997, p. 1A).

Although the driver of the car, Darrell Brett, a millionaire neurosurgeon from a lucrative Portland practice, claimed that June was belligerent and that he hit her by accident, a Portland jury didn't see it that way. After three hours of deliberation the jury found that he had committed civil battery and awarded June $1 million in damages. This, however, wasn't the end of the surgeon's days in court. He faced still another lawsuit brought by a Portland area pharmacist who contended that the surgeon made ethnic slurs against him when he called for confirmation of a prescription. This case was settled out of court.

Brett's behavior seems outrageous, yet it is all too familiar to people who have been the targets of bullies in relationships, in the workplace, in sporting arenas or in stores, at airports, on our nation's highways, in neighborhoods, and to parents whose children are continually harassed in schools. Bullies frequently begin their cruel targeting of others as early as elementary school, leaving considerable emotional pain in their wake.

Rita and Bill Head of Marietta, Georgia, know that pain. Their son, Brian, endured bloody noses, broken eyeglasses and name-calling for years. When he was fifteen, Brian walked into a classroom and yelled, "I just can't take it anymore," and shot himself to death in front of his peers. In an interview with Diane Sawyer on *Good Morning America*, Brian's mother tearfully read a poem Brian left: "For all my life I have lived with the words that haunt me, the words of America's children" (Nissen et al., 1999).

Like thousands of parents across the nation, Bill Head was concerned for his son and told him to tell his teachers about the taunting behavior of his classmates, but "figured it was normal kids' stuff" (Mulrine, May 3, 1999).

The emotional pain is also known by Leah Parsons and Glen Canning, the parents of Rehtaeh Parsons, a teen who was sexually assaulted and then became the target of cyberbullying and harassment by her peers and took her own life in April of 2013. They, like many parents who have lost their children to bullycide, are fighting for prevention and for the rights of victims.

Bullying is not merely, as many minimize, an occasional stinging comment made by significant others at the breakfast table, a passing bad day with the boss, children wrestling with others on the playground, or learning the hard-won lessons of sibling rivalry or conflict resolution with one's peers. **Bullying is frequent and systematic cruelty deliberately aimed at a person by a person or persons with the intent of gaining power over another by regularly inflicting psychological and/or physical pain.** As stated by Peter Randal, "The bully wins something that he or she wants. Sometimes this is just the pleasure of watching someone else in pain or seeing their fear; often it is the extortion of something valued like their property or giving up their rights to holiday leave or even parking slots" (Randall, 1997, p. 15).

Despite the catchphrase that many of us grew up hearing, "Sticks and stones may break your bones, but words will never hurt you," being the target of bullying definitely hurts and is sometimes lethal. Unfortunately, Brian Head is one of hundreds of youths who commit suicide after repeated bullying by classmates.

Several research studies report that 75 percent of our nation's youth had been bullied during their teen years. According to a report from the National Association of School Psychologists, every day in America over 160,000 children miss school because of fears of bullying, and, in a study sponsored by the Centers for Disease Control and

Prevention, 81 percent of the students surveyed *admitted* to bullying their classmates in one form or another.

According to a study conducted by the American Association of Suicidology, more than 20 percent of the high school students surveyed said that they had seriously considered attempting suicide in the preceding twelve months. Teasing, bullying and social rejection top the list of triggers in completed suicides.

Our lack of awareness often causes us to be both deaf and blind to the pain experienced by our nation's youth and, as a result, our young people too often become the prisoners of their sadness and depression, seeing little possibility for change and no way out. Those who have attempted suicide frequently let us know that they didn't try to kill themselves because they wanted to be dead, but rather because they didn't want to continue living the way they were living.

A fourteen-year-old boy who had been bullied for some time and committed suicide to escape the hurt left these words in a suicide note to his mother: "I could take a gun and shoot all the boys, but I'm not a bad person. I'm not going to name the bullies either. You know who you are. I was laughing on the outside and crying on the inside. Mom, after my death, go to the schools and talk with the kids. Tell them to stop bullying each other because it hurts deeply. I'm taking my life to show how much" (Moharib, 2000).

It is not surprising that the perpetrators of this hurtful behavior regularly deny their actions or minimize the effect their systematic cruelty has on others. What is surprising to us is that millions of people in the United States today seem to lack awareness that bullying is a serious and costly problem worthy of attention. In fact, many friends and acquaintances that have been consistently supportive of our past work in areas of psychological trauma and its effects *laughed* when told that we were working on a book on bullies. "Really? Bullies? That surprises me. You usually write about important issues." "Why are you wasting your talent and energy on that?" "Oh come on. That's silly. Bullying isn't serious. It's just part of life, it doesn't really damage anyone. People just need to toughen up!"

Being the target of bullying causes strong feelings of fear and shame, increases vulnerability, lowers self-esteem, and leads to anxiety, depression and feelings of powerlessness that often increase victimization. Sadly, victims blame themselves for the bully's behavior and frequently others blame the victim as well: "If he'd just stop being such a wimp . . ." "If he can't take the heat, he should get out of the kitchen." "He just needs to smarten up." "If he'd lose weight, he wouldn't be such a target." "She's attractive, she should expect guys will focus on her." "She made her bed, she'll just have to lie in it." "If she'd just ignore it, they would stop." "Those people should learn to expect to be a target once in a while. It comes with the territory." "Just focus on your work. Don't let them get to you."

Others dismiss the entire problem with the statement, "Well, she didn't mean to hurt you, did she? I mean, what she did was mean, but it wasn't intentional." It is true that some individuals bully as a way of defending themselves from perceived attack, have poor empathy skills or are just trying to become "one of the guys," but these explanations don't go very far in alleviating a victim's pain. A schoolmate, boss, coworker, friend, significant other or fellow citizen is still responsible and accountable for the pain they cause others. Explaining away bad behavior has become a justification for "looking the other way," and supporting a code of silence that has reached epidemic proportions in our society.

Unfortunately, being the target of bullying has become part of the fabric of many of our lives and we have become numb to its devastating effects. Perhaps because it has become so much a part of our daily lives, the U.S. has been years behind other countries such as Sweden, England, and Australia in focusing on the problem.

For many in the United States, the seriousness of the issue first came into focus with increasing schoolyard violence culminating when two youths in Littleton, Colorado, taking revenge on classmates who had been taunting, teasing and shunning them, shot and killed thirteen students before turning the guns on themselves. A study conducted by the National Threat Assessment Center of the Secret Service concluded that two-thirds of the attackers in thirty-seven school shootings felt persecuted, bullied, threatened and attacked. The bullying was often severe and had occurred over a long period of time.

And now, bullying has caught up with the twenty-first century. A popular Internet site, www.schoolrumors.com, recently closed down briefly for technical reasons after having received seventy thousand visits in a few weeks. "Kids said horrible things," says Allan Weiner, principal of Cleveland High School in Reseda, California. "Bullying used to be confined to a school setting. Now it's worldwide." Weiner said one student was suicidal after untrue tales of her alleged sexual skills were posted. Another student received harassing phone calls after she was cited as a slut complete with name, address and phone number" (Peterson, USA Today, April 10, 2001 p. O6D).

"Toughening up" isn't the answer. Gaining awareness and taking action is. Lack of awareness and consequences for cruel behavior, consistent minimizing and silence are the bully's most valuable weapons.

Bullying Defined

As stated earlier, bullying involves intentional, repeated hurtful acts, words or behavior. Bullying behaviors are varied: name calling, humiliating, spreading rumors, gossip, public ridicule, scapegoating and blaming, isolating, assigning nonjobs or undesirable work areas in the workplace, denying vacation or holidays, punching, hitting, kicking, threatening, taunting, ostracizing, sexualizing, making racial, ethnic and gender slurs and harrassing, imitating and stalking through the use of technology and social media sites.

In early childhood, bullying is usually random. In youth and adulthood, targets are selected. Bullies will always find something about a person to focus on: being too fat, too thin, wearing glasses, doing good work, being in a wheelchair, wearing the wrong clothing, being too passive or too independent, being the wrong color, ethnic background, sex, religion or socioeconomic background, having the wrong sexual orientation, liking the boss, being friendly, being quiet, etc.

When bullying takes the form of two or more individuals targeting a victim, it is sometimes referred to as "mobbing." In the 1960's, ethnologist Konrad Lorenz used the term "mobbing" to describe the behavior that animals use to scare away a predator. "Later, Dr. Peter-Paul Heinemann, a Swedish physician, focused his research on a behavior he was seeing children direct at other children, previously referred to as 'bullying.' He used Lorenz's term 'mobbing' to emphasize the seriousness of the behavior that could drive the victim to such isolation and despair that she or he committed suicide. The book was published in Sweden in 1972 with the title, *Mobbing: Group Violence Among Children* [title translated]" (Davenport, Schwartz and Elliott, 1999, p. 21).

Contrary to the belief that the bully will stop his/her behavior given time (the "boys will be boys" adage), bullies don't stop without consistent intervention, compassionate confrontation and consequences. Bullies fear being required to face their own insecurities through confrontation and being forced to be accountable for their behavior and its consequences. However, without compassionate confrontation and accountability, they just become better over time at what they do.

The Bullying Cycle

In order to feel empathy we need to experience positive attachment and kindness *from* other human beings. As we grow older, in order to receive positive attachment, we need to begin to experience empathy *for* others. It is an interchanging, interdependent circle. It takes one individual willing to be consistently kind while setting firm limits and boundaries that can assist an individual in breaking a bullying cycle. "The unifying thread is our fundamental yet developmentally vulnerable capacity for empathy. Empathy—fully expressed in a community of nurturing, independent people—promotes heath, creativity, intelligence and productivity. In contrast, apathy and lack of empathy contributes to individual and societal dysfuncton, inhumane ideologies, and often brutal actions." (Szalavitz and Perry, 2010, p. 288)

Throughout many years of working with hundreds of adults and youth, and guiding them through change that interrupts cycles of bullying behavior, we have found that it is important to assist them in understanding the triggers that begin a bullying cycle. We have presented the bullying cycle in the form of a circle because we have found that, once triggered, the cycle often runs its course before it ends. On the outside of the circle, we have presented some feelings and beliefs that can be triggers for bullying behavior. On the inside, we have given examples of feelings that may occur as a result of beliefs and behaviors. Bullies may not be aware of these feelings but with consistent guidance they may develop insight into their behavior and be helped to find ways to interrupt the cycle.

As the bullying cycle progresses, the intensity of the feelings and behaviors also becomes stronger. The first circle represents distortion in thoughts and beliefs, and difficulties that the bully experiences with empathy and self-regulation. The second circle represents changes that occur in the cycle with consistent, empathetic, caring, firm limits and interventions that hold individuals accountable for bullying and pro-social consequences for hurtful behavior directed at others. In the first circle one sees negative thoughts and beliefs fueling the need for inappropriate control and power.

In the second circle there is a shift in feelings and beliefs, more trust in self and others and a shift to more positive pro-social behavior.

Trigger: Perceived Judgment

After: Pro-Social Consequences

Project blame unto others — Feeling: Shame, powerlessness and fear.

Make decision to lash out — Feeling: Fear and anger

Lash out with harmful behavior — Feeling: Anger and distorted thinking

Waiting for response from target — Feeling: Rage, "I'll get you"

Receive response from target, fear, anger etc. — Feeling: Anxious

Decide on more retaliation at target, fear, anger, etc. — Feeling: powerful, fearless

Waiting for response — Feeling: Powerful, righteous and arrogant

Involve others for more sense of power — Feeling: high, adrenaline pumping, anxious

Stops behavior for a short of time — Feeling: In total control, fearless

Feeling: Guilty and ashamed

Feeling: Fear, arrogant, anger — Intervention from outside source

Feeling: Anxious, arrogant — Given pro-social consequences

Feeling: Fear, Mistrust — Experiences the change of behavior

Feeling: Hyper-vigilant, mistrust anger — Back to old behavior, distortion, mistrust

Feeling: Compliant, more trusting — Given more pro-social consequences

Feeling: Some confidence, more trust — Compliance

Feeling: Pride in self, uncomfortable, with new behavior, feelings — Experiencing the change

Feeling: Powerful in helping others, kindness, self-respect, trusting self and others — Continues with positive behavior

The bully can cease the negative behavior until another trigger and the cycle begins again.

It takes firm and compassionate intervention, healing guidance and for the bully to experience a difference in feeling for the change to begin. There should be movement from a life of irresponsibility, anger, rage, mistrust, disrespect, fear, terror, shame, and dishonesty to a life of balance, trust of self then others, responsibility, empathy, acceptance, forgiveness and being loved and loving. Each and every person has the ability to change if he/she makes the choice. Ask for help.

We have learned from many with whom we have worked that as they experience positive change in connection with others, and pride in pro-social behavior, they become excited about making more changes. A shift occurs from mistrust, disrespect, distortion in thought, rage, mistrust, fear, anxiety and a need for inappropriate power and control, to a life of balance, trusting first in self then others, the development of empathy, acceptance, kindness, forgiveness, responsibility and accountability, and the joy of feeling loved and loving.

Bullying in Schools

The National School Safety Center calls bullying "the most enduring and underrated problem in American schools." "As many as 8 percent of schoolchildren miss a day of class monthly for fear of being bullied. And in a nationwide survey, 43 percent of children said they were afraid to go to a bathroom for fear of being harassed" (Mulrine, 1999).

Boys Are Creative and Sensitive and Have Feelings, Too

Jim didn't fit the "macho" image required of him to fit in at his junior high school. He liked to read and played the piano instead of football. The "cool" kids teased him mercilessly. At least once a week, the "jocks" that lived in his neighborhood would gang up on him as he walked home from school. Sometimes they would tear his glasses off his face and toss them back and forth to each other over his head while shouting, "Hey, four-eyed *wuss*, where are your eyes?" Sometimes his glasses would get smashed in the process. He was on his fifth pair.

He was afraid to tell his folks, afraid they wouldn't believe him or if they did, afraid of retaliation. He'd tell them he accidentally broke his glasses. After the first time, his mom and dad lectured him endlessly on responsibility. He'd been grounded for a week each time and the last two times had to pay for the new glasses out of the money he'd saved for a new bike doing odd jobs for the neighbors.

Early in life, children are classified and pigeonholed into subgroups or cliques in schools and neighborhoods according to looks, interests or behavior: "the popular kids," "the jocks," "the brains," "the preppies," "the geeks," "the freaks," "the nerds," "the emos," "the posers," "the nobodies," "the faggots."

Boys live in fear of not complying with the unspoken rules of how to belong: act cool, don't show your feelings, act tough or macho, bully or get bullied, be good in sports, don't appear too sensitive or "bookish," look good, and never cry, ask for help, or appear to be too close to your mom.

In *Real Boys' Voices*, William Pollack describes the survival techniques that boys learn early to subscribe to the "Boy Code," and the need they feel to wear a mask throughout their lives. "When boys wear this mask, they completely repress their inner emotional lives and instead act tough, composed, daring, unflappable, laughing off their pain. They may wax strong and silent or lash out with fists and fighting words" (Pollack and Shuster, 2000, p. 33).

Without the mask, they run the risk of being bullied relentlessly. Often the mask requires that they bully or actively support their buddy who is bullying. Some can't take the constant pressure and abuse, see no way out, and become depressed and suicidal or strike out with fists and weapons.

"The Boy Code, which restricts a boy's expression of emotion and his natural cries for help, has silenced the souls of our sons and paralyzed our natural instincts to reach out to them" (Pollack and Shuster, 2000, p. 4).

Girls Are Smart and Strong, and Come in All Shapes and Sizes

A twelve-year-old girl killed herself after being teased, threatened, and bullied relentlessly for a significant length of time by sixteen- and seventeen-year-old girls. The twelve-year-old died after taking one hundred painkillers. Another girl, fourteen, hung herself after similar attacks by female schoolmates. Neither girl retaliated or confided in another. They just took the abuse until they couldn't take it anymore. Both girls were singled out because they were overweight, passive and shy.

Not all girls play with Barbies, dress like her, or look like her. In fact, if Barbie was a real person, she probably couldn't stand up with her proportions. Yet, girls still are pressured to fit into a particular image of what it means to be female. Girls are under constant pressure to belong, to be part of a group, to be attractive (not too fat or too skinny), to wear the right clothes, and later, to attract the attention of boys. Girls who don't fit the image, are too shy to fight against group norms, or can't find a group to belong to are often targets for bullies.

In general, girls bully each other differently than boys. They tend to spread vicious rumors, intimidate (whispering insults and laughing with each other loud enough for their target to hear), ruin another's reputation, or tell others to stop liking a girl with whom they want to get even. They tend to use social exclusion as a primary weapon rather than direct emotional or physical aggression, although studies indicate that girls, too, are becoming increasingly more physically aggressive in the last decade.

Studies indicate that female gangs often arise in groups of girls and women who have been oppressed, and that they resort to aggression and fighting as a way to obtain power over their environments, finally obtaining their own power. We are living in a culture where those who were once victims are frequently brutally fighting back (Campbell, 1995; Chaudhuri, 1994).

Bullying in Relationships

Bullying on the playground is frequently the beginning of a history that culminates in domestic violence in adulthood. Many studies indicate that early bullying behavior is strongly associated with emotional and sometimes physical abuse in relationships (Jacobson, 1992).

Joy's Story

When Joy married Sam, she knew he had a long history of cruel behavior directed toward other children throughout their school years: shoving younger or weaker children and harassing teachers in elementary school; taunting and teasing classmates until they cried throughout their middle school years; "rumors" of date rape; and taunting, isolating, and ensuring the expulsion from their "popular group" of those that did not agree with him in high school. Unfortunately, Joy didn't see Sam's behavior as a warning sign.

"I never thought about it," Joy said with tears streaming down her face. "You know, Sam was popular, 'a real catch,' captain of the football team, and Prom King. He never did those things to me and the teachers kind of ignored him. Some even laughed at his cruelty at the expense of others. A lot of the time he was really charming. I thought it was just a guy doing 'guy things' until we married and he started making me feel ugly and stupid. Even then, I thought it was my fault."

After they married, Sam took more and more control, and Joy began giving him increasingly more power over the day-to-day functioning of their lives. "He took charge of the money, teaching me that I was 'incompetent.' By the time we separated, I didn't even think I could write a check properly. When I would eat, he'd imply that I was 'getting too fat,' but when I dieted he said I was trying to be attractive to other men. At first, he'd tell me I was too active in bed, acting like a 'slut.' Then when I no longer showed interest in sex, he'd . . . well . . . I guess it was like rape."

*Joy is literally one of millions of women and men who are bul-
lied emotionally and/or physically in relationships. Most blame
themselves, think it's normal behavior in a relationship, are afraid
to leave or ashamed to tell another living soul about the abuses
they suffer daily.*

Bullying in the Workplace

The workplace, too, is fertile ground for cruelty, resulting in high
rates of absenteeism, low staff morale, health issues, high staff turnover, atmospheres of tension, depression and suicides, workplace
aggression, etc. Employees develop a sense of helplessness, powerlessness and a perceived inability to create change. Hundreds of individuals actually end their lives, seeing no way out of a painful double
bind. On one hand, they feel the financial pressure to keep their jobs,
while on the other, they live with intolerable psychological pain daily
after being targeted by brutal coworkers or bosses. Others have taken
revenge on coworkers, as can be seen in the growing number of incidents of work-related violence.

In his book, *Brutal Bosses and Their Prey,* Harvey Hornstein (1996)
estimates that as many as 20 million Americans face workplace abuse
on a daily basis and that an estimated 90 percent of the workforce suffers abuse from bosses sometime in their careers. Bullying behavior
in the workplace costs organizations millions of dollars in absenteeism, illness, and the inability of employees to function productively
because of the daily stress they experience.

Many estimate that bullying at the hands of coworkers and bosses
is a more devastating problem for employers and employees than
all other work-related stresses combined. Bullies slowly destroy the
foundation of any company where they are allowed to take root.

Bullying in the workplace may take many forms: ignoring a worker's contributions or communications; excluding employees from the

information loop or important meetings; sabotage, such as changing the information on a chart or deleting an important file; starting destructive rumors and spreading gossip; ostracizing, shaming in public, shouting at a worker, sending rude and threatening e-mail or assigning the worst jobs or substandard work areas.

Bullies in the workplace often view innocent acts on the part of coworkers as hostile and personally threatening, and seek revenge for perceived attacks through intimidation or physical means. They crave power and authority and have difficulty empathizing or regulating aggressive behavior. Bullies are frequently triggered by insecurity and experience jealousy of coworkers whom they perceive as smarter, more popular, or more attractive.

Sexual harassment, yet another form of workplace bullying, has typically been a means for men to claim power and declare the work environment as masculine turf. Although one definition of sexual harassment is "the exploitation of a powerful position to impose sexual demands or pressures on an unwilling but less powerful person," much of what is done both to women perceived as more powerful and to men who are perceived to be not "manly" enough, isn't sexual in content but a pattern of conduct that reinforces gender difference.

"About one-third of female physicians recently surveyed said they had experienced sexual harassment, but almost half said they'd been subjected to harassment that had no sexual or physical component but was related simply to their being female in a traditionally male field. In one 1988 court case, a group of male surgical residents went so far as to falsify a patient's medical records to make it appear as though their female colleague had made an error" (Schultz, 1998, p. 12).

Frequently bullies are ineffective in their own jobs and survive by stealing the ideas of another. This was the case in a major health organization.

Joan's Story

Joan was horrified when Tom literally backed her against the hallway wall as she walked back to her office after a board meeting. He screamed at her and repeatedly jabbed his finger in her chest, "You will do as I say," he screamed, "or you will pay the price. You think you're smart? Well, you're not. You will never disagree with me in public again. My job is to do the talking; yours is to keep your ugly trap shut! Who do you think you are anyway? Having opinions is not in your job description! Do I make myself clear?" With that, he stormed down the hall to his own office. Later he came down to her office carrying a bouquet of flowers, apologized for losing his temper, and joked, "Don't you see? You drive me crazy sometimes. People around here always joke that we're like an old married couple. I guess we act like it sometimes."

Tom was the CEO of a major health corporation. Joan had been his administrative assistant for over twenty years. For years he had asked her feedback in virtually all areas, then taken her ideas and presented them as his own. The attack in the hallway followed a board meeting where she had gently corrected him on a piece of information in a proposal he was presenting that she had, in fact, written. This was not the first time. Other employees had watched but said nothing. Some later told her privately that they thought he had treated her unfairly. The incident was not reported.

Most incidents of bullying in the workplace are not reported. The targets of bullying are usually naïve about bullying behavior, blame themselves, and have no training on how to deal with it.

The Unpardonable Offense
of Being Different

Jeremy was nineteen when he was brutally beaten while walking home from his bus stop. Two men followed him in their pickup truck shouting, "Hey faggot, where are you going? Hey queer, we don't like your type around here." Jeremy ignored them, walking faster, but not fast enough. The two men stopped the truck and jumped out. They ran after him and threw him to the ground, brutally beating him until he passed out. His offense: he walked "like he was gay."

A young woman walked down a quiet street holding her child's hand. Four teenagers slowed their car and yelled, "Hey, I bet you would like sex from a real man, not those dorks you live with!" She ignored their continued obscenities and jeers. Each of them took turns leaning out the window and spitting on her before they drove away. Her offense: She was Amish.

A group of popular high school athletes raped a seventeen-year-old girl with a baseball bat and a broomstick. Many of the town's residents held her to blame for all that happened to her in the attack. Her offense: She was retarded.

A man was decapitated and torn to pieces as he was being dragged feet first behind a pickup truck. He had been alive when the torture began. His elbows had been ground down to the bone while he desperately tried to hold himself up away from the road's surface before dying from the trauma. His offense: He was African-American.

Twelve students sat in the back rows of most classes in their high school year after year. Most teachers rarely addressed them. It was as if they were invisible. One was a sensitive poet, yet he flunked English every year. He eventually hung himself. Another was told at the beginning of his high school years that he wouldn't make it in college, even though his grades were above average. Their offenses: They were Native American.

Kids called Alison names every day of her school history. Neighborhood children poked at her with a broomstick as she walked to school. No one would sit beside her in the school cafeteria because "she smelled funny." She worked hard, even won a trophy in sports, but officials took it away because she couldn't attend the honor banquet. She didn't have a "proper" dress to wear. Her offense: She was poor from a single-parent family; her mother was an alcoholic.

George was stopped at least three times a week on his way to work by local state troopers. He was harassed repeatedly. He was late for work because they held him hostage while they checked his car for "violations." There never were any. His offense: He had a long braid and wore an earring.

A seven-year-old boy has artificial legs and no hands, all because his family was told that he couldn't be admitted to the hospital near his home. He had been only five months old when he developed a high fever. He went into cardiac arrest while his family raced to an acceptable hospital seventy miles away. He was revived but gangrene had set in. His offense: His HMO didn't pay for service at his local hospital.

To six-year-old Samantha, school was constant torment. She ate alone every day and cried. One Christmas season when students exchanged presents, she opened her present from her Secret Santa and dog biscuits fell out. Her classmates laughed and barked. Her offense: The most popular girl in the school, already a cheerleader at six, didn't like her.

Most of the victims of bullying listed above never sought help. Most blamed themselves for the acts of violence and intolerance committed against them. Many of the incidents were witnessed by children and/or adults who remained passive, supporting the bullies with their actions or with their silence. Others walked away feeling that it was none of their business. Yet, most of us are horrified when we read these accounts of bullying, intolerance, and emotional and physical torment.

In order to reduce the incidents of bullying throughout our neighborhoods and communities, there must be a significant increase in the level of awareness of the bullying that is taking place around us. If we allow bullying behavior to take root and flower in our schools, homes, workplaces, neighborhoods, and society in general, it will ultimately give rise to even greater fear, learned helplessness, oppression, and hurt.

Bullies have power because we give them power through our apathy and silence. We may wish to believe that the incidents like the ones illustrated above only occur rarely, and yet, at some deep level, we know this is far from the truth. We read about them in our newspapers, see the faces of the victims on our television screens, witness them in our daily lives and, yes, experience them firsthand. Minimizing the extent of the problem allows us to turn away, keep silent, and only increases our belief that there is nothing we can do about it anyway.

We hope "they" will find an answer, when the answer is in the knowledge that "they" is "us." To find a solution, we need to wake up and then wake others who are sleeping. We need to empower each other, our neighbors, and our children.

Empowering Kindness in a Culture of Bullying

Six-year-old Mira ran, bicycled, and pumped her scooter around the track as she pushed herself to make as many laps as she could for her classmate and her dad who had been injured in a car accident. Raising money for this family was Mira's idea and she e-mailed and called countless relatives and friends to make a monetary donation to the family for each lap she completed. Her family, including her three-year-old sister who cheered her on for every lap, applauded Mira for her effort. Mira raised over $1,000 for her classmate's family.

Eleven-year-old Lauren and two of her classmates, Emily and Hanna, worked to raise money for a peer who had cancer and wanted to visit Cinderella's Castle in Disneyland. The girls set up tables at their church and school, and passed out lollipops to those who would give donations. They called their campaign "Lollies for Lily" and raised $1,800.

We could tell hundreds of stories about children and their families like Mira, Lauren, Emily, and Hannah, who are part of a powerful, but often silent majority, who have tremendous empathy, concern, and support for peers and community members. Yet, as a rule, these stories do not make the headlines of newspapers—though they should.

Bullies thrive on attention, power, and silence. As we wrote in an earlier edition of this book, to combat bullying in our schools we must do three things: teach targets how not to become victims; give pro-social consequences to bullies in order for them to change and regain a place in the circle through caring and kindness; and give the greatest attention and power to a once-silent majority, empowering them to become a vocal, caring majority.

The same is true as we begin to confront the culture of bullying and negativity surrounding us daily, as well as a media that is often quick to demonize anything and anyone. In order to change the bullying fabric of our culture and combat the bullying in social media, we need to broadcast and empower positive behavior, and balance our ability to create new and increasingly powerful technological tools and media sites with stronger values that prohibit using those tools for bullying.

Norms are the unspoken rules that govern social interaction. Norms are developed by the power of the "majority." For instance, when we turn on the radio, television, our computers, cell phones, or tablets, we are assaulted with bullying in politics, religion, "reality" shows, and sports. These things have hence become normalized. If you share a differing opinion or political view, the answer is to trash those who share another opinion, and attempt to destroy their reputations through social media. If a peer in school or in the workplace is prettier, stronger, and more competent or captures the eye of your love interest, spread gossip about them or verbally assassinate them on social media. Those of a different race, sexual orientation, economic class or ethnic group are attacked through subtle words or behaviors, or blatantly through media distortion of facts, or by feeling entitled to violate their privacy in the name of humor. If we are envious or jealous of another, attack them anonymously in an attempt to destroy them. We are bombarded with the impression of a culture where it is often more socially acceptable to attack someone for what they do or think than to be kind, supportive, and interested. In other words, we are surrounded by a worldview where bullying seems to be the norm. It will take a majority of us who do not subscribe to that particular point of view to begin to break the silence through our words or actions—in the workplace, in schools, or through the media—and indicate that we will no longer validate the norm of bullying with our silence.

For those in our society looking for positive values and norms, it will take people who are respected in their schools and communities, such as Kevin Curwick, a football team captain at Osseo High School in Osseo, Minnisota, who became so upset at peers being bullied on Twitter that he decided to challenge cyberbullying by starting a Twitter account that would only spread good things in his school community. For example, "'Take a tip from Jake Lange, guys, he knows how to treat his girl right.' 'She knows Harry Potter better than anyone and is willing to try something new.' Kevin began to make kindness cool in a world where words matter." (*http://www.youtube. com/watch?v=Rb-xNEtgYFQ*) Kevin was not looking for notoriety, and began his campaign anonymously. It is encouraging to note that people across the city, nation, and world began to join him in his efforts, which is a testament to those who believe that the silent majority would rather support kindness than bullying, and that it takes only one person to become a leader for change.

Battle of Good Words and Bad Words

By Dennis Saddleman

Out there on the battlefield earth
There was a war . . . there was a battle
Between good words and bad words.
All the spiritual words knelt down
They bowed their heads
They murmured silent words and prayer words
The strong words stood silently with their spears
The strong words were bodyguards to the chief of words
The chief of words spoke brave words to the word warriors
"Today we fight for good words
    we fight for good thoughts
    we fight for our language."
From the west came the dark words
    Swearing words
    Angry words
    Evil words
    Violent words
The leading words took the first clash
The good words fought the bad words
In the battlefield there were stabbing words . . . slashing words
And then there were many fallen words
Soon . . . the battlefield was covered with bleeding words

Hurting words
And dying words
The battle was over
Breathing words sang victory words
Healing words came
They doctored the wounded words
They buried the dead words
And then throughout friends
   Throughout many families
   Throughout the land
There were good words
   Good thoughts
   And good languages.

(Dennis is a survivor of the residential school system in Canada. Thousands of First Nations children—Native American children in the United States as well—were taken from their homes and forced to attend residential schools, many from age five to seventeen. Many of these children were mentally, emotionally, spiritually and sexually abused at the hands of those entrusted with their care.)

2

Navigating the Roadway: A Manual of Strategies for Survival

By uncovering the unconscious rules of
the power game and the methods by which
it attains legitimacy, we are certainly in a
position to bring about basic change.

Alice Miller

Wﾍhen learning to drive for the first time, very few
of us get in the car alone, put the key in the ignition, the
pedal to the metal, and set off for the nearest interstate
highway. Instead, we took courses in defensive driving or learned
from a skilled instructor. We learned the rules of the road, learned
to recognize traffic, road and warning signs, and hopefully stuck to
the speed limit. Initially we avoided high volume traffic areas, were

guided and supported by skilled drivers, practiced, and learned how to skillfully maneuver hazardous conditions, and read and reread driver manuals. All of these careful steps prepared us to pass our driver's test, get licensed, and drive defensively and carefully enough to get to our destinations.

The steps we followed in learning how to drive can be useful in any new situation requiring skills. In this case, the analogy can be used as a manual to help us learn to deal effectively with the bullies in our lives.

In many ways, bullying has become epidemic in our society. Many of us can clearly remember the hurt experienced in a bullying incident in our earliest school years. Most of us have experienced a bullying boss, coworker, neighbor, family member, friend, or significant other. Yet most people have never learned successful strategies to effectively deal with bullying behavior and are still surprised and caught off guard when it happens. Most people become confused and frightened and swallow their feelings; others lose their tempers. Either way, the bully achieves the desired effect: ensuring another is weakened, defensive, helpless, out of control, and out of their way.

We are frequently caught off guard when we are brutally attacked by a bully. Often, we blame ourselves. Confused by the abusive behavior that seems to come out of nowhere, we replay the incident again and again in our minds. Sometimes we react with defensiveness or anger or try to ignore it. Caught up in our own helplessness, we unintentionally escalate the attacks against us. Bullies are fueled by our helplessness and anger.

In order to prevent the injuries to our self-worth that being the victim of a bully engenders, we must follow a four-step approach:

Step 1: Break the chains of denial that have held us captive.
Step 2: Learn not to personalize the bully's bad behavior, empower ourselves with self-awareness and seek the support of others.

Step 3: Learn to recognize the styles and tactics of bullies in much the same way that we would familiarize ourselves with hazard signs on our roadways and highways.

Step 4: Learn the strategies and skills that are necessary to effectively deal with the bullies in our lives. Learn tools that will prevent us from being hemmed in and held as the bully's emotional captive.

In the following pages, you will learn to empower yourself, become familiar with the six most common styles used by bullies, and learn strategies that are effective for adults to use in countering bully attacks. Effective steps to teach our children will be presented in chapter 4.

Empowering Yourself

The most important step in self-empowerment is learning not to personalize the bully's bad behavior. The behavior belongs to the bully. He or she is responsible and accountable for his or her actions. While learning the necessary steps to empower yourself when attacked, remember that you didn't cause the bully's bad behavior.

One of our most effective tools in preventing paralysis and helplessness is self-awareness. Realize that we all make mistakes on our jobs, in friendships and in relationships. We are human, not "stupid" or "worthless." Mistakes are about *doing*, not about *being*. Bullies attack our *being*.

Acknowledging and accepting who we are, "warts and all," allows us not to be confused and blindsided. Bullies are good at using a grain of truth as a weapon in their emotionally abusive behavior. Self-awareness, knowing our own truth, effectively renders their weapon useless.

For instance, if you made a mistake on a report on Friday, be truthful with yourself, accept it, learn from it and move on. When the bully screams at you, "I can't believe you made such a *stupid* mistake on

that report. You are *always* making mistakes. You are such an *airhead*,"
you have already accepted the mistake you made. He or she won't be
blindsiding you with a secret you don't know.

Take time for a quick reality check:

Did you make a mistake on the report?	*Yes*
Are you *stupid*?	*No*
Are you *always* making mistakes?	*No*
Are you an *airhead*?	*No*

The insults he or she is hurling at you are not you. They are her
or his bad behavior. Many times when faced with a bully's abuse, we
defend the attacks on our *doing* and personalize the attacks on our
being. The bully's weapon becomes effective because we are paralyzed
with shame.

Practice self-awareness and make friends with all parts of yourself.
Ask supportive friends and family members to help you with this
process:

Do you have freckles?	*Yes*
Are you *ugly*?	*No*
Did you forget to bring home the milk?	*Yes*
Are you *uncaring and irresponsible*?	*No*
Have you gained ten pounds?	*Yes*
Are you *lazy and unlovable*?	*No*
Do you express your feelings?	*Yes*
Is expressing your feelings emotionally healthy?	*Yes*
Are you a *crybaby*?	*No*
Are you *too sensitive*?	*No*

Bullies are experts at finding our Achilles' heels, those parts of us that are most sensitive, exaggerating them, shaming them, and using them as weapons against us. If there are parts of you that you shame in yourself, like making a mistake or having freckles, make peace with them. Seek out support and a compassionate, honest mirror so that you won't be giving the bullies in your life a weapon to use against you.

Another important part of empowering yourself is to trust your intuition. If it feels bad, trust the feeling. Sometimes bullies are expert at being charming one minute and attacking the next. One behavior does not preclude the other. Don't get caught trying to make sense of it. The energy you spend on rationalizing the bully's behavior will decrease your ability to act on your intuition. If you are feeling attacked, trust the feeling.

Next, recognize that you have basic rights. Write them down. Keep them with you. Memorize them and learn to believe in their truth. Below are a few basic human rights that will help you begin your list. Copy the ones that are helpful for you and add to them. You have:

- The right to have your thoughts and feelings acknowledged and accepted as real. Your thoughts and feelings belong to you, no one else;
- The right to live a life that is free from judgments and blame;
- The right to emotional support;
- The right to live a life that is free from physical and emotional threats;
- The right to be asked to do something, not ordered to do something;
- The right to be heard and treated with respect;
- The right to your own opinions and viewpoints, even when they are different from those of others;
- The right to be loved and cherished.

Seek out support. Since one of the weapons used by bullies is to isolate and alienate, one of the most important aspects of self-empowerment is seeking out a support system that is mutually respectful. We need people who will respectfully listen and offer compassionate and honest feedback when we request it. One of the biggest gifts that life can offer are those honest mirrors who accept us and empower us. We need each other. In our pain, we often don't acknowledge how much we need each other.

Seven Basic Strategies to Deal with In-Person Bullying

Bullies are experts in using intimidation techniques. They repeatedly use behaviors that have worked for them in the past to gain power and control over others, in order to fuel their power needs or get their own way. Many bullies, in fact, have been perfecting their skills of intimidation since early childhood. Bullies depend upon eliciting confusion, fear or feelings of powerlessness in their intended victims. Rendering their targets helpless or forcing them to lose control of their tempers enables the bully to gain control of the situation.

In much the same way that we learned to control the speed of the vehicle in order to avoid potential accidents, swallowing your feelings or losing your temper will put your self-esteem at risk when faced with a bully. Stand up to the bully, but avoid fighting with him. Be assertive, not demanding.

There are seven basic strategies to follow when being tormented by a bully:

1. **Look the bully straight in the eye.** Your natural inclination to avoid eye contact can give you the appearance of being powerless. Bullies thrive on the helplessness of their intended victims. Most people are uncomfortable with conflict and, as a result of this discomfort, take a sudden interest in their shoes while delivering an otherwise assertive message. The message will not be communicated if nonverbal communication says, "I'm really afraid and powerless."

2. **Use confident body language.** Bullies are highly sensitized to fear in their intended victims. Use a firm tone of voice. Be certain that your gestures match your words. Your assertive message won't come across the way you intend if you are shuffling your feet and using a pleading tone of voice.

3. **Choose carefully whether to confront the bully alone or with others who have also been bullied or have witnessed your abuse.** Sometimes bullies depend on the laughter and silent agreement of their peers. When surrounded by a group, they will fight to preserve their "image" at all cost. They need to be right and sometimes you are less likely to be heard when there is an audience. If the bullying is recent and you have equal power (a coworker or a friend), or are in a position of power (you are the bully's supervisor, mentor, etc.), confronting the bully alone can be effective. Confronting the bully alone generally does not work if the bullying has been going on for a long period of time or if the bully is in a position of power.

   If the bully is in a power position as is the case with a boss, or the bullying has been going on for a long period of time, it is useful to have the support of others who have received similar treatment from the bully or have observed the bully's torment of you. To confront the bully with a group of people who have discussed, arranged, and planned the intervention gives the group more power than the bully. It is more difficult for the bully to con, manipulate, or threaten you if you have the support of a group. The bully may attempt to deny or distort what is being said, lie to or charm you, threaten you, or con or manipulate you so that you become defensive. When you become defensive or appear helpless, the bully is in charge.

   If you have any reason to believe that the individual you are confronting could escalate verbal abuse into physical abuse, make certain that you have others to stand with you, or leave the door open with individuals prepared to take action, if necessary, waiting within hearing distance.

4. **Focus on the behavior you wish to have stopped without using labels.** Using labels both potentially inflames the situation and gives the bully an opportunity to derail the conversation by attacking the label. Labels may include: "you're attacking me," "stop putting me down," "your remarks are shaming," "you're harassing me," "stop bullying me." Describe the behavior as simply as possible: "Joe, you're interrupting me." "Sally, I will not allow you to criticize my work in public. I will be happy to listen to your evaluation in private."

5. **Say it simply.** It is not effective, when confronting a bully, to analyze his behavior or motivations. Chose a few brief, direct, behaviorally specific statements and say them repeatedly if necessary.

6. **Avoid absolutes ("you always," "you never"), sarcasm, and attacks to the bully's character.** Avoid fighting words such as "you're wrong" or "you're doing it again." Bullies have an overwhelming need to be right and save face. Absolutes, sarcasm, attacks and fighting words will escalate the battle that the bully is prepared to win.

7. **Be direct.** Speak from the "I" and deliver the message directly to the person for whom it is intended.

Eight Common In-Person Bullying Styles

Head-On Collisions

You're driving down a highway on a beautiful spring day, enjoying the music playing on the car radio. Suddenly you see something coming toward you in the distance. A Mack truck is coming straight at you in your lane of traffic. Your immediate feeling is terror. Your first thought, *Wait a minute! This is a divided highway. Am I going in the wrong direction? How could I have done that?*

These are some of the thoughts and feelings experienced immediately when confronted with the head-on collision bullying style: fear, confusion, self-blame. The person comes at you, seemingly out of nowhere. You are not prepared and briefly think you have done something to deserve the disapproval and abuse that is aimed at you. What possible reason would this person have for coming at you in this manner? What did you do?

Sue's Story

Sue was sitting at her computer busily typing a proposal for an advertising campaign that she and her office partner Bob had been working up for a client. She had stayed late at the office the night before dictating her part of the proposal. When she came in this morning she found a message from Stevie, their administrative assistant, on her voice mail. Stevie's child had pneumonia and she was staying home to care for her. She had called Stevie to give her support, then began typing her dictation.

An hour later Bob appeared at the door, his tape in hand. "Where the hell is Stevie? Is she late again, damn it? What is it this time? Getting her nails done, or is it her hair?"

Stevie was highly responsible and seldom late but Sue didn't argue the point. She replied, "Actually, she has a sick child."

"Yeah, right. The favorite excuse of females," Bob hissed. "Who is going to type up my dictation? I'm not a secretary."

"I thought we could pitch in and do our own. I'm typing mine right now," Sue responded.

"Who asked you to think? Now I've heard it all. Boy, you girls really know how to stick together, don't you? I'll bet you gave her the day off, didn't you? Bet you were out on one of your little girly excursions at the mall last night and thought this one up while

*your nails were drying! Well, you've got another thought coming.
You gave her the day off, you type my dictation!"*

"Actually I . . ."

*"If the two of you want to compete in a man's world, you'll just
have to work for a change," Bob yelled. "Manicured nails and a
fancy haircut just won't cut it."*

"I think . . ."

*"I'm in a mess here that you caused. The proposal is due at
the end of the day. You think? That's a good one. You should
have thought about this before you gave Stevie the day off," Bob
screamed, heading for the door.*

*"Now just a minute. I don't have to take this from you!" Sue
screamed back.*

*"Right!" Bob yelled slamming the door. "If you want the pro-
posal in on time, you'd better get typing. Take responsibility for
your actions. I didn't give her the day off, you did."*

*Sue felt like she'd been hit by a Mack truck. Bob demonstrated
behavior that is typical of the bully that collides with you head-on.
This type of bully yells, puts you down, calls you names, threatens
and interrupts. Later this individual might appear like nothing has
happened. "What are you so upset for anyway? You in a bad mood?"*

These bullies also often use their physical presence and loud tone of
voice to intimidate you, wear you down, overwhelm you and eventually get what they want. What they're *not* used to is people standing
up to them.

Dealing with Head-On Collisions

1. **Stand up to them.** Head-on collisions are typical of bullies who are
   used to people cowering. Be assertive, but don't fight. They don't know
   how to back down and being right is extremely important to them. If

you fight, they will have gained an edge because you're out of control. They lack controls on their own behavior and are actually shocked when others impose calm but firm controls on them.

Use firm statements and always address them by name and remember to look them in the eye: "Bob, I don't agree with you but I am interested in your opinion." "Bob, I don't agree with you but tell me more." "Bob, I don't share your opinion but I would like to know how you see the situation."

2. **If they are standing, and they usually will be, ask them to sit down.** It's much harder for them to keep the steady stream of intimidation up from a sitting position. If they won't sit, remain standing. If you are sitting when they begin their tirade, stand up slowly, not abruptly. It's important that you don't appear to be in a fighting posture.

3. **Don't let them interrupt.** Be calm but firm: "Bob, you are interrupting me." Then, return to the conversation. You can count on being interrupted again. Repeat your message calmly and firmly, "Bob, you are interrupting me."

4. **Don't become defensive, lecture, threaten, or get caught up in a detailed argument of facts.** Follow the general strategies useful for all bullies listed at the beginning of the chapter.

5. **Avoid absolutes** such as "You always . . ." "You never . . ." Don't use words that serve to escalate a fight: "Bob, you are interrupting me again." "You're wrong." "I don't have to take this!"

State your beliefs and expectations simply, calmly and firmly. Don't allow interruptions, and listen to the other's point of view. If name calling begins, respond with, "Bob, I really want to hear what you have to say but I won't allow you to call me names." Return to the conversation.

Contrary to the beliefs of most individuals, those that collide with you head-on frequently respect those who set calm and firm limits on their bad behavior. In fact, many bullies have told me that they wish people would have stood up to them long ago. Unlike many other types of bullies, these bullies usually respond to firm limit setting and are likely to change their behavior with you in the future.

Rear-Ended

Anyone who has felt the jarring impact of a car hitting their automobile from behind knows the serious injuries that can result. Whiplash is a serious injury; so is emotional whiplash. Most people don't see the hit coming and are often rendered briefly numb and mute by the experience.

Those who rear-end others deliver their verbal abuse from behind, screened in humor or sarcasm. This often leaves the intended victim wondering if they've *really* been "hit," even though they are feeling sore and wounded. The victim questions him or herself since the bully is quick to point out he or she is just being "too sensitive" or has temporarily lost his or her sense of humor.

Eve's Story

Sid and Eve had been friends for many years. Sid loved to tell people that the reason their friendship had lasted so long was that they had much in common, never argued, and had partners that respected and valued the relationship they shared. That much was true enough. Even when Eve occasionally felt hostility from Sid, he denied it. He would smile and accuse Eve of being "too sensitive."

Sid had a terrific sense of humor and was always joking around, especially when they were with other people. Eve always laughed with the group, even when she felt hurt by the "joke." Awkwardly, she had tried to express her feelings on one occasion, "You know last night when you told that joke, well, it hurt my feelings a little. I know you were just joking around but. . . ."

"Eve," Sid said with a patient and somewhat condescending smile, "Of course I didn't mean it. You're working too hard. I think you're losing your sense of humor."

Recently, Eve had received a promotion at work, complete with a much higher salary and a company car. Sid was in the same line of work and had made some jokes about women, and especially black women, getting "cushy jobs" because of their minority status. "Us white fellows don't seem to stand a chance anymore." Yet, he seemed happy for her and had even spent time planning a celebration dinner in her honor. He'd invited all of their current friends and even some of their friends from college.

When Eve walked into the fancy restaurant Sid had chosen for the celebration, Sid stood up and banged loudly on his glass with a spoon. When he'd gotten everyone's attention, including other patrons of the restaurant, he crooned, "Well, here is the guest of honor. Look at that power suit. Guess you're going to have to lose a couple of pounds in the rear end, Eve, if you're going to continue to wear those tailored men's suits. You're right up there with the big boys now. Just look at you. Aren't you something?"

Everyone erupted in laughter. Eve was stunned, self-conscious, uncomfortable, but smiled awkwardly and tried to laugh with the crowd.

After they were seated, Sid continued with his jokes. "Hey, guys, did you see the new, sleek, fancy car that our little Eve was given? A convertible, no less. Paul, look out, our new black Malibu Barbie is on her way. Guess she'll be picking up guys in her new toy just like the old days."

Everyone laughed including Eve's husband, John, although he fidgeted uncomfortably. Eve tried to laugh but managed only a weak smile. Suddenly her stomach was hurting and she didn't feel like eating. She just wanted to go home but Sid had gone to so

much trouble and expense. She thought, What's the matter with
me? Sid spent weeks planning this celebration for me. He put so
much thought into celebrating my success. Why am I so irritable?
Am I so tired that I've lost my sense of humor?

Sid's behavior was consistent with individuals who attack others
from behind, camouflaging their bullying attacks behind a smoke
screen of jokes and sarcasm. The best way to deal with these bullies
is to smoke them out.

Dealing with Bullies Who Attack from Behind

1. **Trust your feelings and intuition.** If you're bleeding emotionally,
   chances are you've been attacked. Validate your emotional reality.
   Recognize that you have been the target of abuse skillfully disguised
   as a joke, that your boundaries have been seriously violated and the
   basic essence of your being has been compromised.
2. **Don't laugh at jokes told at your expense.** Abuse is not funny.
3. **Stand up for yourself without getting into a fight.** Remember, the
   bullies who hit you from behind are every bit as lethal as those who
   hit you head-on.
4. **Be prepared for the bullies who rear-end you by acting innocent in
   response to your assertive stance.** "Have you misplaced your sense
   of humor?" "Can't you take a joke?" "You used to like my jokes, what
   happened to you?" "You are just too sensitive." Don't bite. Just keep
   repeating yourself calmly, directly and simply.
5. **State the facts calmly and simply.** "Remember last night when you
   told that joke at the party? You can be really funny. Everyone laughed,
   but I thought I heard a dig in that. Did you mean it that way?" You
   may have to repeat this statement many times if your sense of humor
   or sensitivity is questioned. Stay on track.
6. **Be prepared to confront rear-end attacks every time they happen.**

7. **Don't expect those bullies who hit from behind to validate your experience.** You will have to validate your own experience and seek out feedback from supportive others whom you trust. Even though they don't openly acknowledge the dig, they probably will stop hitting you from behind for a while.

8. **The price rear-enders eventually pay is that people stop wanting to be around them.** The hurt is too deep. If you do withdraw and the bully asks you why, be honest. If their behavior no longer works, change might be in the forecast. Keep remembering, the bully's bad behavior is about them, not about you.

Speed Up, Slow Down: The Controller

Bullies who are both controlling and righteous are often the hardest to communicate with effectively. They have a similar style to those bullies who collide with you head-on with one important difference; they don't lose their cool, their victims do. They are experts at calmly slashing your self-esteem to ribbons, hemming you in with double binds, and eventually generating an angry response in otherwise patient and calm people. The controlling bully often seeks out potential victims that seem sensitive and vulnerable.

These bullies have a style of behavior similar to those drivers on the highway who slow down when they are in front of you, then speed up when you try to pass. They're also like the drivers who pull into the parking space you've been patiently waiting for, claiming that they saw the space first if you say something.

The controlling bully, like most bullies, has a distorted view of reality. Yet, perhaps more than other bullies, they are highly attuned to the behaviors of others. They see attacks aimed at them when there are none and an enemy behind every bush. They are unpredictable: overly protective, loving and putting you on a pedestal one minute, and calmly cutting your ego to shreds the next. In fact, part of their pattern is to build up their intended victims so they *can* calmly cut their egos to shreds the next. They are experts at double binds and inducing guilt. They feel consistently "unappreciated" for their hard work.

To this individual, control is ego survival. If you are in trouble, helpless, or at a point in your life when you have diminished self-esteem and are questioning yourself, he will "rescue" you while making sure you stay down. She or he will prove to you that you are now safe and frequently help you to become independent, then attack you for being "irresponsible, ungrateful and dependent."

If you decide you can't stand the demeaning behavior anymore and decide to leave, he or she will suddenly become super loving and apologetic, letting you know how "completely miserable" life will be if you withdraw. Then, when you become comfortable again, he or she will once again withdraw affection and begin the process of tearing you down.

Sadie's Story

Sadie was in the middle of a painful divorce, fighting for the custody of her children and struggling to make ends meet by working two shifts at a local restaurant. Her husband had an affair and she had left him. He was enraged and was punishing her by trying to gain custody of their children. He was using both her past drinking history, although she had been sober for six years, and her long hours of work against her in court.

She had begun to question her own sanity, was depressed and struggling financially when she met Lou at the restaurant where she worked. Sadie reflected on that time that seemed so long ago, though it had only been three years.

"He was kind and supportive. He patiently listened to my problems. He bought me flowers and expensive perfume and gifts for the children that I never could have afforded. He told me that I deserved to be 'cherished' and made me believe in myself again. He told me I was a good mother and I shouldn't have to work so that I could devote my energy to raising my children. He even encouraged me to think about going to college, maybe sometime take a night class at the community college. I had always dreamed of going to college and he really thought I could do it," she recalled.

Sadie was granted full custody of her children and Lou proposed soon after the divorce was final. Lou convinced her to quit her job, move into his house and begin night classes at the community college. He said he could well afford to support her and would be happy to share child care.

"We were so happy for awhile," Sadie said. "Lou treated me like I was somebody special, he even helped with the housework. I was gaining confidence in myself for the first time in years. Then almost out of nowhere, the complaints began. He said that I was spending too much time at school or with my friends or family. He stopped being affectionate and complained about the money he was being 'forced' to spend. He told me again and again that I didn't appreciate the sacrifices he had made. Finally, he accused me of having an affair with my college professor. When I accounted for every minute of my time, he told me that thinking about having an affair was the same as having one."

"What in the world gave you the idea I was thinking of having an affair?" Sadie exclaimed in disbelief to Lou. "I love you. You know that."

"Well, let's see," Lou countered calmly. "It could be the fact that you get all dressed up and wear expensive perfume when you go to class."

"Lou, you bought me that perfume. When I don't wear it you tell me that I don't appreciate the gifts you give me. I wear it all the time," Sadie said, bewildered.

"Or, it could be the time you spend on your homework trying to impress him," he replied as if she hadn't spoken.

"I feel like I'm going crazy!" Sadie screamed in frustration.

Coping with Controlling Bullies

1. **Depend on yourself for your self-esteem,** not someone else. If you know you are a good person with good intentions and believe in yourself, there is very little another can do to make you a victim. Sadie began to depend on Lou for her sense of self-worth. Giving another that much power is a no-win situation, particularly when relating to a controlling bully. Like most bullies, Lou needed to bring Sadie down to build himself up. Sadie's low self-esteem and dependency fulfilled Lou's desire for power and control. Don't let anyone convince you that they are your lifeline.

2. **Avoid the double-bind trap.** In his book, *Nasty People,* Jay Carter relates the teaching of a Chinese ancient master: "You show up at the master's house for a lesson. The master invites you in and both of you sit down for a cup of tea. Just as you sit down, the master pulls out a large stick from under the table and says, 'This is your lesson for today. If you pick up the cup of tea, I will hit you with the stick. And if you don't, I will hit you with a stick" (Carter, 1989, p. 26).

   When he presents this lesson to his students, Carter says that some think the answer is to drink the tea because you are going to get hit anyway; others think it is to beat up the master. In fact, Carter says, there are only two solutions to the problem: take away the stick or walk away.

   A favorite ploy of the controlling bully is to present you with situations where you can either choose to lose, or choose to lose. For instance, you are asked to choose between him or your family or friends. As with other bullying styles previously discussed, don't argue or defend yourself. Look the controlling bully in the eye and clearly and simply let him know that you're not going to enter the game. "Lou, I'm not going to choose. I will continue to spend time with my family and you will have to choose." In other words, *take away the stick*.

3. **Don't get caught up in "prove it."** Controlling bullies are very good at emotional blackmail and making you think you're in charge of their self-worth, self-respect, etc. Don't bite. You are not the master of their self-worth any more than they are of yours. A boss that is a controlling bully might say, "I know how you feel about this job. You're just on your way to something bigger. I know it's just a matter of time until you leave." The game: *Prove your loyalty. Make me feel important and do what I want.* Look your boss in the eye and respond simply and factually, "George, I've been at this job for six years. I'm here now."

    Effectively dealing with a controlling bully is a bit like being a traffic guard on Boundary Street: "You make your choices. I make my choices." "You have your thoughts and opinions. I have my thoughts and opinions." "You're responsible for your self-esteem. I'm responsible for my self-esteem." "I communicate my feelings. You communicate your feelings." Don't get caught up in the game or you can expect a collision.

4. **What is, is.** Don't try to make sense out of the controlling bully's behavior or analyze his or her intentions.

When confronted with abrupt changes in the controlling bully's behavior, most individuals get confused. They try to figure out what's real and make sense out of the bully's behavior. Is he the caring, compassionate person they woke up to, or the demeaning, accusing, hurtful person who just attacked them? "Maybe she's having a bad day." "Maybe I did something to hurt him." The answer is that the behavior is what it is. When you are being bullied, it hurts. It doesn't matter what he did an hour ago. Look him in the eye and stand up for your-self: "Lou, you made the choice to support me and the children. If you have changed your mind about your choice, let me know directly and I will be willing to explore other options with you." Sadie is not responsible for Lou's choices and she's not a mind reader.

When relating to a controlling bully, don't be held emotionally hos-tage and be held accountable and responsible for his or her choices. Focus on *your* thoughts, feelings, behavior and choices, not his or hers.

Slippery Road Ahead

Have you ever been driving down the highway on a beautiful early spring or fall day and suddenly hit a patch of ice you never expected to be there? You felt your wheels start to skid. This is a very good time to remember defensive driving rules. Always be prepared for changes in weather and road conditions and unexpected hazards.

Patches of ice and potholes can suddenly appear on roads where you least expect them; so can bullying behavior appear out of nowhere from the people you least expect.

Trish's Story

Trish told her family about the wonderful woman she had met the first day on her new job: "She's incredible. She greeted me and made me feel welcome right away. She took me to lunch and it was as if I'd known her all my life. She was open and honest and before I knew it, I felt completely at ease. I can't believe I met her just six weeks ago. I feel like I could tell her anything."

Trish's biggest mistake was trusting someone she barely knew with her innermost thoughts, feelings and privacy. Laurie wanted to be her "new best friend" almost immediately. Six months later, Trish discovered why. By then, it was too late.

Laurie knew that Trish had been hired because of her excellent work history, portfolio and credentials. She also knew that a management position she coveted would be opening up in the company within the year. If Trish's work performance matched her excellent credentials, they would both be competing for the job. Laurie wanted the job, it was that simple.

Unfortunately, Trish had trusted Laurie with parts of her private life that she had never shared with anyone before in the places she had worked. She had always been careful to keep good boundaries between her professional and personal life. But when the job opened up, top-level managers knew things about intimate parts of Trish's life that she had confided to Laurie. Trish couldn't prove that Laurie got the position because the managers suddenly knew Trish was gay, but she knew who told them.

Getting a Grip on Slippery Roads

This is a good time to remember the rules of the road: Never underestimate changes in road conditions and possible hazards on the highway. Be prepared and drive defensively. In Trish's case, be wary of those who want too quickly to be your new best friend at work.

Laurie fit the pattern of the slippery bully. She wanted something and set out to get it any way she could. She was warm and charming and shared "intimate secrets" with Trish in the hope that Trish would reciprocate, which she did. The only difference was, the details that Trish divulged were real. Laurie's "intimate secrets" were pure fiction. Slippery bullies will skillfully reel a person in like a fish on a hook.

There is only one strategy to use when dealing with these bullies: Don't trust them. Unfortunately for Trish, it was a tough lesson to learn, a case of "hindsight being 20/20." After having trusted a slippery bully too soon there is not much you can do. She wanted the promotion, secret stock tip, information, etc. and she got it at your expense. It's that simple and that painful.

If Trish confronted Laurie, this slippery bully might even boldly admit what she had done. "Trish, haven't you heard that all's fair in love and business? No hard feelings, better luck next time."

Or, if she still needed Trish and wanted to convince her to stay, she might tell her how bad she feels and swear that she was only trying to help Trish come out in a safe work environment, so that she could learn to be proud of herself. "I never in a million years would have expected Tom to be homophobic. I thought his sister was gay." For effect, Laurie might even cry.

The best that you can do after having hit that slippery patch at an unsafe speed is learn never to be unprepared again. Exercise caution, not paranoia. There is not a slippery road around every bend. There is a difference between driving defensively and being wary to the point of panic every time you get in the car. The best Trish can do is learn from her error in judgment, accept the teaching gifts in the experience and move on. She paid a price, but hopefully she learned a valuable lesson in boundaries and judgment.

Sideswiped

A number of years ago, I parked next to a car with a smashed-in side. The side mirror hung limply, held only by a wire. Just as I was getting out of my car, the driver of the injured vehicle was returning to his. He had seen me examining the damage to his vehicle and said, "It's amazing. I never saw him hit me. He was in my blind spot. All of a sudden I was in the ditch. I never saw it coming. It could have been worse, though. I must have sensed his car moving closer even though I couldn't see him. I instinctively moved closer to the side of the road before he hit me."

If you've been blindsided by a bully, you can probably relate to this man's story. Bullies that sideswipe you often appear to be your good buddy while sometimes your intuition tells you his "good will" isn't quite as it appears. Maybe those nagging intuitive voices began when he told you little things that others have been saying about you; for your own good, of course. The problem is we often don't trust our intuition.

Someone tells you the gossip and rumors that this individual has been spreading about you and you feel you've been hit in your blind spot. Bullies that sideswipe are usually jealous or harbor a grudge against you; they don't confront you directly. Both hostile and aggressive, they attempt to destroy you through vicious gossip and rumors designed to "get you back" for perceived attacks on their self-worth.

Gloria's Story

Gloria and Lisa had been working the night shift on the third floor of a local hospital for three years. Lisa loved her job. It was a particularly good job for her because she had three young children and valued the time she could spend with them during the day. She and her husband didn't spend as much time together as they would have liked, but both were committed to sharing child care.

Gloria had never been married and had no children. Although she always encouraged Lisa's stories about her children, she in fact resented hearing them. She felt that Lisa was always "throwing in her face" the fact that she had never married. She hated the "cute, cozy" family picture that Lisa had on display in the nursing station they shared, which was a constant reminder of what she didn't have. Gloria also resented the easy way that Lisa had with her patients and their obvious "adoration" of her.

Gloria had confided to Lisa on several occasions, for Lisa's own good, that the other nurses felt she was "stuck up" and "aloof." "Maybe you should spend extra time with them. You know, show an interest. I know how much you love your children, I love them too, but maybe you could resist going right home after shift a couple of nights and have coffee with us. Spend some girl time."

One day, a nurse who worked on the second floor and liked and respected Lisa told her that Gloria had spread a rumor the nurse felt was damaging to Lisa's reputation, personally and professionally. The nurse said that Gloria had told her friend June in confidence that Lisa was being "intimate" with one of her patients and that this breach of ethics had happened before.

Lisa was sideswiped. Although her intuitive voice had let her know that things may not be quite as they seemed between her and Gloria, she never expected the kind of malicious hostility that had been directed at her. She also felt like she was in a double bind. On one hand, she now felt angry, awkward and distant with Gloria; on the other hand, June had told her coworker this information in "strictest confidence."

Don't Get Sideswiped

1. **Get the facts.** When someone tells you that another is spreading rumors and gossip, attempt to gain their permission to check the story out with the individual allegedly spreading the rumors. Let them know that having the information with no avenue to check it out puts you in an awkward position. If they resist, let them know that you quite possibly will make the choice to check it out without their permission. The bearer of the news may never tell you what people are saying about you again, but that's okay, too.

2. **Speak in private to the person who is allegedly spreading the rumors.**
3. **Relate as directly and simply as possible the information you have been given and the source.** Then ask if this person heard them correctly. Is this in fact what was said?
4. **Expect them to deny it.** Bullies that sideswipe are hostile and angry and, at the same time, they fear direct conflict. They will usually deny what has been said and usually blame the misunderstanding on the person who told you the information. Lisa's response to Gloria in this case might be, "Great. I will let June know what you said."
5. **The bully may continue to deny the information or he may dump on you.** In either case, look the bully in the eyes and let him know directly that you expect him in the future to come to you first with any concerns or perceptions he has regarding you or your life. "Gloria, in the future, I expect you to say things directly to me first."

The sideswiping bully will be more careful about spreading gossip and rumors about you in the future. Like most bullies, these individuals never expect to be confronted with their behavior.

Bullies Are Experts at Their Behavior

All of us have bad days and can lapse into bad behavior on occasion. We are, after all, human beings. Bullies have long-standing and deeply set patterns of behavior that they have been perfecting most of their lives. These patterns have been reinforced because few people have stood up to them in a good way. In other words, they have learned that their behavior works.

Bullies are highly skilled in the act of intimidation. If you argue with them you will most likely lose, or they will keep escalating their behavior. To them, their survival depends upon winning. They must win at all costs. On the other hand, if you swallow your feelings, personalize their attacks and become helpless and powerless, you will continue to be one of their favorite targets. When attacked, don't fight with the bully, question their motivation or personalize their behavior. Look them in the eyes, and stand up for yourself.

Study the behavioral styles of bullies and effective strategies for dealing with them as seriously as you would a driver's manual. Keep yourself emotionally and physically safe and always ask for support from those you know you can trust.

In the next chapter we will present bullying through technology, or cyberbullying. Although the bullies are similar in many ways there are some special considerations.

3

The Making of a Bully: Their Own Stories

The moment you live something, you
are teaching it whether you want to or not.

Dadi Janki from Pearls of Wisdom

Nancy's Story

"I remember being afraid a lot. Fear was constant.
My mother was loud, impatient and unpredictable. She
was nervous and drank a lot. She didn't cuddle or show
affection. I never thought she liked me. When she drank,
she was verbally and physically abusive.

"My father was loud and mean. When he drank he was nice.
He was away much of the time working. My relationship with my
father was one of fear. My father didn't show much affection either.
My parents fought a lot.

"The values that were important were to stick together, do well in school, stick up for ourselves with others and don't attract attention. I was often the scapegoat when things would happen with my sisters. . . . In my younger years in school I was very afraid. I didn't have any friends and I suffered with depression most of my life. I was a victim of my parents' bullying. I was bullied in other relationships and in my marriage. I felt helpless, afraid and unworthy of anything better.

"I, too, became a bully. As I got older, I began to rebel. As a teenager, I felt tough. I discounted people and thought I was better than them. They were weaker than I was, so I had something I could use against them. I felt justified. It was not acceptable to be wrong in my family of origin, so I felt like I always needed to be right. Being right and tough was my survival. I gossiped about others, put others down and triangulated. I had the belief that it was never my fault. I thought things happened to me and that it had nothing to do with my feelings, belief or behaviors. I was afraid that I was a terrible, unloving human being. It was hard to face myself.

"I woke up one day and realized my whole life had been a lie. Nothing that I had learned to think was true was reality. I grew more and more depressed and couldn't function. I needed help and went to treatment.

"The insight that I gained from treatment was that I used the behavior I had seen in my family of origin. In my own struggle to survive, I became what I hated. I didn't know this until I was confronted in treatment and made accountable for my behavior. I eventually risked feeling the fear underneath it all. I had no idea that I manipulated and bullied my parents, my husband, anyone. I just thought I ran the show because no one else would. I saw my mother doing those things and swore I would never be like that, but I was. . . .

"I was in denial. I had distorted beliefs and was extremely defensive because I was protecting my 'shadow side.' I couldn't show anyone who I really was because I would be vulnerable and hurt again. I just couldn't let myself be hurt anymore. I was told that I could change, get well and become the person I wanted to be.

"Through acceptance, understanding and finally trusting others, I was able to see what I needed to change. I asked for and received help from many people: professionals and others who had been like me. I learned to think for myself, to think about what I wanted to say and not just shoot words out. I learned I could be wrong and the world would not end. I began to admit when I was wrong and take responsibility for it. There is freedom in being accountable for what I do and say."

In her story, Nancy describes herself as both victim and bully. She describes a dichotomy in behavior that is often apparent in the bullies we have treated and from whom we have learned. What appears to be a striking difference in her behavior as both victim and bully are actually two sides of the same coin. A child who is insecure and wounded may bully others, and/or set himself up to be the target of bullies. We have never worked with a bully whose behavior didn't have a foundation in victimization. Bullies are not born; they are made. They are not bad children; they are sad children.

In treatment, Nancy was able to move through many of the basic developmental steps missed in her childhood. As with many children who develop bullying behavior, her early childhood was one of anxious attachment, insecurity and inconsistency. As a result, she wasn't able to develop trust in herself and others; to learn empathy, feel security, internalize limits, learn to make choices and know that she was accountable for the choices she made; or to resolve conflicts and build skills that would lead to the development of lasting, healthy relationships.

When children are born there is physical birth and, some believe, spiritual birth, but it takes eight years of life for a child to attain psychological birth. The child moves from "that I am" to "who I am." Children learn who they are as individuals from their parents, older siblings, extended family, teachers, coaches and other adult role models in their lives.

From the first moment of life, children begin taking from the outside and bringing to the inside beliefs about themselves. They learn values, regulation of emotions, and acceptable and unacceptable behaviors that will influence the way they grow up.

As the child grows older, the foundation for aggressive behavior develops and becomes increasingly resistant to change. Children raised in families and communities that are emotionally or physically violent, cold, neglectful, inconsistent, restrictive, punitive and/or indulgent experience the disruption of normal developmental patterns that result in emotional, behavioral and cognitive problems.

On April 22, 1997, a full-page advertisement appeared in the *New York Times* for a special edition of *Newsweek* magazine on birth to age three. The ad featured a photograph of a baby's face. Accompanying the photograph were the phrases, "Every hug. Every lullaby. Every kiss. Every peek-a-boo. Every word. Every touch. Every warm blanket. Every giggle. Every smile. Everything you do in these first three years becomes a part of them" (*New York Times,* 1997).

The Influence of Parents and Other Adult Caretakers

Ann's Story

All her life Ann was abused and bullied at home by both of her parents. She lived in fear all of the time. Like most children from abusive families, she tried to be a "good girl" and to make her parents happy. She thought if she could be good enough, her parents would stop bullying each other, her brother and sister, and herself. She was told all of her young life that she deserved the abuse, that she was responsible for her parents' anger, thus causing the family violence.

When Ann's father drank, he was violent, and when he wasn't drinking, he would constantly tease and threaten, "If you don't behave, I will put you in a foster home." He lied, telling her she was adopted and would be sent back where she came from. Ann lived in constant terror that she would be separated from her brother and sister.

Ann was thirteen years old when she worked in a drive-in restaurant to help support her family. A seventeen-year-old boy would come in and stay for hours, ordering Coke after Coke. He was nice to Ann at first. He told her she was pretty, that she was nice and would bring her little presents. He asked a lot of questions about her family. She would tell him things that she had never told anyone about her family and he would sympathize with her, becoming angry that anyone would treat her so horribly. She believed that he had a genuine interest in her well-being and was a true friend. Although she never accepted his offer, he would offer to drive her home every night.

After several weeks, the boy began to change. He began telling her that he knew who her parents were and that nobody liked them. He began saying mean things to her about her brother and sister and told her that if she didn't accept a ride home from him, he would tell her father and the boss that she was a whore. Ann became fearful of him, began avoiding him and continued to refuse his rides. He escalated his threats, terrorized her, threatening, among other things, to have her brother beaten. She would cry and beg him to leave her alone.

Ann was afraid to tell anyone about the threats. She was afraid that others would believe him and not her. She believed that if he told her father she was a whore, she would suffer more abuse or finally be given away. If her boss found out, she would be fired and be the failure her parents always told her she was. They would be angry and blame her once again for being the bad person that made their life miserable. She lived in terror that he would have her brother beaten and it would be her fault.

One night, after being bullied and threatened yet again, Ann accepted the ride home. The boy raped her that night and left her many miles from home. It was a cold and snowy night and she had to walk home in tennis shoes. She was numb, in shock and blamed herself for the rape. When she got home her mother was drunk and began screaming at her for being late. Her mother accused her of terrible things, slapped her in the face and pushed her around.

Finally, Ann's grandmother stepped in and stopped her mother's abuse. She took her into the bathroom and held her, asking what happened to her. Ann could not tell her grandmother the truth, so she made up a story as her grandmother attended to the frostbite on her feet. Her tennis shoes had to be cut off because they were frozen to her feet. Her grandmother worked all night to get the blood circulation back to her lower legs and feet. Ann was terrified, numb and totally shut down emotionally. Throughout the long night, she just laid on her grandmother's bed, staring at the ceiling.

The next morning, neither of her parents showed the slightest concern about her condition. Ann's grandmother made her stay home from school but Ann insisted on going to work so that she wouldn't lose her job. When she got to work, her feet securely wrapped, her boss took her aside and told her that the young man had told him that she was a slut and that he had slept with her many times. Her boss fired her, saying, "I don't allow sluts to work for me."

Ann was devastated and terrified. She sat on the bench for hours staring into space. She felt hopeless and helpless. She told herself repeatedly that she was "bad," just like her parents had always said. What had happened was finally proof that she was "no good" and would never amount to anything. She found a job the next day at a discount store and never told her parents what happened.

This incident was a turning point in Ann's young life. She concluded that she was such a bad person that it was useless to keep trying to be good. She would never make her parents happy—who cares, why try? She believed that she was so bad that even God no longer loved her. She began to hang out with older kids that were bullies. She was angry and told herself that no one would ever terrorize, threaten or hurt her again. She became sarcastic, loud and defiant. She got into fights with other girls and developed the reputation of being a "tough girl." She began arguing with her parents and fighting back. She hung with a small gang of kids that drank, although she never drank.

Ann didn't tell anyone about the rape for many years. She continued to be "tough" and began to believe that no one could ever hurt her again. Yet, when she was alone, she would cry so hard that she would lose her breath and she suffered from frequent panic attacks.

The only person that Ann really believe cared about her was her grandmother. When she would come to visit, she would never leave her side. She cherished the time with her grandmother and when she would leave, she would sob and cry. She was so tired of being tough that she would make attempts at being the "good girl" again but as soon as she felt the least bit threatened, the "tough shield would immediately come down. She was tough on the out-side and terrified on the inside.

Ann lived behind her mask of toughness for years, hurting and bullying others, until she finally reached a breaking point in her late twenties. Her panic attacks steadily worsened and she was exhausted. She fluctuated between attempts at being the "good girl" and the "tough bully." She became suicidal, finally ending up in a psychiatric hospital, where she began treatment. Ann was fortunate that her psychiatrist was one of few professionals who understood her panic as well as the underlying dynamics of her bullying behavior. The doctor was compassionate, proactive and not afraid of her anger. He became the "honest mirror" she needed to reflect back to her the worthwhile, compassionate survivor she was.

Often, when witnessing the "tough" behavior of children and youths like Ann, many see them as "bad" children rather than victims of mental, emotional and sometimes physical abuse. They have become bullies as a protection against the pain of developmental trauma. They are hurt and angry, and they frequently bully the same way they have been bullied, or they have been "bigger" than their parents, never having learned the lessons of emotional regulation or the internalization of caring yet firm limits.

It takes eight years of life to develop psychological birth. Children are not born with empathy, the ability to regulate emotions, or caring and firm internal limits on their behavior. They learn these lessons through mirroring and internalizing the emotions and behaviors of their adult caregivers. The actual physical structure of the baby's brain as well as her neurochemistry are reflective of this mutual interaction—the caregiver's response to the infant's emotions, needs and behaviors.

I had the following experience one time when I was at my son's house for dinner. His children, Logan and Canaan, had been too excited with the coming of spring, playing outdoors and having Granny home from a recent trip to take their usual naps. Needless to say, by late afternoon they were a bit cranky. At one point ten-month-old Canaan crawled over and began to play with one of Logan's favorite toys. Logan, usually even-tempered but nonetheless two, began pulling the toy from Canaan's grasp. The struggle was on, Logan screaming, Canaan screaming. Finally Logan, in full temper and frustration, hit Canaan. His father appeared, "Logan, I know Canaan is playing with your toy but it is not okay to hit him. Look, he's crying. You hurt him." He picked still-screaming Logan up and held him firmly in his lap, gently yet firmly repeating his words, "I know you're frustrated but it's not okay to hit Canaan. I'm going to hold you until you calm down." Logan screamed and struggled, while his Poppa held him tight. Very soon, Logan fell asleep, his father lovingly rubbing his back.

Later, at the dinner table, Canaan experienced what my daughter-in-law lovingly calls a "meltdown." He was so tired from not getting his usual nap that he was hypersensitive to everything around him and inside him. Peanut and Olaf, the much-loved family dogs, had been sitting next to Canaan's high chair and Logan's chair hoping that a morsel would be dropped, when they heard a noise outside and began to bark furiously. Canaan, half asleep and suddenly startled by the loud ruckus they were creating, sat bolt upright and began to cry. My daughter-in-law, concerned about the sudden fear in her ten-month-old, responded immediately, loosening the belt on his high chair and hoisting him into her arms. "Poor little guy, you've really had it, haven't you?" she said, holding him tightly and carrying him over to the couch. She positioned him in her lap and began to nurse him, gently stroking his small head, "Poor little one. It's okay. It's okay." Soon, Canaan was fast asleep, his mother still gently stroking his head.

At the sound of his brother's crying, Logan, in much better spirits after his brief nap, said to me, "Grammy, Cannon cry. Scared of
doggies." He jumped down from his chair and ran over to where
his mother was comforting Canaan. "Poor Canaan," Logan said. He
gently began rubbing Canaan's back as his Poppa had his back only
two hours earlier.

Attachment: The Development of Trust, Self-Worth and Empathy

Early adult caretakers have an enormous influence on their children. The interaction between the child and his or her primary caretaker is the greatest protection against later aggressive behavior. This
relationship is the foundation for the development of attachment and
empathy, regulating and balancing emotions, and the ability to learn.
The reciprocal relationship between a primary caregiver and a child
serves as a foundation upon which all other relationships are built.
Mutual interactions between infants and their primary caregivers create psychological and physiological states in children that are similar
to those primarily responsible for their care.

Healthy attachment to a parent allows children to take from the
outside and bring to the inside a feeling of self-worth, the ability to
self-soothe in emotionally difficult situations and the internalization of
healthy limits that keep aggressive impulses in check. Trust built from
the consistency, unconditional love and security of adult caretakers
becomes the secure base upon which trust in self and others is built.

Through healthy attachment to adult caretakers, children develop
empathy (i.e., the ability to feel what others might feel in a similar
situation). The seeds of caring, concern and attachment that later bud
and flower into a child's ability to empathize with the feelings of others
are sown in the very first months of life. The foundation of empathy
begins when the primary caretaker of the child accurately assesses

her/his child's needs and immediately and consistently responds to them with empathy. The infant's joy or pain is mirrored in the parent's face. In a few months, the infant becomes the toddler that begins to show the nature of the connection that has been shared with the primary caregiver. As stated so well by Robin Karr-Morse and Meredith S. Wiley in *Ghosts from the Nursery,* "This emotional attunement is the cradle of human connection. Tiny interactions between each infant and his mother create threads of empathy that together form the warp and woof of the tapestry we call community, a tapestry that is weakened by each thread that is frayed or broken" (Karr-Morse and Wiley, 1997, p. 189).

Selma Fraiberg (1959) presents the case of a little girl, age three, who enjoys the pleasure of squashing caterpillars on the sidewalk and gleefully examining the remains. That same child at age six becomes upset and sad at the thought of a dead insect, bird or animal. What happened inside the little girl was not the automatic miracle of development, but rather the careful and patient teaching of parents that has now been internalized by the child as empathy, compassion and a developing conscience. If that same child, however, at the age of six showed an extreme response, losing herself when animal or human was hurt or sad, or still enjoyed smashing caterpillars or intentionally hurting animals, we would have cause to be concerned about the adequate progression of developmental learning in the child's life (Middelton-Moz, 1989).

Regulation of Emotions

The ability to soothe self in emotionally difficult situations is learned early from the comforting words and behaviors of early caretakers. Infants in the first few months of life learn to internalize the consistency, care and love of early caretakers in order to develop self-confidence and security in brief times alone. This learned ability to trust in parent, then self, becomes the first step in developing a boundary between "not me" and "me." The gentle soothing of caregivers becomes the self-soothing in times alone. Children take from the outside and bring to the inside the security that someone is always there, first outside and then inside.

A child learns to regulate emotions through their caregiver's responses to his behavior in the earliest weeks of life. "The baby left to cry for long intervals or the baby whose cry is greeted with a slap is undergoing a very different experience emotionally and neurologically than the child whose cries result in immediate soothing. A caregiver's predictable responses to the baby's distress signals and her sensitive pacing of activities to engage her/his infant when the baby is alert are not only patterning the emotional behavior we can observe, but also are actually building connections and modulating neurochemicals in the baby's brain. This becomes the biological foundation for the child's later efforts to maintain emotional balance" (Karr-Morse and Wiley, 1997, p. 200).

As children grow and mature into adolescents, then adults, they will be exposed to situations that will generate strong emotions of fear, frustration, jealousy and anger. The physiological and emotional patterning that occurred in their first relationships will be the foundation for regulating strong emotions later in life. Returning to the example given of my son and daughter-in-law with two cranky children when Logan was overtired, frustrated, then enraged, he was firmly held by a loving father until he could calm down. When Canaan was overtired, frustrated and afraid, he was held, comforted and soothed by a loving mother until he calmed down.

This process, which will be repeated frequently with Canaan and Logan during their earliest developmental years, will create the physiological and emotional road map inside them that will guide their ability to calm themselves when strong emotions such as anger, frustration, jealousy, or fear are generated in them throughout their lives. They will literally carry their parents' firm and loving presence, emotional strength, guidance, and limits within them.

Frustration, rage, and fear can overwhelm a child, adolescent or adult who has not learned the skills of emotional regulation. Self-destructive behavior, freezing, or aggressive behavior are the result of a child's effort to handle emotions without a healthy internalized experiential map that was lovingly created in the first years of life.

Learning Right from Wrong: The Development of Conscience

Children are not born with a conscience (that voice inside that tells us right from wrong). They take from the outside and bring to the inside, i.e., internalize, the kind and consistent limits on their behavior set by adult caretakers. The healthy and secure caretaker patiently and lovingly limits the child's aggressive behavior by teaching the impact of his behavior on others, "Logan, I understand your frustration, but I won't allow you to hit your brother. It hurts him." These firm yet loving limits soon become the compassionate and firm conscience the child will carry into adulthood.

Conscience and empathy do not grow automatically as our bodies do. They are internalized through the lessons taught by the adults involved in the child's early care. The caregiver that tells the child that he cannot have a toy at the grocery store, then gives in after the child screams, wails and strikes out, giving the child the toy while, at the same time, berating her or him for being a "selfish brat," "bad," or "nothing but trouble," teaches the child lessons that the caregiver never intended. The lessons are that the child's drives are stronger than his caregiver's limits, that fighting and demanding pave the way to getting what is wanted, or that love and acceptance is the price one pays in order to gain power and control.

The development of an internal sense of right and wrong, conscience and empathy for others, starts in the first months of life and continues throughout adolescence. It is one of the most difficult stages for parents and other caretakers who have unresolved traumas in their own development and need the child to be a parent, to meet their expectations, or to project on the child an unwanted part of him/herself (Middelton-Moz, 1989).

Children need to learn that they can be angry, have personal power, needs and independent desires, without being injured or abandoned and without injuring or controlling others. If their adult caretakers allow for the child's emotions and separate desires, while lovingly guiding their expressions with limits, the child as an adult will have a loving, yet firm conscience. They also need to be able to repair conflicts with their caretakers in order to have the ability to be empathetic and resolve conflicts with others.

Many children like Nancy and Ann learn that to survive they have to repress their feelings of anger and emotional needs. They learn that feelings are too powerful and can injure those around them, and that expression of normal feeling leads to abuse and/or abandonment. Some children learn to repress feelings and needs and frequently experience periods of depression ("acting in") or begin bullying others, constantly needing to protect the vulnerability they feel. In order to survive, many others learn to project their feelings of helplessness and powerlessness onto those around them ("acting out").

Children in neglectful or permissive families—where children are left to raise themselves, are raised by other children or who experience few consequences for their behavior—may have to prematurely develop extreme internal limits or constantly need limits from the outside because they don't have them on the inside. These children, then adults, continually blame others for their behavior and use the external world as their conscience. According to Patterson (1986), ineffective, coercive parental discipline that does not appropriately manage children's aggressive behavior inadvertently contributes to the increase in those behaviors.

Most of us know children, youths or adults who appear to have little sense of right or wrong, or who seem to have little empathy for others in their lives—bullies. We also know individuals who seem to have a rigid, non-empathic internal policeman who holds them responsible for everything, including the actions of others around them—perpetual victims. There are some who repeatedly blame their behavior on others and those who believe others are always "out to get them." There are also individuals who know right from wrong, take responsibility for their choices and feel empathy for others without taking responsibility for the moods and behaviors of others. All of these individuals learned lessons regarding limits, responsibility, and care for self and others early in their development.

The controls and limits given to children by their caretakers during early stages of development will later become the consciences they will have as youth and adults. It is an exchange of teaching and learning. The firm, patient, loving, kind voice of an adult caretaker will be mirrored in the internalized, kind, and firm limits the child will place on herself or himself throughout life. These children will then teach their own children or the children entrusted in their care the same kind limits.

Most individuals are aware of the price of abusive parenting as exemplified in Nancy's and Ann's stories. Many, however, are unaware of the effect of inconsistent and permissive parenting. When we asked children to write letters for *Welcoming Our Children to a New Millennium* (Middelton-Moz, 1999), one of the questions we asked was, "What do you want from adults in the new millennium?" Sadly, we expected some of the answers that we received, "I want someone to say hello to me when I get home from school." But some of the answers that we didn't expect from a large number of children and youth were, "I want the adults in my life to be bigger than I am," or "I want a parent, not a buddy," or "I want people to start being held more accountable for their behavior, adults and children."

Children who are "bigger" than the adults in their lives are insecure and fearful. When children push against limits, they're just doing their developmental job. The job of the caretaker is to kindly and firmly hold to the limit so that the child can take from the outside and bring to the inside the internal limits necessary for emotional growth. When a caregiver consistently withdraws the limit or doesn't follow through, the child loses. The child will continue to "up the ante" with the caregiver, as well as other adults in his life, attempting to get the limits he so desperately needs.

One of the things that we have consistently heard from the people we have treated throughout the years, some who have been willing to share their stories in this book as their way to help others, is that the breakthrough in their treatment occurred when they were confronted with and held accountable for their behavior. Compassionate and firm limits and an "honest mirror" allowed them to feel safe enough to work through their pain and move on to happy and healthier lives.

Larry's Story

Larry came from a typical, middle-class family. He was the youngest son. He described his family members as "responsible, hard-working, honest, loving and supportive of each other." He described himself as "wild, always in fights, stealing, drinking and uncontrollable."

Larry said that he separated himself from his family at an early age. He shared that he had no adult role models, he did nothing that was expected of him and he made his own rules. He said that he displeased his parents and other family members. "I was a total nut. If I wasn't in street fights, I was in jail doing a couple of days here and there; nine out of ten times my family found out from the neighbors. I was just totally out of control and nobody wanted to be around me because 'trouble' was my middle name."

Larry said that he wanted to be left alone and be on his own. He said he couldn't care less if anyone wanted to help him out. He was causing pain to his family and didn't want anything to do with them. He said his behaviors were so wild that there was no punishment. *"Just trying to think up a punishment for me was unreal. They really didn't know what to do with me so I was basically allowed to do whatever I wanted. They tried, but nothing worked.*

"I had a great time in school but I was also the class troublemaker. When I got into too much trouble, everybody in the class paid, even though the teachers knew that I did it. I fought a lot with other kids. I took their jackets, their lunches, anything to intimidate them. Some of my teachers tried to help but I rejected and resented their attempts. In the fifth grade I began to bring booze to school with me in little bottles. They moved my desk out into the hallway to punish me. I spent a good part of the fifth, sixth, seventh and eighth grades in the hall.

"I remember once that I was a victim of others' bullying behavior. I stole a kid's bike. Two days later a friend and I were in a different part of the neighborhood when around the corner come about ten guys. They caught me and just about killed me for taking that bike. I could hardly walk. I had black and blue bruises all over, black eyes, the works.

"I would do things at school to get laughs at the expense of others. I abused the teachers unbelievably. Sometimes the whole class had to stay after school because of my behavior. I was not liked by many kids, just those hanging around me. In my peer group I was known as 'wild man.' People in my peer group had much more

stability than I did but I could not have cared less. They had their sights on the future and I couldn't have cared less about tomorrow until it came. I had no goals and didn't care about school.

"I hung out with a little group of guys, but that broke up, so I started hanging out with older people who were all heavy drug users. This was the beginning of even more major bullying behavior: armed robbery; attacking people from behind; picking out victims, knowing by their looks how they would handle themselves. The one rule in the group was 'don't rat on your friends.'

"The one saving grace in my life was that I was a hard worker. It helped me to stay in denial of all my problems. My defenses were that I had a job and was making good money.

"I started using alcohol at the age of ten and was drinking steadily by age thirteen. Even though there is no history of addiction in my family, I believed that I was born an addict. I was in detox centers many times. I was so out of it that I didn't know if I would make it or not. I would get released and hit the first deli for a beer. I have been in three rehabilitation centers. The first two were a thirty-day vacation: very little confrontation; no one holding me responsible for my behaviors, feelings and beliefs; and no one teaching me the choices that I needed to make in order to change my life.

"The third center did confront me. They held me responsible for myself, showed me the consequences of my behavior and taught me what I needed to do differently in my life in order to be an honest, responsible and kind person. I needed a lot of help from a lot of people to get well. It took time to change from what I was into a healthy person."

Thinking about his young life in retrospect, Larry said with some sadness, "What I see now that was strange was that nobody confronted me to the point of scaring me. I wish someone had. I lost a lot of my life doing harmful things to others and to myself."

Larry, like so many children who were "bigger" than the adults around them when they were really small, became more and more aggressive as he fought harder and harder for limits. He was a little boy without effective role models who could guide him, direct him and help him to pass through the developmental mileposts. He did not have the verbal or physical abuse in his home that Nancy and Ann experienced, yet he, too, was a victim of adults who abdicated their roles.

"Firm but fair parenting behavior is frequently associated with the development of mature prosocial behavior and successful moral reasoning. Of importance to bullying, however, is the fact that those parents who provide insufficient or imbalanced responsiveness and control, those who are authoritarian, permissive, or uninvolved, are likely to have children who are aggressive and socially incompetent (Lamborn et al., 1991), particularly when stresses are present" (Randall, 1997, p. 82).

Impossibly High Expectations

In her book, *The Drama of the Gifted Child*, Alice Miller wrote, "The bigger the hole in my mother's heart, the bigger the jewels in her crown have to be" (Miller, 1981, p. 7). Many adults, because of early injury to their self-esteem, hold their children hostage to impossibly high expectations and their own unmet needs. They need their children or the children entrusted to their care to be proof of their own self-worth. They need them to be "the best athlete," "the perfect student," "the beauty queen," "the perfect boy or girl," "the smartest," "the toughest," in order to bolster their own self-worth.

Many of us have witnessed the unreasonably high expectations of injured and insecure parents in the sports arena. Children are bullied by their families while they are at practice or playing a game. Parents and other family members will yell at their children from the bleachers or from behind the fence. If their child misses a ball, family members might call the child "stupid," "lazy," "good for nothing," "sissy," etc. When my oldest son was six and playing in Little League for the first time, a mother left the stands and slapped her child in the face for missing the ball when he was up at bat.

Children cannot live up to impossible expectations set for them, they can never repair the wound in their caregiver's heart or self-worth, yet they judge themselves relentlessly against the backdrop of those expectations.

Dan's Story

"I was my mother's son, her special child, the son she always wanted. I was expected to be what she needed me to be in order to be her son. She and I were very close. She doted on me and I loved it. She resented authority and I learned to. Eventually, I resented her telling me what to do.

"I never developed much of a relationship with my father. He was distant. My parents' relationship was loving, yet strained. They didn't share a bed and slept in separate rooms for years. I was told that they were separated before I was born. Their families pressured them to get back together for the sake of my sister and me.

"I excelled in elementary school and was one of the brightest students in my class. I had friends and participated in music and sports.

"In high school, I found myself challenged academically. I wasn't one of the top students anymore. I no longer felt special and began to feel ill at ease with students who seemed more self-confident than me. I felt like an outsider. I had good times, but there was always an undercurrent of insecurities that seemed to absorb me as time went on.

"In my senior year, my insecurities and emotional problems increased. I would spend what seemed like hours hashing over things in my mind that I should have said in conversations with others, especially girls. Some mornings I worked myself up into such an emotional state that I would become sick and miss the beginning of school. I felt excluded and only supported by a few teachers. I felt self-conscious and increasingly inadequate and excluded by my friends.

"I realize that my bullying behavior began when I was about twelve years old. I was verbally abusive. I started out bullying my mother when she would criticize me for not doing what she wanted me to do. I would get into a war of words with her about who had said what. I badgered her about what she had said or not said. I made her communication the cause of my actions or inactions. I verbally bullied anyone that disagreed with me, wouldn't do something exactly the way I wanted it done, said something that I felt was an attack on the self-image I needed to protect, and/or was someone that I could intimidate and get away with it.

"In later years, if one of my coworkers would dare to question the validity of what I said, I'd belittle their comments and provide evidence of why I was right and their comments were without merit. I would try to 'win' a discussion with my wife by questioning her about what she said, using her responses as a means to negate the validity of her thoughts and feelings.

"I would feel threatened by people and would bully them to prove them wrong and me right. I would feel highly energized and hyper when I was bullying others. After each bullying incident, I would feel powerful but also empty. I sensed that I didn't really want to 'win.' I didn't feel empathy for the person that I felt threatened by or empathy for the feelings they experienced when I bullied them. At the time in my life when I bullied and

intimidated others I had feelings that were mixed: I felt fearful, empowered, anxious, entitled, resentful, threatened, righteous, guilty and inadequate.

"If others attempted to bully me, there were no winners, just those who were willing to continue the fight indefinitely. I bullied anyone who personally attacked me. I always felt justified. If anyone used silence, it would make me even angrier and more strident. I wish someone had effectively confronted me. I wish that I knew then what I know now about my behavior, beliefs and feelings. I bullied to create a distraction, to avoid having to accept my own imperfections and hide from my own insecurities.

"Finally, everything caught up with me. My mother died, I was almost fired from work, I was depressed, I had an eating disorder, my personal hygiene declined, I procrastinated at my job and I wasn't getting my assignments completed on time. I went to see a psychiatrist for six months but reacted poorly.

"Then, I went to treatment where I was confronted and my layers of denial and delusions were peeled away. I learned to identify and discharge my feelings. I learned that I ate to bury my feelings and used my work to attempt to gain self-esteem. When I couldn't use work to feed my self-esteem to distract me, I ate more. I developed an awareness of what I needed to change. I was confronted for trying to tell people what to do and how to do it. I was confronted for picking on someone or being disrespectful to others. I would have my mind racing on what I was going to say next, rather than listening to the person talking to me. I was taught that I had new choices and that I could change and be a healthy person. I have worked hard and asked for help from many sources. I feel better about myself and no longer bully others or myself. Each day is an adventure."

Dan, like Nancy, Ann, and Larry, was offered an honest mirror in treatment. He learned to appreciate the person he was and that he could never have lived up to the projection of perfection his injured mother needed him to be.

Like many children faced with impossible adult expectations, Dan felt that the child he was had been rejected in favor of the child he was "supposed to be" and whose image he could never live up to. He saw himself as unworthy and his world as an untrustworthy and hostile place. The more insecure he became and the more he loathed himself, the more he misread, as all bullies do, the intentions and social cues of others. His internalized sense of unworthiness and lack of trust for a punitive and hostile world contributed to his lack of empathy for others and his bullying behavior.

"Using questionnaires designed to diagnose depression and assess the risk of suicide, Dr. Kaltiala-Heino found that depression was roughly as common among bullies as it was among victims. And severe suicidal thoughts—known to be common among children who are victimized—were even more prevalent in bullies" (Gilbert, 1999).

Values That Contribute to Bullying Behavior

"In Mary Romeo's high school health class, the subject is 'fun things kids can do during their weekends.' Romeo mentions movies, music, theaters, trips to New York. One jock holds up a hand to interrupt her, 'Miss Romeo,' he says, 'we might as well end this discussion because over the weekend we get drunk, we have as much sex as we can have, and on Monday we come back to school. That's what we do'" (Lefkowitz, 1997, p. 138).

Many adults ask, "What has happened to our children's values?" The answer we have heard from many youths is, "If you want something different, model something different. We learn from you."

One wise adolescent girl told us, "Adults are always worrying about the values of young people today. If they are really worried about our values, maybe they should try putting elders in our living rooms instead of TV sets. We are learning the values we're being taught. Our elders today are television sets. One of the biggest problems facing youth today is abandonment. Nobody's there."

We recently saw a bumper sticker that relates well to this youth's concern: "Television: Thief of Time, Thief of Mind." Many studies have indicated that television violence contributes to youth violence, particularly if the youth liked the violence they were viewing (Pearl, Bouthilet and Lazar, 1982; Walker and Morley, 1991; Grossman, 1995).

"In effect a child begins to 'store' the idea of particularly aggressive actions alongside memories of familiar situations that are frustrating. Psychologists call stored patterns 'algorithms.' . . . The algorithms for aggression in young children are formed because of the repeated exposure they get to powerful role models who show them how to change things their way through the use of violence" (Randall, 1997, p. 20).

Yet the problem of aggression in children can't be linked solely to television, video games, or violent lyrics in music. The problem exists when television is the most compelling role model in the child's life and/or the actions of caregivers in the child's life support aggressive behavior and intolerance.

Children who lack consistent models at home frequently search for them in their extended families or in the broader community: a teacher, policeman, spiritual leader. Many of the bullies we have treated lacked these important mentors. They will find them instead in rock stars, gang leaders, cult leaders or Hollywood antiheroes. The unhealthy role models have increasing influence on the lives of our young people.

Many children today come home to an empty house and spend many hours alone in front of a TV set waiting for an adult caretaker to arrive on the scene. Often the first greeting they receive is criticism for not doing their chores or homework. They are told to be accountable for their behavior, yet may spend hours listening to their adult caretakers blame each other for what is or isn't done or maybe for their children's behavior. They teach the importance of community, equality and tolerance, but can be overheard gossiping about a neighbor or talking about "bitches" or "queers." They may be taught the importance of family, yet their family may not eat one meal together all week.

Rather than learning values that support connectedness, interconnectedness and conflict resolution, many children learn values that support aggression, disrespect and "everyone for themselves." The long road to psychological birth takes eight years. Children take from the outside and bring to the inside teachings about self, people and life. Many wise elders have said, "Before you take an action in your life, turn around. When you take the time to look before you act, you will see the children following you."

The way a child learns to respect is to be respected and to watch adult caretakers treat themselves, others and all of creation with respect. I talked to a parent in a grocery store recently who had just hit her child for hitting his brother. This child is not learning to use words and not strike out, but learns instead that you can hit if you're bigger (Middelton-Moz, 1999).

We have heard adult caregivers cautioning their children, "You can't let yourself be stepped on. You've got to fight back. Look out for number one. No one else will." Many parents discipline their children for fighting with siblings, lecture them against hitting, yet encourage them to hit a classmate that has bullied them. Another parent might tell a child to care for others and share, and yet cut in front of everyone in the grocery line. The message that is taught is the one that is seen, the example that is set, not the one that is heard.

Many caregivers teach their children the benefits of communication and to resolve conflicts in a healthy way, while engaging in "cold wars" or verbal assaults with their partners. Again, that which is modeled is learned. Children pay attention to actions far more than words.

Children learn how to express anger and resolve conflicts from observing the expressions of anger seen every day in their homes, neighborhoods, schools or on the playground. They learn from political campaigns, television, video arcades, magazines, and books how to express their feelings.

Many youths have told us that the values they are learning in their families and communities are often ones that lead to competition and aggression rather than connection and cooperation. The following are some convictions that can lead to competition, bullying and aggression, rather than connection and cooperation. Check your own way of life against this list and consider the actions of society at large:

1. I need it right now. Gratification has to happen immediately.
2. Might is right.
3. Don't get involved.
4. It's important to beat out the other guy before he gets ahead of you.
5. Get ahead any way you can.
6. Women are objects.
7. Men don't feel.
8. My beliefs are right and yours are wrong.
9. Aggression is the appropriate way to handle disagreement.
10. Money and objects are more important than relationships.
11. Good guys finish last.
12. You're not accountable unless you get caught.

13. Money is power. You can get anything you want or solve any problem with enough money.
14. Talk about people, not to people.
15. Blame others for your problems.
16. I can only be heard if I talk louder, or show you who's boss.
17. Childhood is overrated. Grow up fast so that I can get on with my life.
18. Look out for number one.
19. Those are your kids, not my kids.
20. Your problems are none of my concern.

4

A Message to Parents, Extended Family, and Concerned Adult Community Members

"The mother gazes at the baby in her arms, and the
baby gazes at his mother's face and finds himself therein . . .
provided that the mother is really looking at the unique,
small, helpless being and not projecting her own expectations,
fears, and plans for the child. In that case, the child would
find not himself in his mother's face, but rather the
mother's own projections. This child would remain
without a mirror, and for the rest of his life
would be seeking this mirror in vain."

Donald Woods Winnicott

A Model of Healthy Parenting
and Forgiveness

Seventeen-year-old Taylor, covered with sweat, kept punching and punching. "I hate you! I hate you!" She said again and again at the picture of her once best friend smiling back at her. A few days earlier, in hurt and anger, she had taped a picture of Sherri on her punching bag in her basement workout room. She hit and kicked the bag, again and again, day after day. Tonight again she had been punching and kicking the bag for what seemed like hours. "How could you have done this to me? You were supposed to be my best friend," she yelled, pummeling the bag and then leveling a high kick at it for good measure. Exhausted and sobbing, she collapsed on a chair. A few hours before, she thought she had gotten out all the anger. She and a couple of her friends had gone to Sherri's house. With a piece of brightly colored chalk she had written a note for Sherri in big bold letters in her driveway. "SHERRI, YOU ARE A SLUT, A WHORE. I HATE YOU!"

Upstairs, Taylor's mother, Rebecca, was going through her own emotional turmoil. When Taylor was a small child, Rebecca had spoken to all of Taylor's friends' parents. "I want you to know that Alan and I need all of your help. I want you to promise us that if you are ever aware that Taylor is doing anything that concerns you, anything that could be hurtful to her or if she is doing anything to hurt anybody else, please call us. Please let us know. We all have to promise to look out for each other's children. As parents we need each other's eyes and ears to keep our children safe."

Tonight, one of those parents had called her. Ann, Sherri's mother, said, "Remember when Taylor was a little girl and you told me that if she was ever doing anything that concerned me, you wanted me to call you? Well, I'm calling now. "

Ann had told Rebecca that she and her husband, Mitch, were very concerned. "Sherri has seemed depressed for days. First she wouldn't talk to us. She told us nothing was wrong, but she would isolate herself in her room when she came home from school. Then, she didn't want to go to school at all. She said she was sick. When Mitch and I came home from visiting a friend tonight we found a message left in our driveway. The message was for Sherri. It said she was a 'slut and a whore.' It said 'I hate you Sherri.' After a lot of encouragement, Sherri told us that Taylor had been ignoring her at school for days, and had gotten the other girls in school to ignore her, too. She wouldn't tell us why. I think Taylor is bullying her. It's not like Taylor. We are concerned about both girls."

Rebecca knew that Taylor had been out of sorts for days as well. She, too, had said nothing was wrong. Rebecca knew she had been spending a lot of time in the workout room in the basement. Rebecca assumed it was because she and her husband, Alan, had separated six months before and that Taylor was still having difficult time. She also thought that maybe Taylor and Troy, her boyfriend of a couple of years, could be having difficulties because she hadn't seen much of Troy for a few weeks. She had asked Taylor about him but she just kept saying, "Nothing's wrong, I just haven't been feeling well."

Ann and Rebecca agreed that it was important for everyone, the girls and both sets of parents, to come together in the next day or so to talk things out. Ann said that she would be there and so would Mitch and Sherri; just call and give them a time. Then, Rebecca called Alan to share Ann's concerns. Alan came right over. They talked for an hour or so, sorting out their feelings about what had taken place, before talking to Taylor.

When they went down to the basement, they found Taylor still crying in the chair by the punching bag. They saw Sherri's picture taped to the bag. They each hugged Taylor and asked her to join them upstairs because they wanted to talk with her. Once upstairs, they told Taylor about the phone call they had received from Ann and mentioned how concerned they were about both girls. They asked Taylor if she had written the message in the driveway. After a long silence, she nodded. They explained how depressed Sherri was feeling, and that she didn't want to go to school. They asked her if she had gotten the other girls to ignore Sherri at school.

"I didn't ask anyone to ignore her," she cried. "I just told them what she had done and they were angry at her, too."

"What had she done?" Rebecca asked softly.

Taylor remained silent.

Alan tried, "Your mom and I love you very much. We are worried about you. Writing a message like that was mean and hurtful. It's not like you. You are a loving person and have always been a kind and supportive friend."

Taylor erupted, "Well, maybe if Sherri had been a kind and supportive friend I wouldn't have written a message like that!" She began to cry.

She told them that she and Troy had a fight. "We just hadn't talked for a few weeks. We were letting things calm down. Then all of a sudden I find out that he was with Sherri after the last game. I can't believe Sherri would do that to me! I thought she was my friend."

Rebecca and Alan spent many hours that night listening to and comforting their daughter. They let her know that they heard her and understood her feelings, but they couldn't support her actions. They told her that they had arranged a time for Taylor and Sherri to meet with both sets of parents to talk things out. Taylor was enraged, and said emphatically, "You can't do that to me. I am your daughter and you are supposed to support me! I'll apologize to Sherri for the message and tell the girls to stop ignoring her but I'm not talking to her!"

"We are supporting *you*," Rebecca said softly, "We are not supporting your actions and it is your responsibility to speak with her and her parents. We will be there to support you and Sherri, so will Ann and Mitch. I also want you to take Sherri's picture off the punching bag. Your hurt and anger are justified, but not your actions."

Taylor ran out of the room and went to her bedroom and slammed the door. She did not speak to her parents the next day. She was furious!

They all met two days later. All parents offered their concern for both girls and helped each of them to express their feelings and tell their stories. Sherri explained that Troy had told her that he and Taylor had ended their relationship. They had met after the game and one thing led to another. She apologized to Taylor, let her know that she wasn't seeing Troy anymore, and that she had not meant to hurt her. Taylor apologized for her actions. Taylor and Sherri had cleared the air and the bullying stopped, but they did not part friends. Taylor stayed angry with her parents for many weeks to come.

Taylor and Sherri, both longtime athletes, were on the same soccer team. Several months after the difficult meeting in her living room, Taylor felt the pain of the loss of their friendship and that the distance that had grown between them had gone on long enough. She asked Sherri to meet her after a practice. They went out for a hamburger and finished talking things out. They grew to be best friends again.

Two years after the bullying incident, Mitch ran into Rebecca in the grocery store. "You have quite an amazing daughter," he said smiling. "She came to our house last week and said she wanted to apologize to Ann and I for her actions and to thank us for our phone call and our support. You can be very proud of her. You have raised a loving and compassionate human being."

The girls grew up, graduated, and eventually started their own families. Troy and Taylor worked on their relationship, are happily married today, and are the parents of a toddler. Taylor is grateful to her parents for their modeling. As a new mother, thanks to them, she is glad she will know what to do if her child bullies another child or is a target of bullying.

Parenting: The Most Rewarding and Difficult Job We Will Ever Do

There is no such thing as a "perfect" parent. Parenting can be both challenging and rewarding. It has become more difficult in days of swiftly advancing technology. In seconds, the message Taylor wrote on a driveway can be sent into cyberspace for hundreds to see. The painful incident that occurred between Taylor and Sherri happens in countless ways in every neighborhood and school. Unfortunately, the outcome is often tragic. For many youths, like Sherri, the bullying escalates and continues.

Youth across the globe feel isolated, ashamed and alone. Far too many youth who are targets of bullying commit suicide every year. Far too many that bully don't get the help and support they need to change. Parents, who have not done their own emotional work, too frequently take sides with their children, become defensive, and block any chance of intervention. Sometimes parents join their children by bullying, retaliating, or succumbing to feelings of powerlessness because they can't protect those they love. Instead, there are things we can all learn from Ann and Mitch and Rebecca and Alan.

1. **It *Does* Take a Village to Raise a Child:** Rebecca and Mitch realized early that they needed support and help raising their children. Both, like most parents today, lived away from family support systems. Grandparents, uncles, and aunts were spread out across the country and weren't available next door or down the street to be another pair of hands, eyes, or ears. To remedy this, the couple worked to create a community of caring adults to be the support system needed, while volunteering to do the same for other parents.

There was a time, in the not so distant past, that if a child hurt or was hurting another in one part of town, the parents knew about it before the child got home. The concept of a village raising a child has changed dramatically in the last forty years. Families, for the most part, are more isolated, more focused on "my children" and "your children." Feedback regarding children, once solicited, is far more often met with defensiveness, retaliation or "mind your own business." Rebecca and Alan were able to support their daughter because Ann and Mitch communicated their concerns. Ann and Mitch did so because they were invited to be part of a community that could surround and protect the children.

Our children need to be surrounded by all the healthy role models that we can offer them, in childhood and in teen years, "As we increase distrust of others by keeping children inside, by not allowing them to play spontaneously in their neighborhoods with their friends, by rigidly structuring their lives, we are also destroying the community bonds that keep us all healthy" (Perry, 2006, p. 235).

2. **Working Together on Behalf of Our Children:** Too often, when parents divorce, or partners separate, children become hostages in a cold, or sometimes hostile war. Children the need the support of both parents. About one out of every two marriages ends in divorce (PEW, 2010). This number does not reflect the growing trend of adults who have made the choice to raise children without marrying. Most divorces and separations occur in the first seven years of marriage (Shino et. Al. 1994). This means that a high percentage of youth are in need of parents who can work out their differences enough to jointly and consistently parent their children. In cases where a child has been abused by a parent and the abusive parent refuses treatment, this is not possible. In most cases, it is the passive aggressive, or righteous war, where there are continual battles over who is "right," sometimes tense silence for days, or a war, where one or both partners seek

revenge, that leads to inconsistency in parenting. In these wars, it is the child's learning and development that is taken hostage.

When there is inconsistency, our children fall through the cracks. This is particularly true in the case of bullying, where targets are afraid to tell, and bullies fear exposure, depending on the silence and isolation of their targets. As stated in earlier chapters, we have learned that bullies frequently come from environments where consequences for behavior were never given, or where discipline was harsh and inconsistent; where aggressions and power, rather than empathy and compassion, were allowed and even rewarded, and the reactions of others were not determined by one's own actions. Therefore, skills in healthy interaction, self-regulation, and self-control were not internalized.

In Taylor's case, she began a bullying cycle that was interrupted because two sets of concerned parents intervened before it escalated. Because of that very important life lesson gleaned through parental support, intervention, and modeling, she learned: 1) Sad, hurt, and angry feelings can be absolutely justified while acts of bullying are not; 2) Living in anger doesn't protect one's heart and doesn't make an individual feel as powerful as using her/his voice and, in time, choosing to work toward forgiveness; 3) There is a tremendous feeling of empowerment when one can sort out feelings, make healthier choices, and find one's voice; 4) Friends can make mistakes and relationships can be repaired; 5) Even when there has been conflict, hurtful actions, and betrayal between partners, trust can be rebuilt if both parties are willing to be the architects and the carpenters; 6) Valuable lessons about bullying can be stored and used later in parenting the next generation.

3. **Working Through Our Issues—A Priceless Gift of Love for Our Children:** At one time or another, most parents have acted out a scene from a painful part of their own growing up years rather than effectively parenting children; times when words come out of our

mouths that we promised we would never say, or when we find ourselves escalating to an emotional level that is evidence that we are no
longer in the present time zone but reliving pain, anger, or powerlessness from the past. I witnessed such an incident last week in the
park. Two four-year-old children were playing on a slide. A little boy
pushed a little girl out of line. The little girl's mom came immediately
to comfort her child who was in the dirt crying. She picked her up and
brushed her off, "Wow, that really hurt didn't it? The little boy was in
a hurry to get to the slide and pushed you down." She then turned to
the little boy and in a calm nonthreatening voice said, "Tina got hurt
when you pushed her on the ground."

Suddenly, the mother of the little boy came up and began yelling,
"Don't talk to my child. Your child runs to get ahead of him every
time. It's about time he began standing up to her! He had every right
to stand up for himself."

The mother of the little girl picked up her daughter, continued comforting her, and said to the boy's mother "I'm sorry you feel that way.
I will have to disagree. These are two four-year-old children and we
could have helped them work it out, I'm sorry we can't seem to do that."

It was obvious that the little boy's mother was working out an
issue that had little to do with her son. Too often, parents of children
who have bullied another child come to their child's defense and, in
doing so, deprive their child of valuable lessons of empathy, cause
and effect, and accountability. Likewise, the parents of the targets of
bullying can focus anger and blame toward the bully and forget to
attune their child's needs, fears, feelings of powerlessness, or actions.
Children can get lost in the parent's past.

Rebecca, Alan, Ann, and Mitch tuned into their daughters' feelings
and listened and supported each to find her voice. Taylor would not
have become "that loving and compassionate human being," Mitch
referred to without the life lessons that both sets of parents modeled

and helped her learn. Taylor could not have found her voice through the mire of her guilt, pain, and anger if both sets of parents hadn't supported her to speak. Rebecca could hear Ann's words because she didn't need her daughter to be a reflection of her own worth. She could deeply feel Taylor's pain, because she could separate her pain from her daughter's. She could hold Taylor accountable for her actions, while also holding her in her heart, because she could tolerate Taylor's anger and stand firmly as the consistent parent she needed.

In effective communication "the receiver of the message listens with an open mind and with all of his or her senses. Her reaction is dependent on what was actually communicated, not on a predetermined and rigid mental model of what was expected. This exchange occurs in the present moment without preoccupation with internal events of the past" (Seigal, 2003, p. 82).

Ann called Rebecca with concern, not rage. She didn't need to blame. She could separate her daughter's pain from her own. Because she was able to remain in the present, she could support both girls to grow and learn.

The good news is that no matter how painful or traumatic our childhoods, we can grow, change, and become caring and supportive parents. The brain has neuroplasticity, the ability to change and grow throughout life, not just in childhood as once believed. What changes our brain is experience. New experiences can create new neural pathways as long as we live. As stated so well by Daniel Siegel, M.D., clinical professor of psychiatry at UCLA School of Medicine, "Research has shown clearly that no matter our challenging past, if we can make sense of how our early experiences have shaped us and learn new models of security, we can offer our children the security of attachment" (Seigal, 2013, p. 161).

4. **Attunement and Empathy:** "The chalice of this infant's heart is filled to overflowing, and as she grows she will seek opportunities to share

her love with others. And how will she do this? By following the model she has been given. She will be there for others in the way her caregivers have been there for her" (McClure, 2012).

All children are born with the capacity to be compassionate, empathetic, cooperative and loving human beings. Children need to be treated empathetically and loved by those who show caring and empathy, and for others to reach their full and glorious potential. Without attuned and loving caregivers, children are like a beautiful score of music sitting on a piano bench. Without the musician, it never reaches its full potential. Together, the musician and music co-create the sound that was meant to be heard. The artist must read the music to create the song, and without the artist the song never reaches its glorious potential.

It is through the attunement and continual presence of adult care-givers that children learn, first to be aware of their own emotions, and then to be empathetic to the feelings of others. From the first moments of life, the connection between parent and child provides the blueprint for the child's future relationships with others. The concern in our mother's eyes when we skin our knee becomes our concern, first for ourselves, and then for the hurts of others. A parent's genuine interest in our explorations, and pleasure in our joy, translates into a belief in ourselves and a willingness to explore again. Over time, it creates our support and interest in the exploration of others.

Just as in a plane when we are gently cautioned to put our own oxygen mask on first, before attempting to help another in need of our assistance, it is impossible to tune into our children's feelings before we have processed our own. As parents, it is difficult to hear that our child has bullied another. It is easy to react with guilt, denial, embarrassment, fear, anger, blame, or defensiveness. The reality of our child as we may wish to see her/him is challenged. Rebecca and Mitch took the time to support each other to sort out and vent their reactions and emotions before talking with Taylor. In that way, they could choose an appropriate, rather than "knee jerk" response to the information they had been given. Also, by first processing their own feelings, they could effectively attune to Taylor's.

5. **Modeling Compassion:** Compassion is the deep concern we feel for the welfare of others. It is the desire to help and to alleviate the suffering of another. Research shows that compassion is deeply rooted in our brains. Our own compassion fosters compassionate behavior in our children (Keltner, 2004). As stated by one granddaughter, reflecting upon the teachings of her grandmother, "My grandmother taught me how to live and she also taught me how to die" (Middelton-Moz, 2005). It is through our actions, and not our words, that our children learn to care for themselves and then others.

When hearing from our child that he/she has been wounded by the unkind actions of another, an immediate response is to protect, to defend and, too often in the case of bullying, to retaliate and blame. But are retaliation, anger, and blame the life lessons that we want to teach our children? In Sherri's case, her parents were deeply concerned about their daughter, yet were able to extend their concern to Taylor as well. In reaching out to Taylor's parents, Mitch and Ann were not only showing compassion for their own child, but modeling compassion for others as well; a life lesson that would serve both girls throughout their lives.

Unlike Rebecca and Alan, many parents would respond to Ann's call with anger, blame, and denial. Through the action of compassionately reaching out, Ann and Mitch were modeling compassion regardless of the response on the other end of the phone. Fortunately for Taylor and Sherri, both sets of parents modeled concern and compassion for both girls and, in so doing, assisted them in working through a difficult time in their friendship; a model of caring, communication, reconciliation and forgiveness that Taylor and Sherri will be able to use to resolve conflicts in the future and model for their children. Just as bullying behavior can be passed from one generation to the other, so can compassion. As stated so well by Victor Frankl: "Those that showed compassion to others, comforting others and giving away their last piece of bread offered proof that everything can be taken away from a man but one thing: the last of the human freedoms—to choose one's attitude in any given set of circumstances—to choose one's own way."

6. **An Understanding of Our Children's Developmental Capabilities:** A child of two cannot be expected to have the same emotional regulation, social skills, and cognitive capabilities as a child of ten. An adolescent can't be expected to have the same skills in making healthy decisions and choices, or the same emotional regulation, as an adult. Navigating through adolescence is like driving a Mac truck with a kiddie car steering wheel.

Adolescence is a time when many changes are occurring in the developing brain. It's an exciting, yet often frightening, time period that we share with many other species. In *Zoobiquity* a fascinating book by Barbara Natterson-Horowitz, M.D., and Kathryn Bowers, I was surprised to learn that many other species also have a difficult and exciting transition between childhood and adulthood. In reading the book I found that much like other teenagers: Only the "daredevils of the otter world," adolescent otters, risk swimming in the chilly waters called the Triangle of Death south of San Francisco where white sharks swim and there are treacherous undertows and riptides; adolescent California condors without the teaching of mentors eat garbage, suffer from malnutrition, and will follow false mentors in the form of anything that soars, including hang gliders; and male adolescent elephants, without the presence of male mentors, will become aggressive (Natterson-Horowitz and Bowers, 2012).

Just as we see in other species, adolescence is a time of many transitions, and as researchers have discovered, important developments in our brain. They have found that it isn't raging hormones in teens that cause many changes in behavior, but rather changes taking place in the brain. With increases in novelty seeking, social engagement, and emotional intensity, adolescence provides an important foundation for the years to come, but it can also be difficult for teens to maneuver safely and for parents to provide effective and consistent guidance. Just as the adolescent otters plunge into unsafe waters, adolescents can seek the thrill and downplay the risk. They can impulsively write a bullying message to a classmate and push a button without pausing to consider the consequences of their actions. They need mentoring and guidance. We were meant to live in extended families and connected communities. "Throughout human history, we stayed together as communities with adolescents exploring and establishing independence while maintaining a range of important and instructive interactions with their adult elders. These strands of connectedness are being stretched in today's world, sometimes severing them with negative consequences of isolation and alienation" (Seigal, 2013, p. 27).

We were never meant to live in isolation. We need each other and sometimes we forget how much we need each other. Just as the California condor can follow "anything that soars" when left without adult condors to guide the way, teens desperately need the same guidance. Too often they are judged as "bad kids" or "delinquents" when they are experiencing the same normal development as adolescents of every other species. Too often, they are judged and removed from the circle when they desperately need to be surrounded by caring and compassionate adults who can provide guidance.

Rebecca and Alan intuitively understood that they needed a circle of support around their children, other mentors to help guide them.

Both sets of parents instinctively knew that many of the behaviors their children were showing—slouching shoulders, rolling eyes, dependence on the acceptance of peers, avoiding eye contact, anger at parents, impulsivity—were normal behaviors of an adolescent period of life, and surrounded them with concern, limits, love, and support rather than judgment.

More Tips for Parents

1. **Sit Down to Dinner Together:** One of the most important times of the day for children and youth is mealtime. It is a wonderful time when families can sit down together, enjoy each other, a meal, and conversation. It is a not the time for technology, so make sure that the television is off, cell phones are turned off and put away, and iPads, iPods, computers, and whatever technology will be invented by the time this book comes out, are in their docking stations and silenced. It is a great time to recharge their batteries and our families. The family dinner table is not the place or time for discipline or arguments but rather conversation, storytelling, and exploration. Mary Gordon, founder of Roots of Empathy spoke about her family dinner table, "At the dinner table, the rule was that the conversation must focus on ideas . . . not gossip or mundane events. But the table rung with laughter and spirited debate" (Szalavitz and Perry, 2010, p. 9).

   Researchers have confirmed what parents have instinctually known since almost the beginning of time, sharing a family meal is good for the brain, the body, the mind. and the spirit. Many studies link regular family dinners with many behaviors that parents desire most in their children and youth: lower rates of substance abuse, teen pregnancy and depression, higher grade-point averages, lower obesity and eating disorders, resilience, and self-esteem" (Fishel, retrieved 2014).

2. **Communicate with Your Youth and Teens and Ask Questions:** Youth and teens who have bullied or been bullied frequently deny, are

fearful, experience guilt or shame, feel isolated and alone, and keep secrets while suffering in silence. They need the four Cs: our complete attention, concern, connection and communication. Healthy communication on the part of parents can lead to the fifth C, change; ending hurtful behavior and isolation, communication of important lessons, empowerment to find one's voice, support to sort out confusing feelings and a healing salve for a shamed spirit. Ask questions: What were the good things about school today? What was your least favorite thing? What is it like for you riding the school bus? Have you ever received a hurtful message online? Have you ever sent one? It is not only important asking the questions but also really listening to the answers and using them as a springboard for more dialogue. Also, be aware that asking questions is communication not interrogation.

It is important that we can attune to our children; really listen to what they are saying verbally and non-verbally, rather than planning what we are going to say next. As stated earlier in the chapter, our communication needs to occur in the present rather than being filtered through the judgments, sadness, anger, or mental models of the past. We need to communicate in the present rather than through a time warp.

Children also need our words to match our behavior. If we are saying we understand, yet are looking away or rolling our eyes, it is our non-verbal cues that will be communicated to our children. The communication that will come across loud and clear and be believed and/or internalized is our nonverbal behavior, rather than our words. Our communication is right-brain-to-right-brain and left-brain-to-left-brain. The center for receiving and sending non-verbal communication is located in the right hemisphere of the brain and so is our emotional regulation. The left hemisphere specializes in literal, linguistic, and logical information. When our words are saying one thing and our non-verbal communication is saying something else, the result is confusion. Our non-verbal communication makes the greatest impact. An adult may say, "I believe you, Jeffrey," but the sneer on her face or the doubt in her eyes will be what is understood and believed on an emotional level. It is important to pay close attention to the nonverbal communication of our children as well as our own.

3. **Model Healthy Values and Consistent Limits Regarding Bullying Behavior:** Our children learn by our modeling, not merely our words. If parents, educators, extended family, and community do not model healthy values, our children will not learn them. If we bully, judge, gossip, and put others down, our children learn to do the same. If we allow our children to hurt others without setting kind and compassionate limits on their behavior, we are teaching them that power, rather than kindness, is the value we want them to learn. Children learn from our interactions with them and others, the values that will be the internal compass will direct their interactions with others.

4. **Support Youth and Teens Who Are Being Bullied to "Find Their Voice":** When our children find the courage to speak with us, or if we hear from a teacher, a neighbor or friend, that he/she has been bullied, it is important for us first to assist them to "find their voice." We need to attune to their experience and their feelings. Rather than telling them to "fight back" we need to first let them know that bullying is absolutely not their fault. There is never a "good reason" to be put down or bullied. We need to be their coaches and advocates in friendships, on the playground, in cyberspace, and to support them to find their voice. We also need to help them own who they are, identifying and understanding their buttons and triggers, so they don't give the bully the weapon of using their buttons against them. To say to your child, "Don't let it bother you, you are just like everyone else," when your child is the only Native American in a dominant culture school, is not supporting them to own who they are. Instead, when he/she is a sensitive child, a talented child, a child with red hair or

freckles, a gay teen, etc., it is more useful to help empower her/him, by first listening and hearing their story and tuning in to what he or she needs from an adult, then arming them with the knowledge and power of everything they are as well as skills in advocating for themselves. We can do this by helping them find role models that are like them in history or in our communities. Teaching them to advocate for themselves and to seek out the support of caring friends and adults in the caring majority is essential.

When the bullying becomes a pattern, it is important to notify the school and ensure protection from harm by insisting on compassionate and safe schools. It is also important to attempt to reach out, as Rebecca and Alan did, to the parents of the child who is bullying in order to attempt to help resolve the situation in a good way, and model compassion for all involved. This does not always work, but does in many instances.

In all cases, we must insure that we arm our children in a good way with both internal and external caring and loving supports. They need to be wrapped in the caring arms of the compassionate majority.

5. **Limit and Monitoring the Use of Technology:** In the last several weeks, while writing the sections on bullying through technology, we have become increasingly aware of the use of technology in families to the exclusion of personal interaction. We have witnessed situations where couples and families, out for a meal together in a restaurant, have spent the majority of their time on cell phones and tablets rather than communicating with each other. One family of five that we observed did not speak one word to each other during the hour and a half they were in the restaurant. Both parents and one of the teenagers spent the entire time texting, communicating only to the waitress to order their food. The remaining two youth, one appearing to be about twelve and the other a young teen, spent the entire time playing games on their tablets.

"By their own admission, many young Americans, aged eighteen to twenty-nine, say they spend too much time using the Internet (59 percent), their cell phones or smartphones (58 percent), and social media sites such as Facebook (48 percent). Americans' perceptions that they spend 'too much' time using each of these technologies decline with age. Conversely, older Americans are most likely to say they spend too much time watching television, and among all Americans, television is the most overused technology tested" (Newport, 2012).

We have also witnessed young mothers with infants on their laps, busily texting rather than attuning to their children.

A majority of young people have televisions in their bedrooms and use their cell phones texting rather than spending time with family or texting until the early hours of the morning rather than unwinding or getting much needed rest. Many report sleeping with their cell phones under their pillows at night, afraid that they miss a text or call.

"The average young American now spends practically every waking minute—except for the time in school—using a smart phone, computer, television, or other electronic device, according to a new study from the Kaiser Family Foundation" (Lewin, 2010).

The 2010 study also found that heavy users (those using technology sixteen hours a day) had lower grades and were more likely to report that they were sad or bored, got in trouble, or had greater difficulty getting along with parents than lighter users (three hours a day or less) and were not happy at school (Rideout, Foehr, and Roberts, 2010).

As stated earlier, attunement, connection, and communication with adult caregivers is essential for the development of empathy, compassion, and the ability to read the nonverbal cues of others. The growing use of technology to the exclusion of building personal

relationships and necessary community and extended family supports, will limit important brain development in our children.

A friend, the father of a boy in his late teens, recently told me of
an interaction that had taken place at his home. He had asked his
son if he could meet some of the friends he was communicating with
online. Six young people in their late teens came to the house. One
young man, Todd, seemed to only be able to talk about his body. He
had talked on and on about his workouts, his bodybuilding techniques, and his pecs. He seemed particularly attracted to Donna,
another teen in the group, and appeared intent on impressing her
with his physique. Sarah had been showing signs for a while that she
was tired of his endless chatter about his body, and eventually got up
to leave the room. Todd held out his arm, attempting to block her
exit. My friend, astonished by the young man's actions said, "Todd,
Sarah obviously wants to leave the room. Don't block her path. That's
not cool. We don't treat others like that in this house." To this, Todd
seemed confused but complied. My friend engaged him in a conversation, and it was apparent that he hadn't read any of her recent body
language and seemed quite curious.

Todd said, "I probably would have understood that she was getting bored with my talk and wanted to leave if she had texted me."

Technology, the Internet, email, cell phones and smartphones, and
social media sites have opened up important new vistas of learning
and connecting with others across the globe, yet technology, as a
replacement for personal connection, can be an addiction that dis-
connects us from one another. We need to balance its use in the lives
of our children with family discussions, playing together, time spent
outdoors, and reading books to our children along with family and
community connection.

"Brain development is use-dependent: you use it or lose it. If we
don't give children time to learn how to be with others, to connect,

to deal with conflict and negotiate complex social hierarchies, those areas of the brain will be underdeveloped" (Perry, 2006, p. 239).

Limiting the use of technology to no more than three hours a day and making sure that the television is off, and cell phones, tablets and the like are placed in a basket or back in their docking stations during meal times and before bedtime is essential for individual, family, and community development.

6. **Know the Rules Regarding the Use of Media Sites and Educate Your Youth and Teens About Why They Are Put in Place.** It is important for our children and youth to know that using technology and social media sites is a privilege, not a right and comes with rules for safety and good cell phone and cyber citizenship. Navigating the cyber superhighway can bring an abundance of good information and healthy connections with others in cyberspace. You wouldn't, however, let the youth in your life drive a car at twelve or at sixteen without first taking driver education and receiving their learner's permit or driver's license. The same is true in being offered the privilege of using cell phones and navigating the Internet. Some rules and tips:

- **Don't let your child ignore website age restrictions.** Most media sites are not open to children below the age of thirteen. Do not support your child lying about his or her age. The rule is in place for a reason.
- **Educate your children on cyberbullying and harassment.** Communicate with your youth before allowing them to use media sites that it is not acceptable to gossip, bully, harass, or make hurtful remarks to anyone. Parents can help youth learn healthy conflict resolution skills and the importance of taking a "cool down" period when they are angry or hurt before responding to someone online. It is also important to avoid sarcasm or remarks that might unintentionally wound someone.

- **Help them be part of the caring majority that doesn't take part in another's attempt to bully or harm someone else.** Have discussions with children and youth about the importance of kindness. Use examples of bullying incidents that have taken place in school, or that are mentioned in newspaper or magazine articles, as a starting point for discussions.

- **Remind your children to safeguard personal and family information.** Never give out personal information or family plans and schedules on the Internet to people that they don't know well in real life. Understand that people with malicious motives can access personal information about them or family members by information they post. Remind them not to "friend" everyone, only those that truly are their friends. While a large number of "friends" might be enviable, it can also increase the likelihood of problems.

- **Help your youth understand the very "public" aspect of media sites and that they should not post anything that they would not like all of their peers, their parents, or others to see.** Also help them understand that the messages they send and post can remain in cyberspace for a long time. An unwise post from the past could harm a student's chances of getting into his college of choice, or even prevent him from getting a job down the road. Once posted or sent, the sender loses control of who sees it or uses it. Parents can go to Google.com and enter their child's complete name in the search engine in quotes to see what is posted about them or other family members. Parents can search their own online reputation as well.

- **Teach your child to guard their passwords like they are gold.** Parents should discuss safety with their youth before they begin using technology. One safety measure is not to share their passwords with anyone, other than their parents, not even close friends. This includes social networking sites, instant message programs, computers, online gaming accounts, or cell phones. Help them understand that friendships can change, as can social networks.

- **Caution your children about letting someone else use their cell phone.** Help youth understand that loaning their cell phones to others when they are not close by, or leaving the phone unattended, can result in someone sending images or texts to others that they would never send. Several instances have occurred where a "friend" has used another's cell phone to send bullying texts or images to or about someone else using the owner's entire contact list without their knowledge.

- **Tell your child that responding to every text or post is not necessary.** Youth often feel they need to do this, but it often just escalates the problem. Let them know that it is best not to respond to negative comments about them or, when appropriate, help them post an assertive message to stop the behavior. It is also important to teach them to delete any message that spreads rumors, gossip, or has content that bullies someone else. They may respond proactively letting the person know they are not interested in being a witness to bullying. Help them choose to support the person being bullied.

- **Help your child with the awareness that communication online can be easily misunderstood.** What may be an innocent message can be read in many different ways. It may be teasing, angry, friendly, playful, sarcastic, or aggressive. Without nonverbal cues, it is sometimes difficult to assess what someone is saying accurately.

- **Keep technology with Internet capability in common areas of the house.** Computers and tablet use should be allowed only in the family room, kitchen or living room, particularly

when youth are young, before they have earned more freedom
with technology.

- **Monitor your child's online use.** Until they build trust in
  their teens' cyberspace "citizenship," parents should frequently
  keep tabs on their children's online comings and goings. Much
  is available in the way of software for helping you do this. Many
  tools for monitoring can be found online or by consulting your
  wireless provider. Tracking software can be installed that records
  every site visited or every message that is sent or received. If
  monitoring is something that seems reasonable to do, always be
  honest with youth, explain what you are doing, and why. Also,
  allow them to earn your trust as they get older, or have proven
  that they practice healthy cyber citizenship. Monitoring can be
  resumed if youth abuse online privileges, have bullied others, or
  who have engaged in behavior that has put them at risk.

- **Use blocking software to keep children safe from inappropriate material.** Blocking software can also be used that
  screens material or blocks sites can also be used to protect early
  users who are curious and might inadvertently have access to
  sites that could be risky or harmful.

- **Know the media sites and apps that your teens may be
  visiting or using.** Some popular sites include Facebook, Ask.
  fm, Twitter, My Space, Spring.me, Kit.com, Snapchat, Instagram,
  YouTube, and Mashable. Sites change names, new sites emerge,
  and new apps are created all the time. Become familiar with the
  sites and apps available and ask youth which sites they prefer
  and why. Also, become knowledgeable about the rules of each
  site and discuss them. It can also be helpful to enlist youth in
  open discussion about cyberbullying that may have occurred
  on various sites and talk to them about their feelings and viewpoints about what has occurred. Many strong teens have found

a positive voice and become leaders in monitoring postings and tweets as well as becoming members of the compassionate majority in using technology in positive communication. Explore the compassionate actions of those teen leaders and the values they are modeling. Help them discuss norms around appropriate and inappropriate behavior.

- **Model and promote open communication.** Create openness and space for discussion around difficult issues such as racism, homophobia, bullying, and harassment. Ask questions often: What are your favorite websites? What do you like about this site? Have you ever been contacted by someone online who you didn't know? How did you respond? How do you keep yourself safe online? Have you ever been bullied or upset by someone online? Do you ever worry that someone else is being bullied? Have you ever bullied or said something online that you wish you could take back?

- **Let your teen know that if he or she is the target of cyberbullying, or if he or she is being harassed online, to let you or a trusted adult know immediately and keep a record of the messages sent.** Print copies of the messages and websites. Use the "save" feature on instant messages. Don't hesitate to let the school know and to call the police if your youth is a target of illegal behavior.

- **Be aware of the signs that your child may be a target of cyberbullying:** isolation, low self-esteem, fear of going to school, withdrawal from peer group, depression, abrupt changes in behavior, becoming easily angered, aggression, appearing upset after being online or viewing a text message, hiding what they write, or abruptly shutting the computer when an adult comes in the room. Support your child and seek help if he or she expresses thoughts of harm to self or others.

- **Assist your child in learning to support others who are being bullied and speak out against bullying.** Engage your children in discussions about bullying. Use concrete examples of bullying incidents and ask your children how they might feel about being the target. Role-play interventions they might use to support the target.
- **Enter into a contract for Internet and cell phone use.** Excellent contracts, written by Sameer Hinduja, Ph.D., and Justin Patchin, Ph.D., can be found at www.cyberbullying.us
- **Keep up to date on Internet safety.** Helpful information about Internet safety can be obtained from many websites. Some that we have used are cyberbullyinghelp.com, stopbullying.gov, and connectsafely.org. Other sites also exist and can be found by searching the term "Internet safety."
- **Help youth and teens understand personal privacy and the laws regarding sexting.** Even though many adults are "sexting," they may be unaware that many tweens and teens are as well. It is important to review the laws on sexting with your youth who have Internet and cell phone privileges. Don't threaten them; instead, teach them to respect themselves and educate them on some of the difficulties that can arise if a "sext" is sent. Have an open discussion with them on "sextortion," "revenge porn," coercion, and harassment using some of the examples in Chapter Six.

Keep communication open. Some of the signs that your tween or teen is sexting are: He or she hides their phone or says they have lost it when you want to see it. He or she keeps the door closed constantly, and when you knock they don't want you to come in. He or she has sudden changes in personality, or becomes secretive about his or her online activities. If you have reason to be concerned, you might want to remove the texting option on their cell phone until you can trust that they are not putting themselves at risk. By far the best option is to educate without judgment, remain calm and interested, have frequent discussions and keep the lines of communication open. Particularly for younger youth, it is important for them to leave their cell phones in a common area at bedtime. You might wish to have a basket where technology can rest while your children do the same.

- **Communicate with the school often, and actively support compassionate and safe schools.** It is extremely important that our children attend schools that are compassionate and safe. Talk to school personnel about their policies and programs regarding bullying and Internet safety. Compassionate schools are often schools that actively teach, model, and practice healthy values, and are trauma-informed. If your school's atmosphere is not safe or founded on healthy values, become an advocate for change. Becoming an active part of the school community for our children is investing in their future.

In the words of Benjamin Franklin, "We may not be able to prepare the future for our children, but we can at least prepare our children for the future."

5

PART ONE:
Cyberbullying and Youth
"The Hit and Run"

"Life is a fight, but not everyone's a fighter.
Otherwise, bullies would be an
endangered species."

Andrew Vachss, Terminal

Seventeen-year-old Kevin Curwick, from Osseo, Minnesota, was tired of witnessing his fellow schoolmates being attacked with hurtful words on Twitter. Although Kevin, an Osseo High School football team captain, was never a target of cyberbullying himself, his concern for his classmates caused him to stand up and take action against cyberbullying by anonymously starting a Twitter account, @OsseoNiceThings, to lift their spirits by tweeting positive things like "nice artist but even a better friend" or "puts others before herself." Kevin's kindness inspired peers throughout the world to join his efforts. *www.usatoday.com/news/health/wellness/story/2012-08-17/teen.../1*

When others discovered who started the site, Kevin, a person who never wanted anything other than to show kindness and respect anonymously, became a celebrity on talk shows like the *Today* show and *The Ellen DeGeneres Show*, which demonstrates that kind words and actions can become more noteworthy than hurtful words, and standing up and speaking out, more powerful and popular than silence. Kevin's action in his school proved that many of those who had remained silent actually felt strongly about speaking up yet needed "permission" and a peer role model to do so. Peers supporting peers is a powerful way to stop cyberbullying in our communities.

Most of us have become used to the luxuries and benefits of our rapid acceleration into technology. In the middle of a presentation we can ask Siri to find the most up to date research on a particular topic. We can access the weather for the week without waiting for the local news, or find classmates through social media that we haven't been in touch with since high school. We can immediately have access to role models like Kevin Curwick and new technology can provide all of us with a window to the world that most adults had never dreamed possible. The vast web at our fingertips can provide youth with a venue to engage in sharing music and art, and mobilizing for social change. For many youth and adults, advances in technology have been a saving grace that have helped them feel less isolated or alone.

History of the Information Superhighway

Since the mid-90s the Internet has had tremendous impact on the world. Today, people from all over the world connect and share information about themselves and their personal lives on social media. Generally, they are alone in their room with the keyboard, a monitor, a mouse, and a computer or tablet. Most of the information is shared through words, pictures, web cam, and face-to-face on the cell phone. People can correspond with each other as they have never been able to before. We can stay in touch with our loved ones, family, friends, business peers, and acquaintances and can make many new friends through social media. Those who are in the United States military and are serving anywhere in the world can keep in contact through social media. We are now, as a world, in close contact with each other 24/7. The choices for people to stay in contact are many. Some include: blogs, micro-blogs, forums, message boards, virtual worlds, social marketing, tagging, writing sites and digital storytelling, scrapbooking, podcast portals, and wiki's. New sites are constantly being opened. Some of the most popular sites are: Facebook, Twitter, LinkedIn, Myspace, YouTube, Flicker, WordPress, Typepad, and Indymedia. These sites are growing rapidly with many more to come.

The Internet had its earliest beginnings in the 1950s. In 1990, more than 1,500 web servers were online and the Internet became the "Information Superhighway." Today, the world has become a very small place because of the global sharing of information. The ease and availability of finding and using information for education is a positive result of this phenomenon known as the Internet. The origination of the Internet, social media, e-mail and texting was to provide worldwide information at a faster pace than we had ever known. Since the mid-1990s, the Internet has had tremendous impact on the world culture. Today, people from all over the world connect and share information about themselves and their private lives on social media.

The first smartphone was invented by IBM in 1992 and was called SIMON. Text messaging began in 1992, but became a way of life in 1999 when users could begin using mobile networks other than their own (Cooke, Harriet, 2012). Although instant messaging had much earlier beginnings in the 1960's, a turning point was when AOL launched AIM, which attracted millions of users, 53 million by 2005. The first search engine was opened in 1998 by Google. In the

year 2000, 70 million computers were connected to the Internet. In
2002, Friendster social network opened in the United States and had
3 million users within three months' time. In 2003, My Space and
LinkedIn were introduced. In the same year there were more than
3 billion webpages. In 2004 Facebook, podcasting, Flicker, and Digg
were introduced and YouTube began storing and receiving videos.
There were 8 billion plus webpages at this time. In 2006, Twitter was
introduced and Facebook was open to anyone over age thirteen. Apple
introduced the iPhone in 2007 and it was the first multimedia smart
phone, revolutionizing the way we communicate. In 2009, Facebook
ranked as the most used network worldwide. It was estimated at that
time that one quarter of the world's population was using the Internet.
In 2010, Facebook grew to over 4 million users and the Internet sur-
passed newspapers as the way people chose to receive their news. In
2011, social media were accessible from virtually anywhere in the
world and became a part of billions of people's daily lives. The sharing
of so much private information from people through social media
became a concern for many at this time. People began to show a concern for invasion of their privacy. As of 2013, Facebook users were up
to 1.11 billion, Twitter had 500 million registered users, Flicker had
87 million users and 8 billion stored photographs, Instagram—100
million users and 4 billion stored photographs, Linkedin had 225
million users, MySpace—25 million users, Pinterest—48.7 million
users, WordPress—74 million blogs posted, Dropbox—100 million
users with one billion files uploaded daily, Google—343 million users,
with 156 million blogs. An Australian survey found 34 percent of
users logged on at work, 13 percent at school, and 18 percent in the
car. 44 percent used social media in bed, 7 percent used it in the
bathroom, and 6 percent on the toilet. It is estimated social media
users will double by 2015, nearly 60 percent of our world population
(Curtis, Anthony, 2013).

The cyber world knows no boundaries. The ease and availability of finding and using information for education is a positive result of this phenomenon known as the Internet. The origination of the Internet, social media, e-mail and texting was to provide worldwide information at a faster pace than we had ever known.

Cyberbullying and Youth

Texting has become the most common mode of communication for a majority of teens and many adults. Most adults and youth that we have asked about their experiences with technology have related extremely positive experiences. Yet, the misuse of our advancing technology, including cyberbullying, is all too real and is devastating for thousands of youth and adults.

We define cyberbullying as intentional, frequent, and systematic cruelty deliberately aimed at a person or persons through electronic devices and social media, with the intent of embarrassing another and/or gaining power over another by regularly inflicting and causing psychological pain and/or harm. Cyberbullying may include: posting or sending hurtful messages; taking embarrassing pictures of another without their knowledge and posting them on social media websites or sending them to others; spreading rumors through e-mails, text messages, Twitter, and other social media; creating a Web page with the intention of hurting or embarrassing someone; impersonating someone with the intent of acting or presenting themselves in a way that causes the person harm or pain; or playing online game devices while being abusive, intimidating, threatening, or hateful.

In their research, Sameer Hinduja and Justin W. Patchin (2009) found that most often those who bully in person also bully online and those who don't bully in person aren't as likely to bully others online. Similarly those who are bullied offline are more likely to be bullied online. "Youth who reported bullying others in real life in the previous six months were more than 2.5 times as likely to report bullying others online. Similarly, youth who were victims of traditional bullying in the previous six months were more than 2.5 times as likely to be victims of cyberbullying" (Hinduja and Patchin, 2009, page 59). We also learned that kids who had been bullied in person were almost three times as likely to be cyber-bullied."

Motivations for Sending or Posting Hurtful Messages

The reason that a youth might send or post hurtful messages to and/or about another covers a wide range of motivations. Some examples are:

- Youth who carelessly respond to a message in anger or humor without the intent to cause harm and were not considering the consequences of their actions when responding.
- Bullies who wanted to exert their power and control over others by inflicting hurt, fear, and harm.
- Group of teens who are bored and bully online as a form of "fun" and "entertainment."
- Popular teens who are threatened by the popularity of those considered to be rivals, and bully to intentionally "remove their competition" in order to maintain their place in the peer group.
- Girls who are jealous of another girl and may see attractive or popular girls as competition for popularity or attention from boys, and bully as a form of "lateral violence." Lateral violence occurs when members of an oppressed group turn their aggression on the members of the same group (Middelton-Moz, 1990).

Types and Extent of Cyberbullying

Judy, Samantha, Ruth, and Joyce were spending an overnight at Joyce's house. Ann, a friend of Samantha's, had not been invited. Judy did not like Ann and had been envious of her since elementary school. She was also angry with her because she felt that Ann had shown an interest in Aaron, a boy Judy liked in math class. While at the overnight, Samantha agreed to call Ann and ask her questions about her interest in Aaron while the others listened. Ann, of course, thought she was only talking to Samantha, one of her dearest friends to whom she could confide her deepest feelings and secrets. At the end of the conversation, the others came on the line and let Ann know they had heard every word. They laughed at her for her interest in Aaron and other personal secrets she had expressed to Samantha. The next morning Ann found her private feelings posted on Facebook and Twitter. Ann left school complaining of a sick stomach and didn't return for the rest of the week.

The bullying of Ann by her "friends" is only one type of bullying using electronic media. Ann was tricked into divulging personal and sensitive information that was used to bully her and cause her embarrassment and pain.

Another type of cyberbullying is impersonation. Most of us have received e-mail messages from friends or family members alerting us that our e-mail has been hacked because they have received suspicious messages supposedly sent from our address. Usually, our e-mail address has been used to send junk electronic ads, known as spam, to our entire e-mail list. Imagine, instead, that our e-mail account has been compromised and those impersonating us are using our e-mail address to send hurtful and sometimes vicious messages and embarrassing material in our name to many of our peers and family members. Perhaps an entire Facebook account has been set up in our name containing hurtful messages and denigrating pictures of us, or belittling and embarrassing postings.

Other forms of online bullying include posting or sending cruel, threatening or vicious messages to, or about, someone to hundreds of people; "tweeting" or posting damaging photos or material; or posting or sending rumors or gossip, all intended to cause hurt and pain and/ or damage reputations.

Sometimes cyberbullying takes the form of using electronic messages full of anger, threats, or vulgar language, or stalking an individual online. This form of bullying sometimes extends to stalking offline as well.

Extent of the Problem

Countless surveys on cyberbullying are conducted each year and statistics vary widely regarding the number of children, teens, and adolescents who bully using electronic technology or are targets of cyberbullying. Size of sample in data collection, those conducting the research, interpretation, location, and target populations result in a wide disparity of statistics regarding the extent of cyberbullying. Most research findings agree that the majority of youth use technology responsibly and do not bully. That said, far too many are targets of cyberbullying.

Some data shows that a significant number of youth report that they have harassed someone online (McQuade and Sampat, 2008).

In 2006, national law enforcement leaders estimated that more than 13 million children and youth ages six to seventeen were victims of cyberbullying (Fight Crime: Invest in Kids, 2006).

No Bullying.com reported the following statistics in 2014:

- Fifty-two percent of young people report being cyberbullied.
- Twenty-five percent of adolescents and teenagers report that they have experienced repeated bullying via cell phones or the Internet.

- Embarrassing or damaging photographs taken without consent of the subject have been reported by 11 percent of teens and adolescents.
- Of the young people who reported cyberbullying incidents against them, one third of them reported that their bullies issued threats online.
- Over half (55 percent) of teens and adolescents who use social media have witnessed outright bullying via that medium.
- An astonishing 95 percent of adolescents and teens who witness bullying on social media report that others, like themselves, ignored the behavior.
- More than half of the young people surveyed said that they never confide in their parents when cyberbullying happens to them.
- Only one out of every six parents of teens and adolescents are aware of the scope and intensity involved in cyberbullying.
- More than 80 percent of teens and adolescents use cell phones, making them the most popular form of technology and therefore a common medium for cyberbullying.
- The most common type of cyberbullying tactics reported are mean, hurtful comments as well as spreading rumors and gossip.
- Cyberbullying affects all races.
- Girls are at least as likely as boys to be either cyberbullies or to be targeted although boys are more likely to be threatened by cyberbullies than girls.
- Childline, a free counseling service based in the United Kingdom especially for adolescents and teens, reported in their most recent annual report that cyberbullying concerns rose by a whopping 87 percent in 2013 over the previous year.
- Victims of cyberbullying are more likely to suffer from low self-esteem and consider suicide.

Effect on Targets and Witnesses

Copeland, et. al. (2013) conducted a study of 1,420 participants who had been bullied between the ages of nine and fourteen. They found, after controlling for childhood psychiatric problems and family hardships, that there are multiple direct effects of being bullied, including depression, generalized anxiety disorder, suicidal ideation, agoraphobia, and panic disorder. The effects were found to extend into adulthood.

In a 2013 Youth at Risk Behavior Survey, cyberbullying was associated with depression, suicidal ideation, psychological distress, skipping school, weapon carrying, lower self-esteem, social anxiety, self-injury, and suicide.

A fifteen-year-old girl was raped by a boy she had known since middle school and when she told her friends what happened, she said they turned on her, posting ugly messages online and sending texts accusing her of lying about the assaults. "I never actually attempted suicide, but there was a time when I considered it. I was so depressed and felt so hopeless. I felt like a zombie walking down the halls of the school with everyone staring at me and judging me."

Cyberbullicide is suicide directly or indirectly associated with victimization from cyberbullying. In their research, Hinduja and Patchin (2009) also conducted research linking suicidal ideation to online victimization. In the past years many have been directly or indirectly the victims of cyberbullicide. The following are only a few of the many young people who have tragically ended their lives after being bullied online, and for some offline as well:

- Fifteen-year-old Audrie Pott hanged herself after her family said she was sexually assaulted by friends and a photo of the assault appeared online.

- Clara Pugsley committed suicide in the woods near her home after incessant bullying on her Ask.fm page. Users would call her "slut" and "ugly" in the months leading to her suicide.
- Thirteen-year-old Megan Meier's mother found her hanging in her bedroom closet after being cyberbullied by an adult neighbor who created "Josh," a teenage boy and his Myspace online profile. After almost a month of developing an online relationship with "Josh," whom she corresponded with exclusively online and to whom she was attracted, "Josh" told her he didn't want to be her friend anymore "because she was not nice to her friends." Posts on Myspace followed, calling Megan a "slut" and "liar." "Josh" wrote that the world would be a better place without her. The neighbor said she made up "Josh" to find out information about what she was saying about her daughter online.
- Erin Gallager, thirteen, committed suicide after being continually bullied on Ask.fm. Two months later, Erin's fifteen-year-old sister, Shannon, committed suicide as well.
- Fifteen-year-old Joshua Unsworth's body was discovered in the garden of his family's farmhouse after allegedly being bullied for months leading up to his suicide.
- Seventeen-year-old Daniel Perry was blackmailed on Skype and jumped to his death from a local bridge. Daniel was harassed often on his Ask.fm page with posts telling him to kill himself and that he should cut his throat.
- Fourteen-year-old Hannah Smith was found hanging by her sister. Hannah was routinely bullied anonymously on Ask.fm.
- Phoebe Prince committed suicide at fifteen after suffering months of bullying online and off by classmates. After her death, bullying continued when crude comments about her were posted on her Facebook memorial page.
- Sixteen-year-old Jessica Lang hung herself after being bullied about her appearance and weight on Ask.fm.

- Thirteen-year-old Ryan Halligan committed suicide after being bullied in school and online. He was repeatedly bullied including being sent homophobic remarks. Ryan was continually threatened, taunted, and insulted.
- Twelve-year-old Rebecca Ann Sedwick's body was found in an abandoned cement silo. Her family told reporters that she had been relentlessly bullied on Ask.fm.
- Twelve-year-old Jeffrey Johnston was an honor student who loved reading and had a wide circle of friends. A boy began trashing him online, telling everyone he was gay. His friends began shunning him. The bullying continued and, when he was thirteen, a video game that had been designed by Jeff and a friend was hacked into and the site was used to post vicious comments about Jeff including that he was fat, ugly, and that he laughed at friends behind their backs. Postings also said that he was a "faggot who needed to die." At fifteen, his mother and brother found Jeff's lifeless body in his closet.

It is important to note, again, that most youth, teens and adolescents do NOT cyberbully. Patchin and Hinduja have conducted extensive research studies on cyberbullying. "Our most recent study found that about 30 percent of teens had been the target of cyberbullying and about 19 percent admitted that they had cyberbullied others—both numbers higher than the ten-year averages." (2014).

Those who are cyberbullied experience tremendous fear and pain, as do many of the silent majority who witness the bullying of others and feel that they must remain silent. The majority of those who keep their silence do not support the cruelty.

Twenty-one-year old Josh, his eyes filling with tears recalled a classmate who had been cyberbullied. "I don't think I will ever forget that I did nothing. I don't think I will get over the guilt. I'll never get over it. I still dream about him and the pain that always seemed to be in his

eyes. I knew that he was being cyberbullied for ⟩
remarks about him posted on Facebook and later the ⟙
remarks constantly on Twitter, '#Joe is a queer, a faggot who shoᵤ
not be alive.' It happened daily. I felt powerless to do anything. I didn't
know what to do and was afraid I would be bullied, too, if I said or
did anything. Maybe my friends would think I was gay He eventually
committed suicide and I felt responsible because I had done nothing. I
will never forget him and I will always feel guilty that I was responsible
because I stayed silent. It eats away at me and the image of the caring
person I thought I was.

Take Steps to Stand Up for Yourself

Michel J. Fox said so eloquently, "One's dignity may be assaulted,
vandalized and cruelly mocked, but it can never be taken away unless
it is surrendered." Although these words are true, we understand that
it is extremely difficult to remember them when afraid and terrorized by cyberbullies. They are, however, words of wisdom. In order
to prevent further harm it is important for those that are bullied to
take steps on their own behalf to both prevent injury from occurring
and to stand up to bullies who attempt to take away their self-worth
and dignity. Some things to consider:

Protect your passwords and user names. Never give them out, other
than to your parents—not even to your closest friend. Those who
wish to do harm can use them to post things as if they were from you.
Change your user name and e-mail addresses immediately if you are
being bullied online.

- Use privacy settings to keep your pages as private as possible.
- Know how to block unwanted calls and information.
- Don't post information about yourself, your family, or friends that
  you would not feel comfortable with everyone seeing. Assume that

everyone has access to your profile. Don't say things or post things you wouldn't want everyone to see. Realize that some may use information on your profile to cause you harm. Don't put anything you wouldn't want someone who may wish to harm you to know.

- Give your cell number only to people you know you can trust. Trust is earned and those who put you down or tease you in ways that feel uncomfortable are not trustworthy, even if they respond after you are hurt that they were "only joking." Trust your instincts.
- Don't respond to text messages from numbers or people you don't know, and keep your cell phone keypad locked.
- Set up privacy controls. Restrict access to your media sites to trusted friends and family only. Settings must be configured to ensure protection of your site.
- Always log out of your online accounts. Don't stay logged in when you walk away from online media accounts, e-mail accounts, or your cell phone.
- Delete e-mails or text messages from known bullies or those who may send bullying messages about someone. Delete them, don't read them.
- If you are being cyberbullied, and efforts to set boundaries have not been successful, keep a journal recording detailed information of the dates, times, and messages. Always keep threatening messages and report them to a trustworthy adult who will validate your feelings and will assist you in taking action.
- Do not respond with aggression if you or someone you care about is being bullied. Respond with absolute boundaries, such as: "What you are doing or saying is not cool, please stop." Firmly and clearly let the abuser know you will not tolerate his or her bullying behavior.
- If the bullying continues, or is threatening, tell your parents and/or an adult you feel will hear you, validate your feelings, and assist you in taking action. (Parent, coach, teacher, aunt, uncle, etc.) Remember, you are not alone. There is someone willing to help. Remember the

difference between tattling and telling. Tattling is to get someone in trouble; telling is to keep someone, including yourself, safe. Don't stop until you find someone who will hear you and assist you.

- Report any inappropriate behavior on media sites to the site administrator.

- If you are being cyberbullied by text messages, and the person will not stop when you set clear boundaries, turn off your phone or give it to an adult you trust and report the abuse to your provider.

- "Google" yourself. Remove any personal information or photos that can be used by anyone who may wish to target you.

- Increase your awareness of cyberbullying and raise awareness in your school.

- Don't be a cyberbully. Be as kind to others as you wish they would be kind to you.

- Don't forward hurtful messages.

- Don't condone hurtful, threatening, or bullying behavior just to fit in. Remember, most of your peers don't bully or think bullying behavior is cool.

- Don't take a bully's words and behavior personally. It is not about you, it is about them. They are coming from a place of fear and powerlessness; don't let them pass it on to you.

Standing Up for You, Standing Up for Me

Many grew up listening to or reading Dr. Seuss books. One of our favorites is *The Lorax*. Three quotes come to mind as we address the issue of cyberbullying. "I speak for the trees. I speak for the trees for the trees have no leaves," exclaims the Lorax. Most who have been relentlessly cyberbullied have fear, hurt, and shame that continues to be magnified and amplified by thoughts regarding the beliefs and reactions of those who have witnessed the cruelty and have remained silent.

Through their silence, they appear to agree with the cruelty. Many targets of cyberbullying feel shame and fear to the extent that they temporarily lose their voice and the ability to take action on their own behalf. They desperately need the voices and actions of others. Those who take action, like Kevin Curwick, lend them a voice and validate them enough to find their own voice again. "To the world you may be one person; but to one person, you may be the world." (Dr. Seuss)

"Unless someone like you cares a whole lot, nothing's going to get better. It's not." (Dr. Seuss) When Kevin Curwick modeled change, those who previously had lost their voices began to speak up, and the climate of his school changed from one that was cruel and unsafe for many entering the doors every morning to one that was welcoming and safe. It took one person to create change. His actions changed the climate of his school and by courageously modeling a different norm, he began empowering others in other areas of the world to make their schools safe places for everyone as well.

As cyberbullying increases, many more are standing up and using their voices against cruelty. Celebrities like Ellen DeGeneres are speaking out on national television, saying, "I stand for honesty, equality, kindness, compassion, treating people the way you want to be treated and helping those in need." Youth, teens, adolescents, and adults are starting movements for change: Love is Louder, STOP Cyberbullying, DoSomething.org, Teens Against Bullying, wordswound.org, It Takes One (ITO) club, to name a few. Many are proving that the once silent majority can be the vocal majority. Because of the efforts of a few, many students realize that most who witness cruelty don't like it and have been bystanders because they haven't known what to do or have been silenced, like Josh, by fear. With action steps and the support of other peers and adult role models, the vocal majority can create safe and compassionate school environments and support those who have been bullied to once again find their voice.

The Cumberland Valley School District in Mechanicsburg, Pennsylvania, recognizes that the most powerful person in a bullying situation is the bystander. The "It Takes One" club empowers those who witness bullying to act against it by standing up and speaking out. The once silent majority is now the vocal majority. As recommended in our chapter on school bullying, the entire school community—administrators, teachers, support staff, and learners—are taught to deal effectively with bullies, targets and the caring majority. Learners are taught to monitor what is happening in their school in order to make their school safe. Bullies are taught to re-channel their behavior into positive leadership behavior. The school teaches everyone to "act against injustice." *www.cvschools.org/services*

Another powerful program The WE WILL GENERATION is a program that is "a student teaching student" model. The focus is on respecting differences, uniting together, and taking action. There is on online curriculum that can be accessed readily at their website. *www.pacer.org/bullying/wewillgen/*

Youth helping youth is a model that has worked in many school environments. In order for youth to be empowered to make a difference, they need the support of the adults in their schools and community.

Among the facts posted by DoSomething.org, 75 percent of the youth surveyed have visited a website bashing another student and 90 percent of teens have seen social media bullying and have ignored it while 84 percent have witnessed others telling cyberbullies to stop. *www.DoSomething.org*

It is important for youth to feel empowered to take action in support of one another by role model peers and adults, and to believe that compassion is the norm in their schools and community. The majority of youth do not want to injure the self-esteem of their peers, and when the power is given to the caring majority, bullies lose the ability to hurt, and instead are encouraged to be empowered through positive leadership.

PART TWO:
Cyberbullying and Adults

Cyberstalking/ Harassment and Trolls

Adults have often been the hidden victims of cyberbullying because many of their stories have not been in the headlines as frequently as the targets of teen cyberbullying. The technical name for cyberbullying between adults is cyberstalking/harassment and another unseen presence to contend with are Trolls. Cyberstalking/harassing is the use of the Internet or other electronic means to stalk or harass an individual, a group of individuals, or an organization. Bullying may include the making of false accusations, monitoring, making threats, identity theft, damage to data or equipment, or gathering information that may be used to harm or harass.

Cyberstalking/Harrassing

Cyberstalking/harassing shares important characteristics of stalking. Many stalkers both on- and offline are motivated by a desire to harm their target. A cyberstalker/harasser may be an online stranger or person whom the target knows. They may be anonymous and frequently solicit the involvement of others online who do not know their targets.

We recently interviewed a man who knows the distress of being cyberstalked and harassed. His name is Bill and he has had several businesses and websites over the past eight years. Last month he was working with an online customer who became unhappy about the price of an item he was quoted. Bill told his customer that his price was firm. The customer became angry and threatened to post online that Bill was dishonest and was running his business poorly. Bill let him know again that the price was firm and that he could certainly look elsewhere for this item. An hour later, Bill noticed that the unhappy customer had begun posting threats to the site he had visited and Bill's other sites as well. Bill was concerned, but was at a loss for what to do. He felt that if he ignored the unhappy customer the bullying would stop. Unfortunately, this was not the case. When Bill opened his online business the following day he noticed that not only were there more threats from the unhappy customer, but threats from customers who had been dissatisfied in previous years. His concern for the reputation of this business and his other online businesses grew. Worse yet, the nature of the comments made him fear for his personal safety.

Bill contacted the administrator of his sites and had him remove the negative, threatening information. He felt that this was all that was necessary because he had experienced an excellent reputation in all of his businesses for the past eight years. The very next day when Bill opened his online businesses, there were more negative statements and more threats. Some of them were, "We will see that you get closed down," "Who you think you are?" "We will see to it that no one will want to do business with you!" With continually growing concern, he decided to seek legal assistance and find out how to press charges on this cyberstalker/harasser. Bill found that many new laws had been put into place to prevent this kind of harassment, and that support groups were available to help targets of cyberstalking.

Not surprisingly, the cyberstalking/harassment took an emotional toll on Bill. He had been unable to sleep since the threats began, he didn't feel much like eating, and became anxious about what "those people" could actually do to his businesses or to him personally. He became hypervigilant, constantly looking over his shoulder to see who was around him. He didn't even feel safe at home. Bill's attorney wrote letters to the cyberstalkers/harassers informing them that what they were doing was against the law and that criminal charges would be filed. Bill knew that he needed to keep a paper trail for evidence, which would provide his legal team the proper tools to protect him. Fortunately for Bill, the legal correspondence seems to have stopped the cyberbullying.

Most people who text and go online are unaware of the damage and harm that can be caused by cyberstalkers/harrassers. As Bill said, "I had no idea that there are people out there who would do this to another person." He was also surprised how frightening it was that he never saw or heard these people who were threatening him and his businesses.

Cyberstalking/harassment involves spying, targeting, hacking, and keeping track of another person's life through the Internet. The motivation can be: boredom, entertainment, power, personal vendettas, or attention. This behavior is generally repeated, unsolicited threatening behavior used by a person or a group of people with the intent to do psychological or physical harm through the use of any electronic environment where communication with others is possible. Cyberstalkers/harassers can hack into a target's personal information and send obscene, hurtful, embarrassing, threatening e-mails, texts, pictures, and instant messages. They may hack into a target's computers and seize their bank, credit card, and other account information to buy things for themselves or to discredit the target. They can digitally change pictures of their target in order to embarrass and humiliate them by presenting them as a sexual object, and send these images to an amateur pornographic website.

Many remain unaware that cyberstalking/harassing is a criminal offense under federal and state law. Assailants who are convicted through anti-stalking, slander, and harassment laws can have restraining orders placed against them, serve probation, or even incur criminal penalties, including jail time (Aftab, aftab.com).

Trolls

Another form of cyberbully is referred to as a troll. Trolls use the Internet/social media with the intent to provoke, antagonize, or annoy. Many of us might remember fairy tales that included a mean old troll. He was usually a hideous curmudgeon who hid under a bridge and would try to scare, annoy, or antagonize those who dared to tread on "his" bridge. Troll story variations might include other locales, such as the woods or in caves, but they all have in common the element of surprise, annoyance, threats, or provocation.

While the trolls featured on the pages of a fairy tale book are harmless entertainment, the trolls that "live" on the Internet are anything but. They share some things in common with the storybook characters in that they approach with an element of surprise, they're annoying, they may be threatening, and they find creative ways of being provocative. Instead of hiding under bridges, today's trolls lurk in blogs, newsgroups, message boards, forums, or other online venues with the express purpose of being annoying; a nuisance who is there to stir up trouble, to try to shift focus, or muddy the proverbial pond. They may try to start an argument within a long-established thread. They may generalize that all contributors to a particular forum, blog, or message board are biased, racist, or of a stereotypical category— simply to try to rile people up, or to get the course of the conversation off track. They may try to monopolize or commandeer the focus of the conversation by causing many of the participants to get off their respective points, while trying to address the methods of the troll.

These trolls will disrupt board or forum for the sole purpose of being an annoyance and drawing attention to themselves. They may pose as a "newbie" seeking help, merely to shift the momentum or dynamics of the group. Oftentimes, they will create so much chaos and distraction, that the group administrator may eventually shut down access to that particular troll who, too often, may have additional aliases so that they can continue to be an annoyance.

The troll can vandalize a search engine or application, or any other site on the Internet, for the sole purpose of attacking and destroying the lives of others. The troll feels no one can see them or hear them and they are all alone. They appear to feel empathy for their targets or follow social norms, boundaries or laws. "I will never be caught" is the belief of the troll. They enjoy saying or doing things that they would never be able to say if they were face to face with their targets. They seem to have few inhibitions because they have no fear or connection to the emotions of those that they are affecting.

We heard about the recent actions of a troll when visiting a beautiful bed and breakfast in British Columbia. The proprietors had an online guest book where those who had stayed at their beautiful home could visit and write comments about their stay. Other travelers, seeking information when making their vacation bookings, often search out the comments of others and base their stay on that advice.

One night, the owners received a call from some people who had recently stayed and enjoyed their visit, "We went to the guest book to write our comments about your lovely and serene place. Your website is full of pornography. There are pornographic comments, images, and videos. I think you might want to check it out."

Aghast, the owners followed up and, indeed, found their site filled with pornography. They contacted their web administrator and had the words, images, and video removed, and worked with him to safeguard that all comments would be screened in the future before being posted on their site.

Those who are experienced participants with newsgroups, message boards, forums and the like, will readily pick up on the presence of a troll, and alert the group as to the troll's presence. The troll could be anyone; a computer geek, living in the basement, seldom seeing the light of day, with little else to keep him or her occupied other than causing trouble; then again, the troll might be a polished professional very much out in the world. The best approach to handling a troll, is to highlight what they are up to by posting "troll alert" and then to ignore the offender. If the troll doesn't get the thrill or attention he is seeking, he will simply go to some other venue to try to stir up trouble there in order to get the "kicks," attention, and chaos he craves.

Who Are These Digital Bullies?

Mental profiling of digital criminals has identified factors that motivate some stalkers. The identified factors are: envy; pathological obsession, either professional or personal; unemployment or failure in their job or in their life; intention to intimidate and cause others to feel inferior; intimidation for financial advantage or business competition, or revenge over perceived or imagined rejection. One type of stalker is delusional and believes he or she knows the target and attempts to instill fear in a person to feel greater status and power. They believe they love them and are "just playing hard to get," or have betrayed them by being with someone else. This type of cyberstalker/harasser is usually not related to the target. Most of the time, contact is achieved through social media. They may suffer from a personality disorder, bipolar disorder, or schizophrenia. Their delusion is the belief that their target loves them even though they have never met. The delusional cyberstalker/harasser is desperate for companionship. Their targets may be teachers, celebrities, judges, doctors, etc.

They commonly target a celebrity or someone they believe to be a high-profile personality. The delusional cyberstalker/harasser can be extremely difficult to stop. Actress, Patricia Arquette quit Facebook after an alleged cyberstalker/harasser posted on her Facebook page. Ms. Arquette stressed the importance of not accepting friend requests from people that you do not know. Ms. Arquette is adamant that people need to understand that just because people are on your "friends list" does not mean that they are safe (Harp, 2011).

Other cyberstalkers/harrassers seek revenge against those they feel "have done them wrong." They know their targets and want them to suffer. They can be angry, unhappy employees, ex-spouses, ex-lovers, neighbors, friends or anyone else that they believe have treated them unfairly. These cyberstalkers/harassers feel victimized and are generally resentful and want to teach their targets a lesson. They are obsessive in their need for revenge. Their beliefs originate from resentments, righteousness, arrogance, blame, and/or feelings of victimization. They focus on instilling fear in their targets through blackmailing or threatening, and by showing their targets that they can hijack their computers. If they have had a romantic relationship at some point with their targets, they are unable to accept that the relationship they once had has ended. They harass their targets for ending the relationship and believe that compulsive harassment will lead to re-establishing the previous relationships by instilling fear and causing misery. While mentally healthy and stable people would never cause harm to one they truly love, these individuals' "love" for their targets is really obsession. They are capable of causing great harm—even death—because they are fueled by anger, hurt, and perceived rejection. Their goal is revenge.

Many people play online games through applications and can play with anyone in the world. Some players are highly competitive and become offended when they lose the game. Some actually feel intense hatred for the person who won and may seek revenge. When they do, they post rude and/or threatening comments to the person. In some cases this has led to cyberstalking/harassing, with the person who lost the online game feeling intense hatred for the person who won, and a need for revenge.

Still others, who do not know their targets, attempt to use fear to make their victims feel powerless in order to increase their own sense of dominance and control. They want to prove to themselves and others that they can actually use the computer to do this. They do not necessarily have anything against their target but simply use the target so that they can gain control over that person and assert their dominance over the other by instilling fear. This can become a challenge to the cyberstalkers/harassers. Generally, the target is chosen at random.

According to Antonio Chacon Medina author of *Una nueva cara de Internet El Acoso (A New Face of the Internet Stalking)*, (Medina, Antonio Chacon, 2013) the general profile of these cyberstalkers/harassers is: cold, with little or no respect for others; predatory, with the ability to wait patiently until vulnerable targets, frequently women or children, appear. The target may be known or unknown.

Stalking has been a crime throughout history. The problem changes with the introduction of social media. Before social media the stalkers/harasser would have to be in the same vicinity as their target. Now they can prey on targets from as far away as another country. This provides these bullies with a much larger range to choose from. They are highly skilled in the act of intimidation as well as having expert knowledge of technology and the use of the Internet.

Cyberstalking/harassing may sometimes consist of an accumulation of behaviors which in themselves are legal, such as calling on the phone, texting, sending gifts, sending e-mails, or posting on different sites. If the cyberstalker/harasser goes offline they may use threats and violence to frighten their targets. They have been known to commit vandalism and damage property, or physically attack their target to terrorize them or, less frequently, sexually assault them.

Cyberstalking/harassing can also occur through anonymous mobbing, much like face-to- face mobbing discussed in earlier chapters. Today's technology allows groups of people online to organize and target individuals. Mobbing can include posting lies and doctored photographs, threats of rape and other violence, posting sensitive personal information about the target, e-mailing derogatory statements about the target to their employers, and manipulating search engines to make up damaging material about prominent targets.

These cyberstalkers/harassers mob by adopting pseudonyms or going off-line entirely. An example of a target of cybermobbing/harassing is the American software developer and blogger Kathy Sierra. In 2007, a group of anonymous individuals threatened her with rape and strangulation. The cybermob published her home address and Social Security number and doctored photographs of her. Terrorized, Ms. Sierra canceled her speaking engagements and shut down her blog, stating, "I am afraid to leave my yard. I will never feel the same; I will never be the same (BBC News, 2007)." These cybermobs tend to become more extreme as members reinforce each other's beliefs. Because of this, they can lose a sense of personal responsibility for their behavior and increasingly dehumanize their targets. They become more willing to behave destructively and more aggressively when they believe they are supported by an authority figure such the mob leader. Internet service providers and website owners are sometimes blamed for not speaking out against this type of harassment, and laws regarding this type of harassment are often unclear.

Cyberstalking/harassing usually consists of online communications yet can, and has, led to offline stalking, violence, murder, suicide, rape, and other physical abuse as well in rare cases. There are also cases where personal property targets have been destroyed.

Targets

Cyberstalkers/harassers could be a relative, co-worker, friend, neighbor, or stranger. They can be male or female. Targets represent all races, cultures, countries, religions, economic backgrounds and/or occupations. Some of the targets are complete strangers. Cyberstalkers/ harrassers target people who they believe they can easily intimidate and control through fear. Like face-to-face bullies, these aggressors can carefully observe their potential target for a long time before attacking, or the attacks can be random when they set their sights on a target they feel is vulnerable.

Again, as is true with face-to-face bullying, many targets of cyber-bullying/harassing who are threatened online believe that the bully is capable of carrying out their threats. Those who are emotionally bullied often feel deserving of the shaming, humiliation and harassment directed toward them.

Cyberstalking/harassing in the workplace, according to overcome bullying.org, consists of spreading malicious rumors/gossip through social networking sites. Many of the targets need to seek therapy to deal with the trauma and, to make matters worse, often lose their jobs because their employer fears for the safety of the other employees. The target of online defamation can be a Fortune 500 company, a grocery clerk, a judge, a teacher, an ex-lover, a minister or priest—or you and/or your family.

Being a target of a cyberstalker/harasser can be a terrifying, traumatic experience. Anyone who receives anonymous messages repeatedly over social media, or via cell phone, that are filled with hatred, threats, or obsession, can experience intense psychological stress.

Cyberstalking/harassing is a cruel and vicious attack from a person or persons you may have never seen and who can hide behind the anonymity of the computer or phone. The bullying that has penetrated our world destroys lives, careers, relationships, and businesses with little or no advance warning. The targets may become so intimidated by the bully that they retreat into silence, which can cause them to feel powerless and helpless. One of the first instincts when confronted by attack is to go behind closed doors so the bully can't continue to penetrate one's life and make things worse. When we most need to reach out, our survival instinct is often to isolate.

These psychological effects on targets can so disrupt their daily life that many escape the cyberstalkers/harasser by changing their employment, residence, or phone numbers or by canceling social media site pages and abstaining from using their computers entirely. "Cyberstalking/harassing is a form of mental assault, in which the perpetrator repeatedly, unwantedly, and disruptively breaks into the life/world of the target, with whom they have no relationship (or no longer have). Moreover, these separated acts that make up the intrusion cannot by themselves cause mental abuse but do taken together have a cumulative effect" (Royakkers).

As with teens, some adult victims of cyberharrasment also commit suicide, or attempt it because the stress on targets can be overwhelming. A classic case of bullying that included cyberstalking/harassment made national headlines because it concerned members of the offensive line of the Miami Dolphins football team. Jonathan Martin, a rookie, abruptly quit the team mid-season. Because of the nature of his departure, there was speculation that he had mental health issues. Soon, however, it came out that Martin had been harassed and bullied, both in person, but more frequently via text and e-mail messages, by his fellow teammate, veteran, Richie Incognito. The mistreatment began early in the 2012 and the frequency and intensity increased. More than 1,000 of the text messages from October 2012 to November 2013 were made public at the end of January 2014. Martin declined to fight back, quit the team, and wasn't sure if he wanted to continue with his football career. Under much stress and mental anguish he said he had considered committing suicide twice. In April, Martin sent his mother a lengthy text message that concerned her. In concern for his mental health, his mother flew to Florida to check on her son. She was so worried, she contacted team officials, and Martin was referred to a psychiatrist who placed him on antidepressants (Shpiegel, 2014).

The cyberstalker's/harasser's target is typically someone who may be new to using social media, and who has little experience with the rules, etiquette, or safety when using the Internet, social media, e-mail, texting, etc. An advantage that targets of cyberstalking/harassing have over the traditional face-to-face bullying is that it is possible to avoid prolonged exposure and suffering by blocking sites, avoiding sites, changing e-mail addresses, or simply turning off their computers. If the cyberstalking/harassing is done through the smart phone media, the target may have to change their phone numbers.

The Cyberbullying Research Center suggests that adults become aware of the laws both federally and statewide on cyberstalking/harassment. If a cyberstalker/harasser affects you in any way, i.e. your health, your safety, your occupation, or any of your family and friends, you should immediately consult an attorney and make sure to keep records of the offensive correspondence, if possible.

Cyberstalking/harassing has been addressed in the United States in the Federal Cyberstalking Law. If you're interested in reviewing this law it can be found at: http://www.aftab.com/index.php?page=the-federal-cyberstalking-law. Cyberstalking/harassment is a criminal offense that also comes under state anti-stalking laws, slander laws, and harassment laws.

There are questions concerning the laws on how Internet use can be traced without infringing on the protection of people's civil liberties. Legal systems throughout the globe have begun to recognize cyberstalking/harassment as an acute social problem that needs to be addressed. How cyberstalking/harassment affects an individual has become painfully clear to legislatures worldwide. The loss of personal safety, employment, and self-esteem of targets has become of great concern globally. Stalking and harassing as a criminal offense is not new. Cyberstalking/harassing is new and needs to be recognized in legal, academic, and mental health circles.

There are now many websites available today to help targets get the help and justice they need. Two sites are: The National Center for Victims of Cyberstalking, *www.victimsofcrime.org*; and Support Groups against Cyberstalkers at *www.talkaboutsupport.com/group/ alt.support.tourette/messages/119862.html.*

Parry Aftab and the United States Department of Justice recommend targets of cyberstalking take the following steps:

1. Tell the person not to make contact again
2. Save all communications for evidence. Do not alter them in any way. Keep electronic copies, not just printouts.
3. Save any information that suggests a violent threat and contact law enforcement.
4. If the harassment continues, contact the harasser's Internet Service Provider. The ISP is provided with instant messages. Most ISP's prohibit using their service for abusive purposes. An ISP can often intervene by directly contacting the stalker or closing the account.
5. Keep a record of your contacts with ISP representatives or law enforcement officials.

Legislation penalizing cyberstalking/harassing has been introduced in a number of states. The Global Cyber Law Database (GCLD) aims to become the most comprehensive and authoritative source of cyber laws for all countries. Many states have in place cyberstalking/harassing laws, or have laws that explicitly include any electronic form of communication within their traditional stalking and harassing laws. All fifty states have laws against either cyberstalking and/or cyberharassment although they may be called something else. For more specific information, visit *www.aftab.com/index. php?page=the-federal-cyberstalking-law*.

Helping Each Other

There is a chapter of the Guardian Angels called "CyberAngels." CyberAngels began in 1995 and was started by Gabriel Hatcher as an online "neighborhood watch." Originally, the CyberAngels monitored chat rooms with the intent of apprehending sexual predators. After that, CyberAngels expanded their focus to educating police, the school systems, and families about online abuse and cybercrime. In 1998, the CyberAngels received a Presidential Service Award. MacSupport.com founder Tony Riccardi was an early member of this chapter of the Guardian Angels.

In writing this chapter on adult cyberstalking/harassing, we had many moments of sadness concerning this new vehicle for hurt. But we are also encouraged by the adults and teens who are working to make cyberspace safer. We are all connected and interdependent. As the Internet makes the world as a whole a closer community, it is important that we join together to use technological advancement to support, rather than harm, those who use it. In order to do this, we must return to balance. Our values, emotional well-being, and physical well-being must be balanced with our intellectual ability as we redefine communicating through technology. The development of empathy comes from human love and connection early in life, and can continue to develop as we grow and mature. We love, because we are loved. We feel the pain of another because someone was available to feel our pain.

As we continue to navigate the world of cyberspace and emerging technologies that change the way we interact with each other, we should remember that we still have choices. We can explore it with the timeless values of empathy, kindness, and trust, to connect with new people and old friends, or we can use it to hide anonymously in the shadows and speak whatever comes to mind without giving a second thought to how it might make another person feel. We can choose to communicate with someone face-to-face, or we can send them a text message and never bother to hear the sound of their voice in reply. These technological tools are miraculous, but we need to use them responsibly. We need to be courageous enough to turn off our computers and cell phones and have dinner with our families, reach out to our neighbors, play outside with our kids, and open our doors to the other children in our neighborhood. We need to advocate for safe and compassionate schools, responsibly monitor the technology that has been created, and take the time to have discussions with children about important topics like celebrating our differences and practicing kindness. Being connected in the virtual world can never substitute for connection in the real world.

6

Bullying Associated with Sexting

Coercion, Revenge Porn, Sextortion, and Textual Harassment

"When a bully is held accountable for his actions,
his future actions will change. Bad behavior
only continues for those who allow it."

Gary Hopkins

Fifteen-year-old Trish couldn't stop crying. She thought he loved her. He had told her so, hadn't he? Now he was blackmailing her, threatening to send her photos to everyone in school if she didn't have sex with him. Why had she sent those pictures? Why? Now everyone would think she was a "slut" and she'd never even had sex.

It had all started innocently enough. She had been attracted to Troy. He was so cool. He was a junior and she was a sophomore. Then he asked her out. She was flattered and excited. They'd gone to the movies and then a second date the next weekend with some friends. It was fun at first, but then he wanted to make out. She wasn't ready for that but she let him kiss her. That wasn't enough for Troy; he wanted more than she was ready to give, but she continued to go out with him. He pressured her more each time, and now this blackmail. She asked herself again, "Why did I send that picture?"

She had been texting with him late one night after everyone in her house had gone to sleep. He'd been so sweet and told her he couldn't stop thinking about her. "I love u so much. If u won't have sex, at least send me a couple of pics." She didn't want to, it made her feel uncomfortable, but it wasn't sex. What could it hurt? Maybe if he had a couple of pictures it would take the pressure off for a while. He loved her, after all, and it was just between them. He was so cool and she didn't want their relationship to end. It's just a picture, she kept telling herself. Finally, she sent a picture of her naked breasts. Then, he'd wanted another one. She sent another, then another.

The next day at lunch he texted her:

> "skip next period and lets go out I really want you those pics drove me crazy its ur fault i love you so much"
> "no IM not going to skip I told u IM not ready to have sex"

"ok ive been patient either u skip with me and we go have sex or I'm
    sending the pics to everyone its ur fault"

"why r u doing this"

"i told u what IM going to do."

"u told me u loved me I knew u were lying this is all u wanted. I dated u,
    kissed u, sent the pics u wanted why r u doing this"

"whatever idc deal or no deal yes or no"

"IM crying now why are you doing this."

"just answer me yes or no now or after school or im sending them. yes
    or no"

"IM crying really hard IM going home"

As hard as it was, Trish did what she'd learned in her class on
cyberbullying. She was ashamed, really embarrassed, and afraid, but
worked up the courage to confide in her parents. They offered their
support and assistance, helping her copy the texts she had received.
Together, they took the copies to the principal of her school the next
day. Afraid and embarrassed, yet also determined, she turned Troy
in. She wasn't going to be pressured anymore and she wasn't going to
let Troy blackmail her.

"Sexting" is the sending or receiving of nude or sexually explicit
photographs or videos through a cell phone, other mobile device,
or via webcams to Internet sites. Some also expand the definition to
include the sending of sexually explicit text messages.

Prevalence of Sexting

A 2013 PEW Research reports about three in four teens from ages
twelve to seventeen have a cell phone (74 percent). That said, there is
a wide disparity in the research regarding the prevalence of sexting
among youth:

Research	Age	Sample	Sent	Received
The National Campaign to Prevent Teen and Unplanned Pregnancy in (2008)	13–19	653	19%	31%
Cox Communication (2009)	13–19	655	9%	17%
MTV/AP (2009)	14–24	600	10%	15%
PEW (2009)	12–17	800	4%	15%
Hindju and Patchin (2010)	11–18	4400	8%	13%
Crimes Against Children Research Center (2010)	10–17	1500	2.5%	7%
MTV/AP (2011) (Naked Photos or Videos)	14–17	631	15%	21%
University of Texas School Of Public Health (2013)	10th Grade	1000	20%	30%

PEW (2013)

The wide disparity of research findings may suggest a difference in the definition of sexting used in surveys, or limitations and differences to the outreach population. Definitions at times limit sexting to the sending or receiving of nude or semi-nude photographs, while others include "sexually explicit" or "sexually suggestive" photos. Still others expand the definition to include sexually suggestive text messages as well. What appears to be clear in the research is that the majority of youth are not involved in sexting as senders or receivers. For those that are, the consequences for a small percentage where bullying is involved, like Trish, can be very painful and, for some that feel they have no place to turn, life-threatening.

Research Adult "Sexting"	Sample Size	Not Specified	Sent	Received
Lookout Mobile Security Survey (2012)	2097	20%		
Pew Research Internet Project (2013)	2252		9%	20%

A poll conducted by U.K.-based mobile news site Recombu among 2,000 adults revealed that almost half (47 percent) of England sends sexy texts to their significant other. Of that adventurous group, about 11 percent have mistakenly sent sexts to the wrong person, such as family members or friends. (Kelly, 2012)

Why Sexting?

The rise in sexting between adults has, for the most part, been innocent; sending or receiving photos from someone with whom one shares an intimate relationship. Between two consenting teens who share a romantic interest, it seems to be a new way of exploring and experimenting with sexual identity and boundaries using technology (cell phones, tablets, computers, etc.) that have been part of their world for most of their lives. The difference is that sexting for youth is illegal in most states. When nude or semi-nude images that are sent and or received are of youth below the age of seventeen in many states and eighteen in others, it is technically considered child pornography. Some states classify sexting between youth as a misdemeanor while others classify it as a felony. Most states are still racing to catch up with creating new legislation as technology becomes increasingly advanced.

For the most part, legislators consider the child pornography laws too harsh for adolescents whose pictures circulate on all kinds of sites and who experiment with their sexual identity and boundaries through the technology they are so comfortable using. States like Utah, Nebraska, and Vermont have changed their laws to reduce the penalty for teenagers who engage in sexting. Fourteen more states are considering legislation that would treat teens engaging in sexting differently than sexual predators or those involved in pornography. (Lewin, 2010) They are instead focusing attention for more severe punishment on those that use "sext" images to bully, blackmail, and seek revenge.

When Sexting Becomes Bullying: Coercion, Revenge Porn, Sextortion, Harassment, and Violence

Research studies indicate that many teens, like Trish, feel uncomfortable when receiving or being asked to send sexually explicit pictures. According to a 2012 survey of 1,200 twelfth-grade girls online, of the 21 percent of senior girls who have sent nude photos or videos of themselves to someone else, 61 percent wish they had not done so. The study found that 37 percent said they did so because they were pressured to do so by the person it was being sent to, 4 percent were pressured by friends, and 36 percent felt that they didn't see any problem with sending someone nude photos or videos, or photos or videos where a private part was exposed. (Kramer, 2012)

According to research published in the July 2012 issue of Pediatrics & Adolescent Medicine, polling 978 high school students in Texas, 57 percent of youth in the study had been asked to send a sext. While the majority of these teens admitted to being bothered by the request, 28 percent of the students followed through and sent a naked picture through text or email.

In another study, 51 percent of girls said they sexted because of pressure from boys whereas 18 percent of teen boys felt pressured by girls. 23 percent of girls and 24 percent of boys said friends had pressured them (2008, National Campaign to Prevent Teen and Unplanned Pregnancy, and *Cosmogirl.com*).

Some teens have expressed the view that they feel "bullied into" sending nude or semi-nude pictures by boyfriends, girlfriends, or by peers. Fourteen-year-old Laura said, "I felt so uncomfortable doing it, but my boyfriend said everybody did it. Some of my friends told me I was being ridiculous, a baby." Unfortunately, these may be the same "friends" who would turn against her if the pictures ended up in the wrong hands and were circulated through the school.

Jessica Logan, a petite, blond-haired, blue-eyed Ohio high school senior committed suicide in 2008 after sexting a nude photo of herself to a boyfriend. When they broke up, he sent the photo to everyone else at her school. She was cruelly harassed for months by the other girls at the school, who called her a slut and a whore, and threw things at her.

Revenge Porn

Although most youth send images to each other with no malicious intent, sexting isn't always "innocent" and can cross the line into bullying as it did in Trish's case. What were innocently taken pictures can become tools for harassment and bullying. In some cases, an individual might consider the photo as a "badge of honor" and will forward it immediately to others he or she wishes to impress. Sometimes, cell phones are borrowed and the images found are sent to others by those who may be envious, jealous, or as a "joke." Once the button is pressed and the picture is sent, the sender has lost control over its use. Some pictures have been stolen from social media profiles and posted to pornographic sites (Godfrey, 2013). The photo sent to a love interest can become a weapon used after a breakup.

Margarite, a fourteen-year-old girl in Washington state, posed naked in front of her mirror. She held up her cell phone and took a picture of herself for her boyfriend, Isaiah. He had asked her for it, told her it was common, and that he had seen other boys' cell phone pictures. However, soon after the photo was sent, they broke up and Isaiah sent it to a girl who had once been Margarite's best friend. He said later that the friend pressured him into it, and she said she was just curious. Their friendship had ended when the two girls had fought over a boy. Still angry at Margarite, she slapped on a text, "Ho Alert!" adding, "If you think this girl is a whore, then text this to all your friends." She then sent it to all her contacts. In less than twenty-four hours, the picture had circulated through four middle schools.

Margarite was not charged with a crime, but Isaiah, Margarite's former friend, and a thirteen-year-old girl who helped forward the picture, were charged with dissemination of child pornography, a Class C felony. Ultimately, the charges were reduced to a gross mis-demeanor of telephone harassment and they were eligible for a community service program. Many youth, however, continued to jeer the girl on MySpace and attack those who spent time with her (2011, New York Times). Even a year later, Margarite was still haunted by the incident and, when asked about it, would retreat to her room.

Eighteen-year-old Phillip Alpert broke up with his sixteen-year-old girlfriend. His girlfriend had sent him e-mails containing nude photos she took of herself with a digital camera. In a fit of anger, he signed onto her e-mail account and sent the photos to dozens of her friends and to members of her family. He was arrested and sentenced to five years of probation and forced to register as a sex offender. He must continue to register as a sex offender until he is forty-three (Ryan, 2010).

The new term for this type of bullying has been labeled "revenge porn." Rather than severe punishment for sexting, many states have passed bills more in keeping with the damage caused by those that use sext images sent in confidence as a weapon to bully. By unanimous vote, the Georgia senate approved the "revenge sexting bill." The leg-islation prohibits someone from texting, sending, or posting sexually explicit photography or videos as a means of retaliation (Wirth, 2014). Similar revenge porn bills have been passed or have been introduced and, in 2014, are pending in twenty-three other states as well as Puerto Rico (NCSL 2014).

Sextortion

Another form of bullying called "sextortion" employs coercion by threatening to release sexual images or information to extort more images or sexual favors from the victim.

In a Maryland suburb of Washington, D.C., fifty boys were involved in pressuring and coercing twenty fourteen- and fifteen-year-old girls into sending them sexually explicit pictures. The pictures were uploaded to a password-protected website. The password was sold to students at the high school and middle school. Pictures were also sold via cell phones and e-mail (2012, Hinduja and Patchin).

A college student in California hacked into 150 online accounts to extort young females into sending him nude pictures and videos. He took control of the young women's e-mail accounts and social media sites. "As digital devices, e-mail accounts and social media accounts now contain the most intimate details of the public's daily lives, the impact of this kind of hacking and extortion becomes more pronounced, troubling and far reaching." The prosecutors wrote in a sentencing memo filed with the court (2014, U. S. Attorney's Office).

No one knows the effects of sextortion more than a teenager in Oregon who was approached the first time for a nude picture of herself when she was twelve years old. Her then-boyfriend told her that he already had a naked picture of her and threatened to share it with others if she didn't send him another using her cellphone. As a naive seventh grader, she didn't question how he had a picture of her, even though she had never given him one. She assumed he had somehow photo edited a picture or entered the girls locker room and taken one. He also threatened to kill himself if she wasn't a "better girlfriend." She eventually sent him the picture he wanted. One picture was not enough, however, and he demanded more and more. Soon, a ninth-grade boy asked her for a picture. He stalked her, exposed himself to her, and attempted to rape her.

Her boyfriend was one of fifteen boys who coerced at least twenty-eight girls to share naked pictures. The middle school boys' "sextortion ring" was a contest to see how many compromising pictures of girls they could collect. Points were given for each picture as well as how explicit they were. The contest went on for a couple of years.

Today, the twelve-year-old target of their sextortion is fifteen and finds it hard to make friends or relax, and is on medication for anxiety. For a time she wasn't sleeping or eating, and would startle easily. Finally, a concerned teacher contacted her parents in whom she was too ashamed to confide (2013, Laboe).

In another prominent case of sextortion, a college student was arrested for allegedly hijacking the webcams of many young women, taking nude images, then blackmailing the victims, demanding more explicit pictures. Among the targets was the reigning Miss Teen USA (2013, Botelho).

Bullying and Textual Harassment with a Cell Phone

Two Ohio boys were convicted of rape after photos of the victim taken on the night of the assault went viral with hash tags like #rape and #drunkgirl accompanying the shared images. New York City high school junior, Temitayo Fagbenle, told *Crimesider* that when she and her friends talked about the social media postings the victim was subjected to after her assault, they were glad the case was getting attention because "things like this happen all the time" (Dahl, Julia, 2013).

Boston College football player Jaryd Rudolph, nineteen, allegedly used his cellphone on February 15, 2012, to record audio of his roommate having sex with a female student and shared it with others, according to CBS News. Six months earlier, the Boston College football team suspended Jaryd. He took a plea in March and was required to complete community service as well as other conditions.

Serious Consequences

Dr. Jill Murray, who runs a private practice in Laguna Niguel, California, specializing in adolescents, teen dating abuse, and domestic violence stated in an interview, "I have two girls who have made suicide attempts and several had to switch schools because of sexting," she said, adding that other patients of hers who sexted and then watched their picture get distributed to other teens, started cutting themselves (Caron, 2011).

Many targets of bullying through sexting report the same psychological symptoms as other targets of face-to-face or cyberbullying: depression, anxiety, PTSD, and suicidal ideation.

A 2010 survey of 23,000 students in Boston area high schools found that sexting can frequently include overtones of bullying and coercion and that teens who are involved were more likely to report being psychologically distressed. The survey found that twice as many respondents who said they had "sexted" in the past year reported depressive symptoms compared to teens who did not. Thirteen percent of teens involved in sexting reported making a suicide attempt during that period compared to 3 percent of non-sexting teens. Lead researcher, Shari Kessel Schneider, made it clear that they have shown a link between "sexting" and psychological distress. She stated clearly that an association has been found but not necessarily a causal relationship. More research is needed (Schneider, 2010).

In some cases, bullying through sexting has been a major contributing factor to youth suicide. The following are only a few of those who have taken their lives after bullying associated with sexting:

- Audrie Pott, fifteen, who was allegedly raped in September 2012, and then subjected to further humiliation when photos of the assault reportedly went viral. She killed herself eight days later.

- Rehtaeh Parsons, a seventeen-year-old, who killed herself in April 2013 after a photo of her allegedly being raped was shared online. Her mother said a boy took a photo of the alleged assault in 2011 and that her daughter was bullied for months after it was distributed online.
- Tyler Clementi, an eighteen-year-old student at Rutgers University in Piscataway, New Jersey, jumped to his death from the George Washington Bridge on September 22, 2010. On September 19, his roommate, Dharun Ravi and a fellow hall mate, Molly Wei, used a webcam on Ravi's computer and a computer in Wei's dorm room to view, without Clementi's knowledge, Clementi kissing another man. Ravi and Wei watched the video on the video stream, via iChat, for a few seconds. Prior to arriving at Rutgers, Ravi had searched for information about his new roommate online. Ravi later referred on his Twitter account to having seen Clementi's communications on the Justusboys website and wrote: "Found out my roommate is gay." On September 21 Ravi posted text messages saying there would be a viewing party to watch Clementi and his guest along with the directions on how to view it remotely. The day prior to the suicide, Ravi urged friends and Twitter followers to watch via his webcam a second tryst between Clementi and his friend, though viewing never occurred.
- Thirteen-year-old Hope Witsell had sexted a picture of her breasts to her boyfriend. According to her family and friends, another girl got her hands on the photo and sent it to students at six schools in the area. Before Hope could stop it, the picture went viral. Hope became a target for eleven-, twelve-, and thirteen- year-old bullies. They even started a "Hope Hater Page" on MySpace. She used her favorite scarves to hang herself from her canopy bed in September 2009.

Sexting becomes bullying:

1. **When you are pressured to send a nude or semi-nude picture of yourself.** A large number of teens acknowledge that they are

pressured into participating in sexting when they don't want to. They admit that they are uncomfortable with it but, like Trish in our earlier example, have difficulty saying "no" because they fear losing status with their peer group, losing the chance for a relationship, or because "everyone else is doing it" and they don't want to be different.

2. **When you are threatened or coerced into sending a sext.** Language that is coercive and threatening includes examples such as:"Either send me a picture or I will no longer be your friend." "You're such a baby, everyone else is doing it." "Send me the picture I asked for or I will break up with you." "Send me a picture or I'll know you don't love me."

3. **When pictures are used to coerce sexual favors or in an attempt to extort more explicit pictures.** In cases of sextortion, sexually explicit pictures are sent to someone in innocence, hijacked from websites, or taken without an individual's knowledge or consent in an attempt to threaten or extort. The "sextortionist" might say: "Have sex with me or I will send your picture to others." "Send me more pictures, even better than the last ones, or I will send the ones you sent to everyone"

4. **When pictures are used for revenge.** Sexually explicit pictures may be sent to others for whom they were not intended in retaliation for ending a relationship, in jealousy or anger, or used as a threat: "If you break up with me, I will send those pictures everywhere." Sometimes pictures sent to someone with innocent intentions can be forwarded to entire contact lists or posted on social media websites after a romantic breakup, as a punishment for a perceived slight, through jealousy or a myriad of other excuses.

5. **When pictures you have sent to a personal friend or intimate partner are sent to others as a "joke" or with malicious intent.** Sometimes pictures sent to someone with romantic or innocent intentions can be forwarded to others "as proof of a conquest" or posted on social media websites under the guise of humor at someone else's expense.

6. **When pictures are taken with a cell phone, tablet, webcam or other technology without consent.** Some bullies think it is funny to embarrass or humiliate another by taking pictures without consent or, sometimes, even their awareness. A teenage girl might be having a fun time at a sleepover and the next day finds a picture of herself as the screen saver on someone's computer, dressing or undressing, in the shower, or in another venue that she thought was private and safe. Perhaps someone snaps a picture of a peer in the shower or dressing after a sports event without his or her knowledge or consent. In some cases, webcams or cell phones have been used to record the sexual intimacies of a roommate. One person's idea of enjoyment and power is often another's embarrassment and shame. Bullies often say, "It was only a joke," after the damage has been done.

7. **When a boss or fellow employee sends a sexually explicit text to a co-worker or employee.** Bosses and co-workers today have found a new way to sexually harass by sending sexually explicit photos, audio recordings, or texts, to employees and co-workers. They may be sent in the form of "jokes" or may be touted as such when the sender is confronted, saying, "I was only joking." This new form of harassment has been labeled "textual harassment." It has become more prevalent because most cell phones today are equipped with a digital camera, audio recorder, and video camera. Some bosses have been known to send sexually explicit texts or e-mails to their employees' homes. People can face serious legal problems for this type of harassment. Some employees are bullying with intent, while others may post such messages without thinking or without consideration of how these messages may affect employees or co-workers (2011, BLR). Many employees are bothered by this type of harassment but let it go on for far too long because they fear losing their job or facing further bullying or ridicule.

Protecting Yourself, Your Peers, or Co-Workers from Coercion, Revenge Porn, Sextortion, and Textual Harassment

Many view sexting as a romantic and innocent interaction between two consenting adults who have become attracted to one another or who are flirting for the first time. In the examples highlighted in this chapter, however, sexting can have serious consequences including revenge porn and sextortion. Below are some safeguards against becoming a target:

1. **Don't allow yourself to be coerced.** True friends or caring and supportive romantic partners do not attempt to coerce others into doing something that makes them feel uncomfortable. Coercion and intimidation in any form is neither love nor friendship, it is bullying. If a partner pressures you by saying, "If you loved me, you would…" The answer could be: "Intimidation is not love." Or, "I love you, and the answer is 'no.' I am not comfortable with your request. I have made my choice. You can make yours." If peers or friends attempt to coerce you using, "Everybody does it." Or, "You're just being a 'baby,'" your answer might be, "I am taking care of myself and am being responsible to myself," or "All the facts point out that 'not everybody is doing it' and I refuse to be pressured." Or "I'm not 'everybody', I'm me." Or "Did someone take a survey? If they did, no one asked me." "Friends do not pressure friends; the answer is 'no.'"

2. **Protect yourself! Be careful who you agree to send pictures to.** "Sexting" can be fun and exciting in a relationship. Take the time to consider: "Could this picture end up in the wrong hands?" "Do I feel comfortable with my family, friends, or others I don't know seeing this picture?" Relationships sometimes end even when it feels like he/she is the 'one' right now. Pictures can be forever. Once it is sent, it is out of your control. Could this picture end up being sent to others accidently

or purposefully? "Does the person I am sending this picture to share my values?" Take time to think before you press "send."

3. **Do not allow sextortion.** Many youth and adults alike, when threatened by those with whom they have "sexted," or by those who use sexually explicit pictures or texts (or the threat that they have them) to extort sexual "favors" or "more explicit pictures," remain silent. They frequently feel intense guilt and shame so they tell no one. The twelve-year-old girl from Oregon didn't tell her parents because of intense feelings of shame. Sextortionists depend on silence. The muteness of their target is their weapon. Silence allows them to continue escalating their demands. If you are a youth, seek out the help of an adult you trust who is in a position to help. If you are an adult, notify the police immediately. The shame and guilt belongs to the person attempting to blackmail you. These bullies are attempting to render you powerless. Follow Trish's example and take a stand. Sextortion is against the law!

   Some who commit sextortion do not know their victims but instead target the person with malware that turns on the victim's webcam. The victim can unwittingly provide images the criminal can use to blackmail the victim. The website *www.welivesecurity. com* provides tips to protect individuals from this type of sextortion. Some suggested tips are: 1) Cover webcams by putting a removable sticker or opaque tape over the camera lens when you are not using it, or unplug stand-alone webcams when not in use. Turn off computers or close laptops when not in use. 2) Use strong passwords. Verify with senders before opening unexpected attachments. 3) Contact the police immediately if you are contacted and/or threatened by a person attempting to extort images (2014, Meyers).

4. **Use your voice if you have become the object of revenge porn or textual harassment.** Those who harass and seek revenge attempt to take away the self-esteem and voice of their targets. They are attempting to render their targets powerless and ashamed. As we have seen

again and again, you *can* find support if you seek it out. In the words of Eleanor Roosevelt, "No one can make you inferior without your consent." Again, the greatest weapon of any bully is to isolate you and render you silent. If you are the target of revenge porn or texual harassment, use your voice. Keep speaking until you are heard. Tell someone you trust immediately! Revenge porn and textual harrassment are against the law.

5. **Don't pass it on.** If you receive a picture that was not intended for your eyes, delete it. If you believe the sender is sending it as an act of revenge, control, harassment, or as a "joke" at another's expense, it is an act of bullying and can have severe social and psychological consequences for the original sender. Be part of the caring majority. Let a responsible person, law enforcement officer, or, in the workplace, your human resources officer know. Also, be aware, without the consent of the original sender, passing it on is against the law in most states in the United States, and in many countries. If the picture is of a youth under the age of seventeen, keeping it or passing it on may be at least misdemeanor, at most a felony.

6. **Be careful what you keep on your cell phone or post on media websites.** In this digital age, very little is "private." A note, a picture, or a text on a media site might be copied, pasted, and distributed. Cell phones may be lost or stolen, media sites and computers may be hijacked. If you are using your cell phone at school it can be confiscated and thoroughly checked in many school districts. If your cell phone or computer is the property of your workplace, they can be confiscated and checked. Many schools and workplaces search the Internet and media sites of those applying for admission or employment. Again, pictures and texts can be lasting. Consider whether you are willing to jeopardize future schooling, job opportunities, or current employment.

7. **Snapchat may be fun, but is it safe?** Snapchat is an app that many use to sext because they feel a false sense of security that it is safe. It

allows a user to snap a picture and send it to another Snapchat user. Once it reaches the user, it can be seen for only minutes before it is deleted and disappears. The sender believes that because it disappears, it is safe to send it. The sender feels no matter what they have sent, their reputation is safe. Unfortunately, the app does not protect the sender from the receiver taking a screen shot with their smart phone. Also pictures don't always "disappear." Many people do not carefully read the Snapchat Privacy Policy. Their December 20, 2013, update clearly states: "users with access to the Replay feature are able to view a Snap additional times before it is deleted from their device. We cannot guarantee that deletion always occurs within a particular timeframe. We also cannot prevent others from making copies of your Snaps (e.g., by taking a screenshot). If we are able to detect that the recipient has captured a screenshot of a Snap that you send, we will attempt to notify you. In addition, as for any other digital information, there may be ways to access Snaps while still in temporary storage on recipients' devices or, forensically, even after they are deleted. You should not use Snapchat to send messages if you want to be certain that the recipient cannot keep a copy (2013, Snapchat).

8. **Stand up for those who may feel they have no voice.** Once a sext has gone viral, some will jump on it and begin their own bullying campaign and harass the individual who has sent the picture or text. She or he then becomes the target of painful and relentless bullying. Don't join in or become a silent weapon for those who attempt to gain power through isolating, attacking, and hurting others. Be the friend, peer, or co-worker you would want others to be for you! When the silent majority speaks up, it is clear that bullying is not the norm, compassion is.

7

Bullying Through Hazing

> "We're very early in this movement to address the most
> common form of violence there is for children, which
> is bullying, and hazing is a type of bullying."
>
> *Stuart Green, Director of New Jersey*
> *Coalition for Bullying Awareness and Prevention*

Hazing, as defined in an Alfred University study, is "any humiliating or dangerous activity expected of you to join a group, regardless of your willingness to participate." It is a form of bullying that has been overlooked by society for generations (Hoover and Pollard, 2000).

Hazing behaviors and rituals have been around for over 2,000 years. The English education system was a contributing factor in America developing its own higher education system. The formation of American higher education created the different class distinctions: freshman, sophomore, junior, and senior. Also, the colleges that were religiously affiliated formed their own class distinctions. The beginning of extracurricular activities had a tremendous impact on the history of hazing. It is important to note that hazing does not just occur at the collegiate level.

The beginning of hazing has been traced back to the opening of Plato's Academy in 387 BC. In America, hazing within the "Greek System" of social fraternities has been well documented. Hazing stemmed from the belief that the newcomer to a higher education system was an ignorant, inexperienced, and crude man who had to be taught to become acceptable before he could become a member of the university. "Before he could taste the sweets of a student's life he should suffer hardships" (History of Hazing, www.greekchat.com, 2002.)

The definition of hazing in higher education is defined as "any action taken or citation created, intentionally, whether on or off fraternity premises, to produce mental or physical discomfort, embarrassment, harassment, or ridicule." The practice is based on an imbalance in power and the principle that new initiates must render themselves powerless and somehow diminished in order to be accepted. In this system, the powerless, if they pass the test of belonging, will eventually be the powerful. Such activities may include, but are not limited to, the following: use of alcohol, paddling in any form, inducing excessive fatigue, physical and psychological shocks, quests, treasure hunts, scavenger hunts, road trips or any other activities carried on outside or inside the confines of the chapter house, wearing of public apparel that is conspicuous and not in normally good taste, engaging in public stunts and buffoonery, morally degrading or humiliating games and activities, and any other activities that are not consistent with fraternal law, ritual or policy, or the laws and policies of the educational institutions.

There have been countless stories on the news and in magazines in recent years about hazing and its shocking consequences including death:

In March 2014, an eighteen-year-old student at Penn State jumped to his death from the rooftop of a hotel in Uniondale, New York. His father, managing editor at ABC News, believes that his son was driven to take his life due to hazing practices he had taken part in as a member of a fraternity. Days before his suicide, his son had sought counseling from a priest and sent messages to relatives indicating that he felt uncomfortable hazing other initiates and didn't feel he could do that. His father found pictures on his cell phone of a blind-folded pledge, with a pistol that looked real, pointed at his head. His son had spoken of other practices including making pledges drink alcohol until they vomited, or choosing between using cocaine or having a toy inserted in their lower body. At the time of the news release, the fraternity had been suspended pending investigation as Penn State has a zero tolerance policy regarding fraternity hazing (Dekok, 2014).

In March 2013, Sigma Alpha Epsilon, one of the largest fraternities in the nation, said it would no longer permit "pledging" as part of the initiation process in joining a fraternity, but would instead offer new brothers membership within days of inviting them to join the fraternity. The announcement came after a string of deaths and injuries resulting from pledging practices (Lovett, 2014).

Thirteen people were criminally charged in the hazing death of Robert Champion, twenty-six. He was the drum major and an initiate to the Florida A&M University elite marching band, the renowned Marching 100, and was beaten, kicked and suffocated by fellow band members during a hazing ritual on a bus following a football game. His parents commented that he had been beaten particularly severely because he had voiced concerns regarding the band's hazing practices (Brown, 2012).

Nineteen-year-old sophomore Arman Partamian was found dead March 1, 2009, after consuming a lethal level of alcohol over a period of three days to gain membership in an unsanctioned fraternity at the State University of New York.

Why would anyone want to participate in such horrific and life-threatening activity? The answer is that some people will go to great lengths to belong to a group and avoid exclusion. One person told us that it wasn't only the need to belong and the acceptance of humiliation in order not to be excluded, but that the learners that belonged to a particular fraternity in his university would receive A's in class because they were members. Many lawmakers have grappled with the question, "Why?" as they debate the need for legislation that would prohibit hazing practices. Many states that have passed laws to prohibit hazing recognize the intensity of peer pressure that prevents hazing victims from providing true consent when participating.

In the past, before its harmful, murderous effects were realized, hazing was considered to be harmless pranks associated with young men in college fraternities. We now know that hazing takes place beyond the college fraternity. Today it is experienced by boys/men and girls/women in school groups, college sororities and fraternities, athletic teams, the military, professional organizations, music, art and theater groups, peer groups or gangs, and cheerleading squads.

Hazing extends far beyond the walls of fraternities and universities and the "pranks" are frequently injurious if not life-threatening. Hazing rituals and activities are often physically abusive, toxic, and/or sexually violating. The activities can vary widely depending upon the participants, groups, and settings.

In the book *Hazing: Ritual of Bondage,* author Richard Lundeen has highlighted three types of hazing: subtle hazing, harassment hazing, and violent hazing. "It is impossible to list all possible hazing behaviors because many are context specific. While this is not an all-inclusive list, it provides some common examples of hazing traditions" (Lundeen, 2013).

Subtle hazing is generally accepted as being harmless. It includes behaviors that the term subtle implies; activities often accepted as harmless although most involve ridicule, embarrassment, and/or attempts at humiliation. Some examples of the subtle hazing are: requirements that initiates remain silent for periods of time. If initiates do not remain silent they may lose privileges granted to other members, giving new members/rookies duties not assigned to any other members. Other practices include line-ups and drills with meaningless outcomes, name calling, or the expectation that pledges will have particular items in their possession.

In *harassment hazing*, activities can cause emotional anguish and/or physical harm. Discomfort is the norm. Some examples of expected activities are: depriving the new members/rookie of maintaining body cleanliness; varying forms of sexual stimulations; sleep deprivation; verbal abuse and threats; implied threats if all requests are not carried out; being directed to perform degrading, crude or humiliating acts; directing new members/rookies to act as "servants," performing personal services such as cooking, cleaning, taking care of their clothes, carrying the books of those considered to be upperclassmen; and, being forced to harass others in order to belong.

The last type of hazing categorized by Lundeen is *violent hazing* and includes behaviors that have the greatest potential to cause physical, emotional, spiritual, and/or psychological harm. Examples of violent hazing activities are: being forced or coerced into using alcohol and or other drugs; being beaten, paddled, branded or subjected to other forms of physical assault. Senior members may brand new members/rookies, using hot metal devices to burn the skin. Other abuses used in this type of hazing include being forced or coerced to ingest vile substances or concoctions, being set on fire, being instructed to abuse or mistreat animals, instructed to be nude in public, put in bondage, abducted or kidnapped, exposed to extreme weather conditions without protection, and/or the expectation that the initiate will take part in an illegal activity.

Psychological or emotional hazing is frequently considered more insignificant and perhaps less harmful than hazing that includes physical abuse. Emotional bullying, however, can leave deep wounds. Abuse can include verbal harassment, and games or rituals that can end up being physically abusive as well. Emotional hazing practices such as yelling at or posting pictures on social media that are less than flattering can leave emotional bruises. Psychological and emotional hazing is anything that may damage another person's self-esteem and sense of self-worth. Many that undertake this practice as entrance into a desired group already have self-esteem issues including negative body images. In hazing, the danger can be exacerbated by the fact that one never knows the extent of psychological trauma a person may bring to the process that would greatly affect the outcome.

Colleges and Universities

In the university and college settings of fraternities and sororities, the term "hazing" often brings to mind images of paddling, drinking games and other antics that some of us will identify with the movie *Animal House*. However, this is frequently no longer a reality. Hazing has become increasingly violent, resulting in the deaths and injuries of many initiates. Because of this, the practice of hazing has created increasingly complex legal issues and a great deal of controversy between advocates of the practice and those that are lobbying for hazing to be considered "illegal" because of the abuses that have occurred.

Criminal charges filed relating to hazing have covered a broad range of behaviors: aggravated assault, aggravated sexual contact, maltreatment, breaking and entering, sodomizing and rape, branding (burning another human being's flesh),exposure to extreme weather conditions without protection, suffocation and drowning. The complete disregard for another human being's dignity, and/or personal safety in many hazing practices is devastating.

Several organizations have been formed to denounce hazing and put pressure on colleges, the military, sports teams, corporations, churches, and others groups to stop the practice. There are groups like the National Save the Family Now Movement that are sponsoring conferences to educate the public and bring attention to this frequently dangerous form of bullying, The National Anti-Hazing/ Anti-Violence Task Force held its first conference in February 2012 at South Carolina State University. There were twelve steps announced at this conference to denounce hazing. An action plan to combat hazing was developed and presented (Buechele, 2012).

This task force was formed as a result of the death of Florida A&M University band member Robert Champion, mentioned earlier in this chapter. Literally thousands of hazing injuries, "accidental deaths," and suicides have been silenced and/or ignored. Today, many still feel that it is a practice that should continue. Even though far too many have literally given their lives to belong to a group, many feel that pledges seeking to enter a group should "be pledged hard" rather than merely admitted to a sorority, fraternity and the like with a piece of paper. Others are relieved that the brutality of some hazing practices are finally receiving attention.

Although it was once believed that hazing was only a ritual for the higher education fraternities and sororities, through much research we have discovered that hazing is involved in many other arenas.

Hazing in Middle School and High School

In Los Angeles, California, in 2012, young soccer players were reportedly sodomized with a sharpened pole. One seventeen-year-old boy was brutally assaulted with the pole by team members when he entered a storage room to return equipment while other team members recorded the attack on their cell phones. A fourteen-year-old reported a similar attack. Hazing in this school, known as the "pole tradition" reportedly has gone on for many years (Winton, 2012).

Another incident of high school hazing came to light on September 10, 2013. Football practice at W.C. Mepham High School in Long Island, New York, was called off a week before the season began due to a serious hazing/bullying incident. Members of this high school football team were accused of sexually attacking some of their teammates. The brutal bullying included rubbing heat-producing mineral ice on broomsticks, pinecones and golf balls, then penetrating their victims while other team members watched. One victim required surgery for his injuries. The community was appalled, some by the crimes, some allegedly by the cancellation of the football season. The star lineman was charged as an adult for twenty-six felonies that allegedly occurred over several nights at the football training camp in Wayne County, Pennsylvania, after the coaches had gone to sleep. He was also a known school bully who would shove kids he had never met into their lockers as he walked by. Some of the school youth were shocked by the incidents of abuse, while others are angry at the victims for telling (Kolker, 2010).

According to the prime investigator in a study completed by Alfred University, high school students could be headed for serious trouble involving hazing. In the study, researchers questioned 1,541 high school juniors and seniors about hazing. Forty-eight percent of the 1,390 students who said they belong to an organized group reported being a part of hazing activities. Dr. Nadine C. Hoover, principal investigator in several surveys and reports on hazing, stated "the numbers are alarming." Most of the hazing that the children are involved in is in connection with sports teams, games, musical groups, and even church groups. Dr. Hoover cited 48 percent were boys and 39 percent were girls who said they had been involved. These students reported being forced to drink alcohol and/or smoke and/or use illegal drugs. The researchers are dubbing this activity as "substance abuse hazing." Twenty-four percent were boys and 18 percent were girls in this type of hazing. The president at Alfred University, Charles M. Edmonson, states that the hazing in the middle school/high school arena may often be dangerous as well as emotionally damaging. The researchers also found that this problem is widespread throughout many middle and high schools in the United States (Wright, 2000).

Hazing in the Military

Hazing occurs in every branch of our U.S. military and takes place at military academies, in boot camps, in special forces training camps, and throughout our military system. Hazing is not exclusive to only the United States military. Czechoslovakia and Russia have hazing in their armed forces. In Russia, there have been many cases of soldiers in the first year dying at the hands of their superiors whom they dub "grandfathers." Hazing in the military also has led to death and serious injury. A large percentage of these cases are never known because of the "code of silence" that are a part of hazing practices.

Two soldiers fighting in the Middle East chose to end their lives after being hazed. Private Danny Chin was dragged across a gravel yard on his back until it bled and rocks were thrown at him in his outpost in Kandahar, Afghanistan. He was called "gook" and "chink." Danny was singled out for hazing because he was considered a "weak soldier." Finally, he put the barrel of his rifle to his chin and pulled the trigger. Another soldier in Afghanistan, Lance Corporal Harry Lew, was punched and kicked. And the contents of a sandbag were poured onto his face until he choked, allegedly because he was caught sleeping on duty. Twenty-two mintutes after the hazing stopped he, too, used his own gun to end his life (Chu, 2012).

Hazing in College and Professional Sports

Hazing is coming out of the shadows in the professional sporting arena. It is happening in the NBA, NFL, NHL, Major League Baseball, extreme sports, swimming, and snowboarding. The Dallas Cowboys and the Jacksonville Jaguars appear to be the leaders among the NFL teams that are attempting to curb these embarrassing, sometimes dangerous rituals. This trend appears to be catching on in Major League Baseball and the NBA as well. These teams are putting an end to the old practice of veterans "roughing up" the first-year players.

Cam Cleeland was a New Orleans Saints rookie when he came very close to losing the sight out of one eye after being hit with a bag of quarters during a hazing ritual. With a pillow case over his head, he had to run a gauntlet of veteran teammates, most drunk, forming a line on both sides of a hallway. Each veteran got a shot at him. He had been kicked and punched all over when a blow with a bag full of coins shattered his eye socket. Today he only has partial vision out of that eye. In the same incident, Jeff Danish made it through the gauntlet only to crash through a plate-glass window. He had to get thirteen stitches in his arm and would have fallen three stories if a safety bar hadn't stopped him from plummeting out the window. That was fifteen years ago. After that, serious physical hazing was put to an end by the NFL yet, as Miami Dolphin rookie, Jonathan Martin, discussed in Chapter Five, can attest, emotional and psychological hazing has continued (Farmer, 2013).

According to the research done in 1999 by Alfred University on the initiation rites for NCAA sports teams, more than a quarter of a million athletes experience some form of hazing to join an athletic team. One in five experienced hazing that would be considered illegal, including being beaten up, tied up, abandoned, or forced to commit illegal acts. Half were required to participate in drinking contests or alcohol-related hazing. Women were more likely to be involved in alcohol-related hazing than any other form. Only one in five participated in positive initiations such as ropes courses (Hoover,1999).

Workplace Hazing

Workplace hazing can lead to serious consequences for employees and employers. Hazing in the workplace may lead to legal consequences such as claims of assault, sexual harassment, discrimination, and intentionally inflicting psychological and emotional distress. Some hazing incidents at the workplace can lead to serious injury. Some examples of hazing in the workplace may include employees engaging in "reckless horseplay," being put under social pressure to participate in unhealthy and unsafe behaviors, bullying, inappropriate sexual behaviors, harassment, and violence.

Firemen, ironically, who are in harm's way daily, are reported to be the most frequently tormented by workplace hazing. In 2008, the City of Tucson, Arizona, paid a firefighter $60,000 after he quit his job because he was suffering from depression related to hazing. He had been tied with duct tape under a running faucet, assaulted, and subjected to name-calling (People's Law Guide, 2012).

Cases involving hazing in the work place come from both the private and public sectors. Again, many do not report it because people are concerned that they would lose their jobs unless they keep silent.

Hazing in Church Groups

In a church in Indiana, thirteen- and fourteen-year-olds were allegedly coerced into drinking a mixture of dog food, salsa, sauerkraut, sardines, potted meat, egg nog, and cottage cheese—after a youth leader had chewed it (Olsen, 2003).

Yes, many report hazing in church groups too! According to the Alfred University Study, 24 percent of those surveyed reported being hazed while joining a church group. Nearly half of those who were hazed said they were forced to engage in illegal activities. "Many more students are involved in church groups than in fraternities or sororities. We know that church groups haze about 24 percent of their new members," said Hoover. "Based on that, we project approximately 237,000 high school students are being hazed to join a church group each year. That is a substantially higher number than hazed to join a college fraternity or sorority, which is approximately 155,000 each year" (Hoover and Pollard, 2000).

Negative Consequences of Hazing and What to Do About It

From many of the stories highlighted in this chapter, it is obvious that some of the consequences of hazing are injury, death, depression, anxiety, low self-esteem, financial loss, and suicidal ideation. These are similar to the findings reported by Alfred University. The study also reported that some felt positive feelings, including belonging, pride, and strength (Hoover and Pollard, 2000).

For many, there are also hidden issues where hazing is concerned. Consider Travis, pledging to his fraternity by holding an empty gun to his head and repeating, "I will die for this fraternity." What his upperclassmen did not know was that when he was eight years old, his father took his own life with a gun. Later that night, after a long rage, Travis was taken to the hospital (Apgar and Szabo).

In 2005, 90 percent of counseling centers reported a rise in learners with severe psychological distress (Gallaghaer and Graham, 2005). Because far too many young people are bringing psychological distress in their backpacks to college already, the triggering possibilities of hazing practices, plus the psychological consequences of hazing, is a recipe for disaster.

In the Alfred University study, 61 percent of teens suggested that there be strong discipline for hazing and 50 percent believed there should be police investigations and prosecution for cases of hazing. They also believed that positive bonding, educational activities and challenging activities would be helpful in prevention (Hoover and Pollard, 2000).

New organizations are springing up letting us know that putting an end to hazing is everyone's responsibility. The mission at hazing prevention.org, for instance, is to educate people about hazing and empower them to stop it when they see it. They teach the importance of taking action rather than being a bystander. They encourage people not to take part in hazing and to report it when they know of hazing that is occurring. They also recommend that people who understand hazing and its effects make it their responsibility to educate others.

Today, the majority of colleges, universities, athletic departments and workplaces have anti-hazing policies. Know the policies in your school or organization.

Forty-four states have passed legislation against hazing. Know the laws in your state, and if your state has not passed legislation against hazing practices, be an advocate for change.

It is important for us, as parents and adult role models, to teach our children early through our love, kindness, and inclusion that being hurt or humiliated is not, and should never be, a prerequisite for belonging. Also, if adults model action, rather than silence, standing up, rather than standing by, our youth will find their voice as well. It is important that they see role models from an early age who will not tolerate acts of humiliation, abuse, disrespect, or disempowerment of others in their presence. It may not be your son who is being humiliated at a Little League game, but if he is alone without protection, stand beside him and hold him up. If his parents, grandparents or other caregivers stand with him, stand in support of them.

Bullies on the Playground

There are people who take the heart out of you
and there are people who put it back.

Elizabeth David

The expression "school bully" has been used for as long as most of us can remember. We have read about school bullies in books and have seen them depicted in movies and on television. The school bully was portrayed as a person to be afraid of. He was depicted as a tough troublemaker who pushed others around, forcing them to do embarrassing things. He was abusive, always getting into fights and destroying property.

School children and even adults in the community were afraid of them. Bullies were characterized as bigger than other children and always from the "wrong side of the tracks." Most of us can remember the school bullies on our childhood playgrounds and in the neighborhoods where we lived. Some of us have vivid memories of being their victims. Those of us who have been their targets know bullies came in all shapes and sizes. They came from all socio-economic back-grounds and were both male and female. Some were the most popular kids in school, the "jock" or part of the "in crowd," others were the least popular kids, the "nerds" or the "outsiders." Sometimes bullies were the most dangerous before and after school when there was little adult supervision. Unfortunately, sometimes taunting from school bullies is accompanied by the bullying comments of those very adults entrusted with the children's care.

Ted's Story

"The Academy was established in a mid-sized Southern town in 1959 as a college preparatory school. It remained small until the mid 1960s when desegrega-tion boosted the student body. To be admitted, one had to achieve good scores on academic tests as the school was at least two grade levels above public schools. I entered the Academy in fourth grade from the public school system. Although I probably could not have been admitted based on my academic level, my father was able to get me admitted based on a business relation-ship he had with one of the founders.

"Most of the students were from 'old families' from Montgomery. I was from Birmingham and entered three months into my fourth-grade year. I was short and skinny for my age and I was also very sensitive. I would get my feelings hurt easily both in school and in my family.

"In fourth grade there was one particular boy who constantly called me 'Janitor.' He would sit behind me in class and repeat, 'Ted does not compute, Janitor computes.' At other times he would remark, 'Sorry Janitor, this school isn't integrated yet.' Interestingly enough, this particular boy came from a very liberal family. I was called Janitor by many people at the school for at least a year and

a half. I remember going home and crying to my mother that nobody liked me.

"In sixth and seventh grade, I was picked on physically by being pushed or hit. Several people would make repeated comments about how I dressed (wearing white socks became out of style and I was slow to adjust). They commented on the tassels on my loafers when I got a new pair. One person said that since the tassels were straight (they were still new), it was like my loafers had an erection.

"During the 1968 presidential election, politics became a topic of discussion in eighth-grade government class. Most of the class supported Hubert Humphrey or Richard Nixon. I and one other person supported George Wallace. I remember clearly that my teacher, in a demonstration of tolerance, told the class that political views were just opinions and that all should be respected. He then said, 'It's only when someone believes like Ted does that we have to be concerned.' He would tease me and ask me if I was in the Klan.

"These are just a few examples. The teasing occurred every day. I think that I must have seemed like bloody bait during a feeding frenzy of sharks. Generally I hated life at the Academy, and looking back it seems that I hated (still do) everybody there and yet, when I think of most of the individuals, I liked them just fine. There were many who treated me nice and were fair.

"Sometimes today I find myself thinking that I've got to 'show them,' that I can be successful. The them is always those people at the Academy. If things are not going well in my career, it is an additional source of shame when I think that I'm not 'showing them.'

"I remember one day about ten years ago I was at the mall with my wife and I saw one of the bullies who had teased me constantly. He was talking to his wife and children. I had heard that he was getting a divorce and the conversation looked like a man and

ex-wife exchanging children after a visitation. I remember think-
ing that I was glad he was getting a divorce and having trouble.
That is a terrible thing to wish on anyone. I was horrified to find
myself thinking like that."

Being the target of a bully, as Ted was, has effects that can stay with
a child into his adult life. In light of recent events, changing desensitized school climates seems more critical than ever. "Eventually
internalized anger is going to erupt," said a Brockton, Massachusetts,
school administrator, Ken Sennett, referring to the feelings of children
and youth who are the victims of bullying (Greenberger, 2000).

Fortunately, the "school bully" is taken more seriously today and
has been identified as a significant problem in schools across the
country and around the world. We now know that bullying happens
everywhere. Yet for many, it has unfortunately taken the deaths of far
too many children, youth, and gifted teachers to finally break through
denial and face the extent of the problem. We have interviewed teachers, administrators, school counselors, and parents who have shared
painful personal stories and deep concerns regarding the increasing
incidents of school violence. Elementary school children are bringing
weapons to schools across the nation. There are growing incidents
of beatings, bomb threats, property damage, blatant disrespect of
authority, and threats made to classmates and teachers. Children are
afraid to go to school and parents are increasingly afraid to send them.

Metal detectors are being installed in schools and resources from
the outside are being brought in to train teachers and school personnel to deal with this escalation of violence. Police officers are becoming increasingly visible on school premises, and in many schools
police dogs are being brought in to inspect student lockers for drugs
and weapons. Some schools have initiated policies requiring children as young as elementary school to wear only backpacks made of

clear plastic so that the contents can easily be examined without the necessity to conduct manual searches. It is easy to understand why the media has begun to portray our schools as war zones. School violence has become a major concern worldwide. Books and curricula are being written, and workshops and seminars are being created to educate and aid teachers and parents in confronting the problem. Bullying has become a popular topic for the media, and Web sites are springing up to assist victims and those working with them.

Educators, administrators, and federal, state and local governments have begun extensive work to increase school safety. Beginning in 1999, all schools in the United Kingdom were legally required to have antibullying policies. The state of Georgia has introduced legislation requiring schools to have similar policies. Their policies include the stipulation that students who bully will be permanently expelled after their third offense. Georgia initiated these policies in September 1999, following the death of Josh Belluardo. Jonathon Miller was found guilty of murder. He had been bullying thirteen-year-old Josh for some time. Then one day as Josh was getting off the bus, Miller punched him in the back of the head. The punch ruptured an artery that killed Josh in sixty seconds. Miller had a history of violent behavior with some thirty-four reported incidents filed against him. The school board and school have come under scrutiny due to their failure to address Miller's violent behavior (*Atlanta News,* May 1999).

In 2000 the Florida legislature put into effect a law that was spawned after incidents of school violence culminating in the shootings at Columbine High School, which received extensive press coverage. The legislature committed to instituting changes to make their schools safer. Starting July 1, 2000, all Florida school districts had to establish plans to prevent school violence. A statewide panel was created as a clearinghouse for security information and to evaluate school safety. Beginning in 2000, Florida schools were no longer graded, as they had been, on how many students they suspended and expelled. This was designed to discourage schools from dealing with potentially dangrous students for fear of receiving a low grade based on expulsion rates. The bill required a one-year expulsion for students who bring weapons to school or make bomb threats.

The state of Massachusetts set aside $1 million to help ten elementary schools implement a two-year Bullying Prevention Program, based largely on the work of Norwegian researcher Daniel Olweus, a leading expert on school bullying. Olweus supports role-playing as a teaching tool in bully prevention in classrooms, better adult supervision inside and outside of the classroom, and closer contact between parents and teachers.

A Brookline, Massachusetts, father of an elementary schoolchild who had been beaten by school bullies on the playground voiced his doubts about antibullying programs in the schools: "I'm not sure that a whole police force, or a whole battery of teachers, could prevent some of these things that are going on" (Greenberger, 2000).

Still, many educators and psychologists insist that, even though bullying is inevitable, programs like Olweus's can work. "I think Columbine is an example of a culture where that sort of behavior was condoned by coaches and teachers," said Michael Nakkula, a psychologist at Harvard's School of Education (Greenberger, 2000). He was referring to the complaints made by the two teenage gunmen that they had been repeatedly teased and abused by the school's varsity football players. This was before they started the shooting spree that ended the lives of many of their peers before turning their guns on themselves.

Schools that receive the Massachusetts grant must set up a Bullying Prevention Coordinating Committee composed of teachers, a guidance counselor, a student, a parent, a community representative, and a janitor, bus driver or cafeteria worker. After training with the Department of Safety, the panelists were supposed to instruct the school staff on how to stop bullying (Greenberger, 2000).

Today, schools across the nation have anti-bullying policies, and states have anti-bullying laws and policies. Some include new legislation regarding cyberbullying, sextortion, revenge porn, and textual harassment. Go to www. stopbullying.gov to learn about the laws and policies in your state.

"Although adults are expected to provide 'individual interventions' between bullies and their victims, the key to changing a school's culture is to focus on everyone. 'The majority of kids are bystanders or onlookers—they feel afraid to get involved,' said Nancy Mullin-Rindler who heads the Project on Teasing and Bullying at Wellesley College. Mullin-Rindler is advising the state of Massachusetts on its bullying initiative. Schools that get state money are required to buy her teachers' guide. 'When kids observe bullying and there's not a successful resolution to the problem, they become desensitized,' said Mullin-Rindler. 'Bullying behavior becomes normalized' " (Greenberger, 2000).

We believe strongly that effective school programs must focus on the entire school climate, not just the bully. We need programs that empower the silent majority, teach targets how not to be victims and give pro-social consequences for bullying behavior. Programs must also focus on underlying difficulties that children bring in their backpacks to school, and assist them with building attachments and understanding, regulating their emotions, and learning values of kindness, cooperation, and compassion. A bully-free program does not just outline behaviors, it provides lessons in connection and interdependence. It is also essential that "bully-free" means that everyone entering the school doors must know they are entering a bully-free zone. This includes administrators, teachers, parents, support staff, students, and all adults. Bully-free must also extend to cyberspace. This type of bullying, as stated in earlier chapters, must be included in school policies, mission statements, and education programs.

Due to differences in age and development, bullying behaviors differ as children move from one level to the next. In elementary school, bullying takes the form of pushing, shoving, spitting, name-calling, tripping, distracting, interrupting, or laughing at others. As these children get older, the bullying can become more sophisticated: verbal and physical fights, intimidation, spreading lies and rumors, excluding others, defacing property and stealing; teasing others about how they look or behave, what they wear, or where they live. Bullies may consistently get others into trouble or make verbal threats of aggression against property or possessions, or target family members or friends.

As children get older and move on to middle schools the research indicates that victims of bullying in the previous school can begin to bully new and younger children. "The incidence of bullying is highest when children start secondary school, because each new cohort is vulnerable to the predations of older children who know the school culture and have already run the gauntlet of acceptance and initiation into it" (Rigby and Slee, 1995; Olweus, 1996). "As children get older, they tend to show less sympathy for their victims, and that in a culture where bullying is part of the status quo, they are more likely to be hardened in the bullying behavior" (Rigby, 1996).

The child who bullies gains a reputation of being powerful, mean, a "hothead" and tough. He or she becomes known as someone to fear and stay away from. Bullies get others to do their schoolwork or help them cheat on tests by using threats or intimidation. They frequently develop the reputation of being liars and use exclusion as a way of getting more power or what they want.

On the Streets Where We Live

Bullying occurs in all schools that do not have effective programs to address the problem: private, public, religious-affiliated schools, boarding schools, trade schools, colleges and universities. It happens in schools where students score high in national achievement tests and communities that have highly educated families with two parents, low divorce rates, excellent parent participation and high socioeconomic status. It also happens in schools where students test low in national achievement tests and communities with high divorce rates, single-parent families, and low socio-economic status.

Most people are in denial regarding the extent and severity of the problem and would prefer to believe that the worst bullying and school violence occur in communities at the low end of the socioeconomic spectrum. Bullying, however, happens in communities at both ends of the socio-economic spectrum and everywhere in between.

For many it has been easier to buy into the stereotype of the "school bully" who lives in noisy communities where people solve problems with their fists, yell and scream, and show anger, rage, and violence. Endemic drinking and drug use and a high suicide rate complete the stereotype of a community that spawns a bully. Many believe that bullying only occurs in cities and towns where a large number of school dropouts openly hang out on street corners stealing the lunch money of small children. We have frequently turned a blind eye to problems of aggression in schools in middle- or upper-class suburbs. In these communities, children may be taken care of by nannies. Here everyone appears perfect with perfect manners and dress in clothes with designer labels and name brands. But in these communities there is also depression and anxiety, violence behind closed doors, fear of failure, stiff competition, bulimic and anorexic youth, high rates of drug and alcohol abuse, and suicide.

Some communities wear pain on the outside, others hide it. The school shootings that occurred in suburban and rural communities made up mostly of middle-class families did a great deal to dispel the myth, "Not in my community. Not on the street where I live."

Some people are still under the impression that bullying is a normal and acceptable behavior that children will grow out of. They make statements such as "Boys will be boys," "They are just being kids," "He/she is just a hothead." "Just ignore it, it will stop." It will not.

In one school we visited, students made their own "public service announcements" as a part of their bully-free campaign. One student filmed adults in his community bullying children, or other adults in the grocery store and post office. Some were yelling, some were gossiping about their neighbors. His caption: "We need bullying to stop everywhere, not just in our schools. We need positive role models who will join us in our efforts to stop bullying."

At School

Our children set off for school carrying a lunch bag, paper, pens, and a developmental toolbox carefully assembled from thousands of interactions with adult caregivers. Families and other adults not only teach children who they are, but they model expectations about people and life. Some of the children come from healthy family systems and are comfortable with following rules, listening and learning, completing assignments, asking questions, regulating emotions and relating to others.

Children from healthy, functional families have, for the most part, experienced a supportive atmosphere of unconditional love, approval for their unique selves, and praise for positive behavior and choices, and they are encouraged to take risks. They have been allowed to have dreams and explore their creativity. These children have learned to accept making mistakes and have had assistance in accepting the consequence of their mistakes. They have learned from these consequences. They have experienced being listened to and have learned to listen to others. Because they have been accepted for who they are, they can accept others for who they are. They have learned to treat others as they would like to be treated and been given healthy physical affection and mirrors that reflected back self-worth. Through learning that they could trust their adult caregivers, they have learned to trust themselves and are developmentally prepared to trust others. They have been taught how to face some difficult situations, ask for help and be aware of their choices. These children can make decisions with assistance and take responsibility for the choices they have made. They have a toolbox that has equipped them for the new social and cognitive experiences they will need to face in school.

Other children going off to school have toolboxes that are not as adequate for new experiences. Many have lived in families that are not as supportive, are overprotective, or have not equipped their children with the internal controls and limits necessary for healthy social interactions. Some of these children have learned to be fearful of making the wrong choices, so they make no choices. They have little confidence in themselves and are afraid of making mistakes. They deal indirectly with problems or don't deal with them at all. They have learned through experience to deny, blame, or distort the reality of new situations. These children may feel victimized by any new situation or by life in general. They fear being confronted or being the focus of attention, and are frequently hypervigilant, wary of people, and of life in general. Many may follow rules and do well scholastically, but they have little ability to regulate their emotions and have difficulty with social interactions. Some, particularly those who have come from overprotective environments and possess few tools in social interactions, become the constant targets of school bullies.

Others who have received few or inconsistent limits for their behavior and have felt bigger than the adults in their lives come to school still trying to receive important tools that will allow them to feel emotionally safe and secure. They are constantly pushing for limits from the outside and often test and bully teachers and peers. This was the case with a number of boys in the Glen Ridge school system highlighted by Bernard Lefkowitz in his book *Our Guys* (1997). He told the story of a number of boys labeled as "jocks" in the class of 1989 and the victims of their relentless bullying. Lefkowitz characterized the boys as children and youths with few or inconsistent limits in their homes or at school. As early as elementary school they were allowed to be bigger than the adults in their lives. Throughout their school history, most of their outrageous behavior was ignored, defended, forgotten with the transfer of cash or rationalized as "Boys will be boys," or "They'll grow out of it." The boys were allowed to terrorize students and teachers alike from early elementary school through high school.

"The middle-school miscreants found many ways to express themselves. One day they smashed the science laboratory equipment, which was reduced to a heap of twisted metal and broken glass. Another day they interrupted their classes with smutty jokes. They treated female teachers and students with contempt. One teacher evoked the experience of many colleagues when she said, 'It's not just one classroom. It's every class. There's a core and you never know what they're going to throw at you. And the other kids watch, wondering if the "core" is going to come after them'" (Lefkowitz, 1997, p. 84).

Other children live in families of bullying, violence, terror, aggression or abuse, and come to school with fears of being ridiculed, punished and/or "found out." They may go to school having recently witnessed incidents of bullying and/or abuse or have experienced it firsthand. They may have heard their mother's screams, their father's rage, loud threats, glass breaking, doors being slammed, or furniture kicked or thrown, or seen police come to their houses, their favorite animal kicked, and their brothers or sisters crying while hiding under the bed. They may have called 911 to put a stop to the insanity.

Children who experience and/or witness bullying and violence suffer from trauma and can react with shock, fear, guilt, confusion, and anger. They learn to keep secrets in an effort to protect their families from ridicule and embarrassment or from fear of being taken away. Some can appear to be tough as a protection against the embarrassment and shame. Some may present themselves as happy, strive for perfection, and focus all their attention on their education. Others are unable to do this and hide behind a wall of anger, bitterness, and defiance. They come to school with survival skills that seem to have worked for them—thus far.

Many children have been taught to be aggressive by role models in their lives. When fearful and/or anxious (which is most of the time), these children use aggression as a defense to protect themselves. Some may find that sports are helpful in calming their anxieties. The physical workout can release endorphins and help them feel calmer. Sports may give them a sense of self-worth and purpose. They can feel good about themselves temporarily because they are finally getting recognition. However, due to the bullying and trauma in their family system, they may only feel the positive sense of self for a brief time before becoming fearful of losing newly won recognition. They may again defend against fear and anxiety by returning to the only behavior they have learned can protect them: bullying, anger, and aggression.

Other children who experience bullying at home can feel inadequate and "left out" at school. They may begin aggressive behaviors in order to achieve temporary power and recognition. The child's stage of development and learned experiences from other adult caregivers are points of reference for how to gain recognition. When children come from bullying homes, they learn the power of bullying behavior. If bullying others gives them temporary power and recognition, they continue the behavior. Because they have no point of reference for negative or positive consequences, any recognition can be positive. If they can get others to do as they want and experience the power of perceiving others looking up to them, these children can affirm to themselves that their behavior works. They no longer feel left out. Until this child is given new awareness and new direction by adult caregivers, there is no reason to change.

Countless studies show that children who are not supplied with an honest mirror are not allowed to develop awareness of their behavior and its effect on others. If they are not helped to view themselves as individuals capable of love and empathy because someone in their lives has not been "just crazy about them," loved them, believed in them, and "felt" who they are or has not helped them develop a new set of behavioral "tools," they will continue their behavior into adulthood. The skills that were honed on the playground will aid them in bullying their partners, friends, coworkers, bosses, clientele, constituents and/or nations.

Theresa's Story

Theresa was from an abusive, violent family. Both of her parents were alcoholics who abandoned their parenting roles. Her father was a physically abusive bully. Originally, her mother didn't drink as much as her father, but was angry and fearful. She took her anger out on her children and, as the years went by, became increasingly full of rage and bullied more as her drinking increased. Theresa was awakened most mornings by her mother's screams for her to get up and do the housework.

Theresa's father regularly physically abused her mother and brother, and bullied, intimidated, and manipulated the entire family. Theresa was blamed for causing her father's violent outbursts, was expected to keep the peace, and was responsible for her brother and sister when her parents were at the bar. Her mother was both bully and victim and did nothing to protect herself or her children. Theresa lived in a world of shame, guilt, and anxiety.

Theresa learned early in her life to protect herself by being "tough," "mouthy" and verbally aggressive to others. Her role models taught her how to intimidate others with her words and actions. She was a tease, sarcastic, and she gossiped and spread rumors in order to inflict pain on others that she felt had harmed her.

"I belonged to a group of bullies made up mostly of boys like my father and brother. There were some girls in the group who came from the same kind of family I did; they had abusive, bullying fathers like mine. I was able to talk to my friends in the group about my home life and they understood. When my parents screamed at me or blamed me for their behavior, my friends were empathetic. I felt loved and protected for the first time in my life.

"The spoken and unspoken rules of the group were similar to the ones I learned at home: be loyal to the group; keep the group's secrets; protect other group members from consequences; respect the leaders of the group (who were always the boys); do as you were told without question; accept teasing and verbal abuse from other group members sometimes; never hurt each other physically; and never show fear or vulnerability.

"We didn't bully everyone, only those that threatened us in some way: rich people, authority figures or people in general that we thought would put us down because of the clothes we wore, where we lived, or who our parents were. But we had standards. We respected, protected, and were kind to smaller children, those that had any disability, and the elderly. We would go out of our way to protect people that we thought needed protecting.

"The boys in the group acted like father figures and told the girls who we could date or hang out with. We couldn't make friends outside the group unless the boys told us we could. We acted like mother figures and listened to the boys' problems about home or the girls they dated.

"*If any of us got in trouble in school, with other kids, authority figures, parents, or the police, other members of the group would lie for us, or clean us up from a fight so that our families wouldn't find out. We looked out for each other. My brother (who was also in the group) and I got into trouble a lot in school and with the police. Most of the time we'd get beat up at home if our parents found out about it. Sometimes we'd get grounded. That was really a joke. We'd just wait for our folks to drink so much they'd pass out every night, then we'd go out and join our friends.*

"*It's hard to believe now, but one of the 'fun' things we did was to have the girls in the group go stand on a specified corner and try to attract boys. Some boys would come over and talk to us. After some time had passed, the boys from our group would come out of the darkness and beat up the boys who were talking to us. At the time the game was exciting. We'd talk and laugh about it for weeks. The game reinforced the rules: One, that we'd better not get involved with boys that were not in the group without permission, and two, it sent a message to other boys that they were not to mess with the girls in the group. I can't believe how distorted our idea of fun was or that we let boys dominate us like that. It's understandable, though, because it was the kind of violence, game playing, and chaos that we lived with at home every day.*

"*At the beginning of high school, my parents decided to move to a different section of town. I was really mad because I had to leave my friends, the only people I ever felt cared about me. That connection was the most important thing I thought I had in my life back then. I had to start a new school where there was no one I knew. I was isolated and lonely. The reputation of the group I was in, as well as my own reputation, followed me to the new school and I was rejected for a while by most of the other kids. I slept a lot, cried a lot, and was really confused. I had no idea what to do. There was no one I could even complain to.*

"Six months after I started the new school, the gym teacher really started to notice me. I was a good athlete and she noticed that. She became an important mentor in my life. I wasn't honest with her about my family, but was able to open up a little about other things. She really showed me that she cared. She was the first person to really confront me on my negative behaviors and beliefs. She spoke in a gentle and understanding voice, and supported my positive behaviors and beliefs. She praised my athletic ability, and I wanted to please her. I began to do better in school.

"I began to feel better about myself and to make a few friends. I wasn't attracted to kids that were bullies anymore. I still had difficulty identifying with people from healthy families, though. I still had a lot of shame and embarrassment about my family. I couldn't have made any changes without the support, understanding, confrontation, and acceptance from that teacher. I didn't want to disappoint her and I didn't. She was the first person in my life that let me know they were proud of me. I wish every child could have someone like her in their lives. I think things would be a lot different for many kids if they did. She really turned me around. I mean, I did it, but I needed guidance and I never had any. I needed someone to teach me the way healthy people thought, felt and behaved, and she was willing. She never made a promise she didn't keep.

"I eventually got professional help. Today in my life there is health and balance. I didn't marry a bully and I didn't model bullying behavior for my children. My grandchildren will not have to live in the pain and shame that I did. I broke the cycle and I'm proud of that. It frightens me sometimes to think what my life would have turned out like if that teacher hadn't noticed me. She believed in me and I learned slowly to believe in myself."

Within a few months of their arrival in school, most children will find their place of belonging in the social constellation. There is a great need to belong to this new unknown environment of school. A child's point of reference in being drawn to and accepted by one peer group or another is largely dependent on how the child feels about himself or herself, behaviors in the group that the child can identify with, or mutual interests. Groups of peers can come from the same neighborhood, the same socioeconomic background, religious background, cultural background, or from similar family systems. It sometimes makes belonging easier, although not in all cases.

Older children form their own groups, cliques or gangs: for example, "the jocks," "the nerds," "the geeks," "the goths," "the punks," "the rednecks," "the rockers." Bullies can be part of any of these groups or may form their own group and/or gangs. For instance, in some schools, the jocks are bullies; in another school it might be the rednecks. In the case of the Columbine shootings, "the jocks" bullied kids that were a part of another group, allegedly goths, who then retaliated by becoming bullies with guns. Frequently one or two members of a group may be bullies and the others are bystanders who don't actively engage in bullying behavior, but do participate passively through witnessing the behavior and doing nothing to stop it.

Each group has its own spoken and unspoken rules (norms) of behavior that members must follow in order to stay in the group. A child finds a sense of belonging in a peer group that allows him or her to continue the same behavior patterns that he has learned and/or that encourage the development of skills the child already possesses.

A person, for instance, moving from Italy to the United States might be attracted to an Italian neighborhood where the language, food, gestures, games, music, and social interaction are the same as he experienced in Italy. It is a neighborhood that feels comfortable. When entering an unknown situation, we tend to seek out what is known.

Like adults, children seek out support, trust and acceptance. Many groups support positive behaviors: healthy social skills, acceptance, sharing and accountability. Others support negative behaviors: bullying, rage, arrogance, blame, dishonesty, and defiance.

Children like Theresa join groups that share similar needs and behaviors to their families of origin while also meeting needs for power, acceptance, and belonging that have not been met by adult caregivers. Their point of reference for loyalty, support, protection, acceptance, and affection is distorted. Fear, for instance, is disguised as respect. Theresa could bring her friends from her original peer group home without embarrassment because they came from similar dysfunctional family systems. They laughed at the same distorted thinking, were used to the same chaos, and were sometimes verbally rewarded by Theresa's parents for sarcastic remarks, aggression and bullying behavior. Her peers could even join the family in blaming others for their behavior. When Theresa began to make friends in her new school, she was embarrassed to bring them home because she feared the judgments from the "normal" families they represented. "If they really knew who I was and who my family was, I wouldn't be accepted. I wouldn't belong," she said.

Groups that tend to bully generally have a leader, usually considered the "toughest" because of their physical size or their ability to intimidate or con others. There are frequently scapegoats and victims that join the group because they are flattered by the attention they receive from powerful bullies, and/or because they are used to being in the role of victim. The pecking order can change within the grouping if another child challenges the leader and proves that he or she is better at intimidating, conning or bullying. The group behavior is frequently a mirror image of the family behaviors of the group members.

Many of the people who had been part of bully groups and shared their stories reported having had strong identification with the behaviors of their groups and were attracted to the level of fear, excitement and power of the group. Again, not all of the children in the group were bullies. Some were victims and others played both bully and victim roles from time to time.

It takes time to learn a new language and the customs of a new and unfamiliar country. It takes the dedication and patience of teacher and student alike, a capacity for learning, care, support, and a compelling reason to learn. The same is true when learning new behaviors and beliefs.

The teacher that came into Theresa's life patiently and gently taught her new ways of behaving. Theresa always had athletic skill and a capacity for empathy and caring. She also had anger, aggression, and skill in bullying. Theresa's teacher encouraged the athletic skill and empathy that was there all along, while confronting the behavior that was having a negative effect on Theresa's life. She helped her believe that she had the capacity to learn and change, taught her new behaviors, and supported and cared for her in a way that temporarily supplied the motivation to learn. "She believed in me. I didn't want to disappoint her. Finally, I began to believe in myself." When Theresa changed her behavior and beliefs, she no longer felt "comfortable" relating to bullies, and her peer group changed.

For many children who are bullies there are no adult caregivers or role models to show concern, understanding, and acceptance while confronting them with their behavior and patiently teaching them a different way to behave. Children who are perpetual victims also come from either abusive, bullying families or have had caregivers who overprotected them to the point where they have never been allowed to make their own choices, resolve conflicts, or make mistakes and learn from them.

Countless studies that have focused on resilient children from difficult and traumatic backgrounds indicate that the number one factor that makes a difference in a child's life is one adult role model who showed compassion, concern, care, and was able to model healthy behavior. All of the bullies and victims who have generously shared their stories with us said that it was just one or two people who cared and believed in them at some point in their lives who made a difference. Because of them, they were willing to dedicate themselves to changing their bullying behavior and make other changes necessary to lead happy and productive lives.

Tackling the Problem

Bullying has been a major problem in schools for many years. Unfortunately until fairly recently, few school systems recognized bullying as a major threat to children, teachers or school personnel. The major approach to the problem was to ignore the behavior and hope it would go away. Today, more school systems have recognized the need to take action.

Many approaches have been implemented with varying degrees of success. A large number of schools have attempted to make schools safer by setting antibullying policies that punish the bully for his or her behavior. This strategy of addressing the problem has proven to be ineffective. Many children who exhibit severe bullying behaviors have been habituated to punishment throughout their lives. Punishments such as school detention, sitting out in the hall, calling parents, or expulsion and engaging in power struggles are usually met by the student with defiance or indifference.

There are many reasons we believe this approach is not effective. Many children who bully in school to the point where the family is notified run the risk of being further abused at home. Due to intense internalized fears of abusive consequences, these children's defenses increase—defenses that are the foundation for the bullying behavior. They may lie, show more defiance or run away, or become more

severely depressed. In a bullying, abusive and/or violent family system, crisis, trauma, shame, fear, anger, and guilt are the norm. In
these families it's terrifying to be the center of attention. Children
have been taught to keep family secrets. If they are seen as bringing
attention to the family through their misbehavior or through sharing their "secrets" with school personnel, children will be blamed
for triggering "outsider" involvement and punished severely for a
long period of time. Again, many bullying children are habituated to
extreme punishment. With more punishment, defenses increase, as
does the bullying behavior.

In other cases when the family becomes involved, children may
actually get a "pat on the back" for the bullying behavior by the adult
bully in the family, "the chip off the old block" distortion. It has been
our experience that in this type of family, some caregivers actually
advise their children on ways they can "get back" at teachers or other
school personnel. Some dysfunctional families believe that any effort
by "outsiders" to intervene or punish their children is out of line and
they will go to any length to defend their children's behavior and protect the family from further attention. Some bullying parents even
act proud of their children's unhealthy behavior and brag about it to
others. The positive attention given to these children gives them the
impression that they have done a good thing. These children hear from
the school that their behavior is unacceptable and is worthy of punishment, yet their families imply through defensive behavior or bragging
that the behavior is acceptable. Children can continue to be confused
and distorted about the behavior and, at the same time, focus on the
fact that they finally received positive attention from their caregivers.

In our work with adults who have exhibited bullying behavior
throughout their lives, it has been apparent that a high percentage of
these adults were confused and baffled that they had so many punishments in their lives as a result of their behavior. When confronted

with their behavior and its effect on their lives and the lives of others, they originally exhibited confusion, blame and defensiveness. Most came from bullying home environments. In some cases both parents bullied, in others one parent was a bully and the other a victim. The victimized parents did nothing to stop the bullying and gave mixed messages to their children about the bullying parent.

It is necessary to help adult bullies become fully aware of their behaviors, beliefs and feelings and to penetrate their denial, defenses and distortions. This is accomplished most effectively in a group process. The adult bullies' need is to learn new, and for them, foreign behaviors, beliefs, feelings and choices.

Still other children who exhibit extensive bullying behavior in school come from homes with few limits. When these children were punished and their caregivers were notified of their bullying behavior, caregivers frequently denied or defended the behavior. They saw their children as the "real victims," blamed the schools and became angry with teachers or other school personnel. We have known parents who have actually moved their children from school to school when confronted with their children's behavior in an effort to find schools that will treat their children "fairly." These children who have been pushing for limits most of their young lives in order to finally feel safe now feel even "bigger" than before. Their bullying behavior increases as they continue to desperately attempt to master a crucial developmental task.

When children who are exhibiting bullying behavior are confronted with understanding and are made aware that they are not "bad kids" while, at the same, receiving the message that their behavior will not be tolerated, many will be open to listening to the choices they have to make in order to change their behavior and be happier in school. Some may take longer than others to take responsibility and make better choices, and a few may never change. Giving children compassionate, honest mirrors can change their lives and, in some cases, save their lives.

Different approaches for making our children safe are currently being implemented. One program that is being used in an effort to intervene on the bullying problem in the United Kingdom is using nonconfrontational small groups. This "no blame" approach to bullying was developed by George Robinson, Ph.D., from West England University, and Barbara Maines, Ph.D., a psychologist in Bristol, England. Under this method the teacher does not reprimand bullies. The foundation of this approach is that the bully is not a "bad" child, but a child whose behavior needs to change. The school encourages the victims of bullying to write out their feelings about being bullied and then read them aloud to a small group of children that includes friends, "sensible pupils" and the bully. The bully is not identified, but it is explained how his or her behavior is hurtful to the victim. Each pupil is asked to come up with suggestions to improve the situation.

A controversial part of this approach is that the bully's parents are rarely informed. Those who endorse the approach feel it is best not to involve the parents in order to prevent them from potentially undermining the school's approach by punishing the children. Despite controversy, the "no blame" approach is being endorsed by a growing number of schools in the United Kingdom.

Another program that is showing a lot of promise is called "Roots of Empathy" and was founded by Mary Gordon. Although Roots of Empathy is not an anti-bullying program per se, it deals with the underlying causes of bullying—and reaches the bully, the target who becomes a victim, and the silent majority. As stated on their website: "Roots of Empathy is an evidence-based classroom program that has shown significant effect in reducing levels of aggression among school children while raising social/emotional competence and increasing empathy." (*www.rootsofempathy.org*)

A program that is currently being used by many schools throughout the United States is called "Bully Proofing Your School," which
is also the title of a book written by the creators of the approach
(Garrity et al., 1994). The program is built on a systems approach to
school bullying. Students, teachers and other staff members at the
school are taught the skills necessary to become a caring community
that has zero tolerance for bullying. Through this program, a caring
school community is created that gains the power to make an impact
on the bullying that takes place. "Our focus is on creating a safer
school environment for all by creating a culture within the school
that does not tolerate acts of physical or emotional aggression by anyone; this environment must be created, nurtured and maintained by
the students. This bully-proofing program has five key components:
Teachers and Other Staff, Caring Majority, Bullies, Victims, and the
Parental Community" (Garrity et al., 1994).

The program emphasizes the creation of an environment where
children can feel safe and secure. When there is a climate of safety, the
fear the bully creates is minimized. Classroom rules highlight community responsibility, inclusion and limits. In this program, accountability is fostered in the entire student community. One of the rules
requires children who witness bullying to help the victim by speaking
out and getting adult help and support.

Staff trainings are conducted to teach specific interventions for
bullies: "We have learned that it does not work at all to engage in
power struggles with the bully. Rather, an adult should help the bully
to rechannel his or her power needs in positive channels. Of course,
this works best when the cultural norms of the school have been
redirected toward caring and kindness" (Garrity et al., 1994).

A major classroom intervention is to empower the majority of
children who remain silent when witnessing bullying behavior (85
percent). The children are taught the elements of bullying. They are

given a survey that includes questions concerning how safe they feel at school, whether they bully or are victims, and some of their supports, peer group, etc. They are also given the results of the survey.

In following sessions the students are taught six strategies to try if they are bullied and four strategies to use when they are witnesses to bullying situations. The strategies are discussed and practiced through the use of role-playing.

Victims are taught skills that will make them less subject to harassment. They learn to be aware of their voice, posture and overall presentation. These skills can help them to be less vulnerable while gaining more confidence and self-respect. Some children are given extra support and help from adults when they are the target of bullying. Victims need an understanding, caring and supportive environment—a small group or an individual setting that will encourage them to talk, share feelings and practice new skills.

A Model Program in Action

We were so impressed by the comprehensive nature of the Bully Proofing Your School approach that we traveled to Englewood, Colorado, to visit the Cherry Creek School District to observe the program in progress. Paul Von Esson, M.S.W., kindly agreed to be our host and guide. Paul had been working with bully proofing in schools for six years. He was trained in the comprehensive program, Bully Proofing Your School. We spent a full school day accompanying Paul to the groups he conducted with the children on bully proofing. From first grade to fifth grade we listened and observed how the program actually worked.

The feeling in the school was calm, secure and happy. There were posters, children's drawings and artwork in the halls and classrooms all about bully proofing. Children and teachers would stop Paul in the hall to tell him that they needed his assistance on a bullying or victim problem. At one point a six-year-old told him how she handled a bullying incident. The children were taught a technique from the book *Bully Proofing Your School* called HA HA SO, which stands for "Help, Assert Yourself, Humor, Avoid, Self-Talk, Own It." The beautiful little six-year-old informed Paul that she had used HA HA SO and it "worked good."

In the classrooms, Paul presented material, led discussions and conducted role-plays. The children and teachers related their experiences or concerns, then received feedback and guidance from the other children, the teacher or Paul. The children were given the responsibility to help each other with their issues and did the task well. They were open with their feelings and seemed excited to share their experiences and ideas with each other. They didn't seem to be the least bit bothered that we had joined them for the day. They shared that they were getting used to visitors because others had come to observe the program. "Even a camera crew was here," one little boy confided. It was obvious that the children were comfortable with the program. This particular school has been engaged in bully proofing for years.

In the afternoon, we visited the third, fourth and fifth grades. The fourth-grade children brought up a problem with the fifth-grade class. Some fifth-graders were bullying several fourth-graders at recess while playing soccer. Paul asked the group if they wanted the fifth-grade class to come join them so that this problem could be confronted. The answer was a loud "Yes!" Paul and the teachers gave the children the responsibility of solving the conflict. Many of them had been involved with the program since kindergarten or first grade. They did extremely well, asking Paul for help when they needed it.

At one point a nine-year-old boy stood up and said that another boy in the class had been bullying him. He said that he had tried some of the skills that he had been taught but "they were not working." He was relaxed and seemed to trust the class to help him. We saw no

embarrassment or anger. When asked how this was making him feel,
he shared openly, stating, "I need help." Paul led a discussion exploring the boy's options. Paul asked if anyone else in the class had had
a similar experience and those who did raised their hands and one
by one stood up to share. Paul asked if the person in the class that
was doing the bullying would be willing to stand up and discuss the
problem so that it could be resolved. Much to our amazement, the
cutest little redhead stood up. Although it surprised us, neither Paul
nor the class seemed surprised that the boy would accept responsibility for his behavior. He took full responsibility for what he had done
and expressed his concern over the other boy's feelings and the fact
that he was upset with him. Paul asked how he was feeling and he,
too, was open.

The class discussed the situation and what these two boys could do
to resolve this problem. Both boys shared that they understood what
they needed to do. Then Paul left it up to them to resolve it. After
class, everybody was laughing and talking and milling around, and I
looked over near the door. The little redheaded boy was apologizing
to the boy who had confronted him. They left the classroom with
their arms around each other's shoulders, laughing and smiling. It
was a pleasure to be in a school where adults cared about the children enough to take risks, ask questions, explore program options,
choose a comprehensive program that encouraged the development of
a healthy community, and finally spend the time and finances to bring
good people in to train them and implement the program. Paul's full-
time job was teaching and maintaining the program of bully proofing.

It was our impression that this program was successful for a large
number of the children. Paul shared that he learned something every
day from the children and was open about his own early mistakes in
perception. He told us that for quite a while the adults felt that they
had to teach the children "the right thing." He learned along the way

that many children often knew the right thing to do, but still used the behaviors that had worked for them in the past. "When we ask kids to give up the ways they had learned to be powerful, controlling and seeking attention, in the name of 'doing the right thing,' it wasn't that they didn't know the right thing to do, it was that it hadn't worked well for them in the past."

Our interviews with the children were enjoyable and rewarding. They spoke frequently about changes in perception and behavior that had happened for them. One of the statements that we heard often from the children was, "I felt somebody really meant what they said. They gave me choices, 'Either do this or this is going to happen.'" Whether referring to a teacher, principal or parent, the children felt that the adult really meant what he or she said. The realization that the adults in their lives were serious about the limits they were setting made the children stop and take stock of what they were doing. Another common theme in our interviews with the children was that they really got tired of being left out. Not having attention or power really bothers children, and in this school they had learned the skills to give voice to their frustrations.

It was a wonderful feeling to have the beliefs we have shared throughout our careers borne out in this wonderful school: Creating safe, inclusive and respectful environments within our schools that allow teachers to teach and children to learn is possible. The goal is to create a warm and respectful community environment where "the right thing" is given a lot of power and the "wrong thing" very little power. It is possible, when the message is "Do what you need to do, these are the choices. Understand that there may be positive or negative consequences as a result of your choices. You will be cared about and given help even when you make mistakes in judgment," rather than "I will make you do the right thing. I am in charge and I will withdraw my caring if you don't do what I say."

As with most problems in society, it unfortunately takes a signifi-cant amount of human loss for people to take notice. The problems created by bullying have recently received enough attention to cre-ate the awareness necessary for action. Hopefully, all concerned and responsible adults in schools and communities throughout the world will be open to listening and learning, so that effective interventions can be the rule rather than the exception. We left the Cherry Creek School District with a warm sense of hope. For many days, the image of the little boys with their arms around each other stayed with us as we imagined them as men, modeling in their families, workplaces and communities the skills they had learned.

Whether using a program that is already in existence or creating your own, there are four components that we feel should be a part of every program:

1. Must involve the entire school community: administrators, teach-ers, parents, support staff, key community members, and learners. A representative from all areas could be part of creating the program or reviewing existing programs.

2. The program must target the underlying causes of bullying behav-ior, not merely the behavior. As stated so well by Bruce Perry, M.D., "People, not programs, heal people." A significant part of the program must focus on attachment, connection, values, and the development of empathy.

3. Education for the entire school community that is age appropriate on bullying, cyberbullying, values, cooperation and building a car-ing community. Education for staff on attachment, empathy, and trauma-informed care. Education for tweens and teens on "sextor-tion," "revenge porn," "coercion," and "textual harassment".

4. The program must focus on empowering and giving voice to the majority of youth. It must ensure that the "silent majority" becomes

the vocal majority in standing up for their peers and no longer remaining bystanders. It must help targets develop the skills not to become victims and give pro-social consequences to bullies rather than excluding them from the community unless there a clear and present danger to the school community. It is also important to focus on empowerment and "catching everyone doing great," rather than an environment that focuses primarily on negative behavior.

To Youth and Teens

*"I learned that courage was not the
absence of fear, but the triumph over it.
The brave man is not he who does not feel afraid,
but he who conquers that fear."*

Nelson Mandela

Danny Keefe was in the first grade when he learned the power of the silent majority. He suffered a speech impediment, caused by a brain hemorrhage at birth, and had become a target for bullies in his school. They called him a "baby" and ridiculed him for wearing a suit and tie to school. Danny was the water boy for the fifth-grade football team. His fellow team members, tired of the bullying directed at Danny, decided to send a clear message to school bullies. They came to school dressed like Danny, and declared a "Danny Appreciation Day."

To Those Who Have Remained Silent and Want to Be Part of a Compassionate and Vocal Majority

Courageous students like Kevin Curwick, the football team captain highlighted in Chapter Five who took action and began sending anonymous Tweets to fellow classmates in support of the targets of bullying, and those who stood up for Danny in the story above, are becoming increasingly vocal and making their school communities safe and compassionate. These courageous members of a once silent majority are letting others know, by making headlines of their own, that bullying is not tolerated by most youth and teens. We need more of your voices, more positive headlines to add to theirs.

Media reports in the past few years have highlighted the actions of bullies whose behavior has become associated with teen suicides and school shootings, Because teens have remained silent in the past, it was easy to assume, one young woman told me recently, "It's just part of school life." An important fact to remember is bullies are in the minority—most students do not support their actions. Websites like *Teens Against Bullying,* created by and for teens, are springing up, letting others know that those who were once silent will not remain so when they see bullying. Hundreds of teens wear orange wrist bands with the words: ACT, HEAL, CHANGE, BELIEVE, EMPOWER, EMBRACE, MENTOR, UNITE. Thousands of others wear pink to lend their voice to The International Day Against Bullying, Discrimination, Homophobia, and Transphobia. The majority of youth and teens across the globe are kind and compassionate. Thousands have deleted bullying tweets, e-mails and text messages, have been appalled by bullying posts on media sites, and have not, in their hearts, supported the gossip, rumors, and face-to-face bullying actions of the few.

In the past, many of the silent majority have not stood up, believing that bullying was the norm in their school. Today, research and the actions of courageous peers are proving that attacking others with words and actions is not the norm. The majority of students in the school community are compassionate, empathetic, and caring. For too long those who didn't support the actions of bullying lost their voice for fear of making the problem worse, becoming targets themselves, or simply not knowing what to do to lend support. Today, that silent majority in many areas of the world are beginning to find a strong and powerful voice and are, in so doing, making it clear that students who act by standing up can create safe and compassionate schools where everyone can feel a sense of belonging.

In order to begin to change the fabric of society as a whole, we need the silent majority to become the vocal and powerful majority. Youth and teens in schools across the globe can take back their schools by taking a moment to experience how targets of harassment may be feeling, and by lending their voice to those who have temporarily been silenced by shame and ridicule. They can respect themselves and others by speaking up and standing by those that have become the targets of a bullying few, and by seeking the assistance of trusted, caring adults when additional support is needed. When peers become the targets of cyberbullying, support them by documenting and reporting what you witness. This is not being a "rat"; it is being a caring community member. Peers who are left unsupported can wrestle with serious emotional problems and feel there are no solutions and no escape from the torment of others. Some feel so isolated, alone, and powerless, that they attempt or succeeded in taking their life. By lending your voice and support, you can save a life.

1. **Become a peer support.** If you notice a youth being bullied in person or online, ask if you can help them out. It's easy to let it pass and

assume someone else will help. Today, decide to be that one person in someone's life. It takes a lot of courage at times to do what's right. Let him or her know you do not support bullying and will stand with them. Don't tolerate cruelty and hate. Bullies thrive on isolating their targets. Let others know you care about them and will listen to them. When they know that the atmosphere in the school is one of compassion where students have each other's back, they, too, consider joining the compassionate majority.

2. **Trust your instincts.** You may be worried about someone in your school or online who you think may be suicidal. Trust your instincts and get help. If it is a friend or peer in school, reach out, find a private place to talk, let them know you are concerned and why, and ask questions, "Are you thinking about killing yourself? Do you have a plan?" These questions will allow the person to talk. Let him or her know: "I care about you and I want to help." Let him or her know you are interested in what he or she has to say. Listen without judgment, remain positive, and show you care. Go together to get help. If you are worried about someone online, and you know them, make a personal connection and reach out. If they are unknown to you, contact the website where the posts appeared. Tell an adult. Again, trust your intuition. Two great resources are: *The Power to Prevent Teen Suicide: A Guide for Teens Helping Teens* (Nelson and Galas, 2006) and *Words Wound* (Patchin and Hinduja, 2014).

3. **Become a peer mentor.** Many schools today have peer mentoring programs where teens help teens by passing on knowledge and helpful advice, acting as sounding boards in difficult situations, and providing encouragement when needed. Adolescence is a time when peers are extremely important. Be a compassionate member of your school community. Pass on what you know. Educate those you mentor on bullying and let them know how important it is to support others, stand up in a good way to bullies, and to seek help if bullied in

school or online. Find out if your school has a mentoring program; if it doesn't, talk to school administrators about starting one.

4. **Use social media to support and hold each other up rather than putting each other down.** More than likely, students are anonymously tweeting negative things about others in your school. If your school does not have a site where you can post positive messages, start one. Learn about those that are in place based on Kevin Curwick's idea: @OsseoNiceThings, @ComplementsCHHS, @ComplimentsDC, and @GRHSnicewords, and many more. Also, find out about others spreading kind and compassionate words on Facebook and Instagram. If your school doesn't have a site, start one. Kevin also felt it was important for those who received a positive post to share it at #niceit forward, spread the kindness. Be part of the solution; share a positive message with instructions to pass on the kindness.

5. **Get support when the bully is an adult in your school, team, or youth organization.** It can be painful to witness a peer being bullied by an adult who is supposed to be a role model. Many youth have asked us, "What do you do when the bully is a teacher and the target is one of our peers, often one that has difficulty standing up for himself? We see the incident, we hurt for them and us, yet feel powerless to do anything because it is an adult with power."

    Our suggestions would be: 1) Document the incident(s). Include time, place, what you saw, heard, and felt; 2) If others witnessed the incident(s), encourage them to document as well; 3) If it is in the school, take your documentation as a group, or only your own if you are the only witness, to an adult you trust to support you and lend his/her voice (a teacher, coach, counselor); 4) Together, peers and trusted adult, take your documentation to the principal; 5) If nothing is done, seek out a strong advocate outside of the school, an adult who you believe can and will support you. Present your documentation to him/her and together meet with the school superintendent to present your concerns.

If the witnessed bullying incident occurs in a youth group, sporting event, etc. by an adult leader, follow the same guidelines only after documentation by witnesses. Take the documentation first to a trusted adult whom you can depend on to support you, and then, together, present the documentation to someone in a position of authority in the organization.

6. **Be Creative.** Use your creativity, your songs, your art, your voice and, most of all, your actions to let others know that bullying isn't cool and you want them to join you in being the vocal majority that speaks out against bullying and stands up for kind and compassionate schools and communities.

To the Targets of Bullying

If you are the target of face-to-face or cyberbullying, know first and foremost that the actions of a bully(s) are not your fault. There is no excuse for intentionally trying to hurt another person. Also, know that even if the majority of peers in your school or neighborhood have not yet found the courage to speak up, it has been proven by many surveys and research studies, that the majority do NOT support the bully. We realize that just knowing this does not erase the pain you are feeling.

It is normal and natural to begin to believe what others say about us. As human beings, we often create our own feelings of self-worth based on the actions and words of others. We often take from the outside and bring to the inside people's unkind words and actions, giving them the power of truth. They come from the others' fragile and powerless places. Know that bullies attack those who are "too popular" and "not popular enough"; those who have difficulty learning and those who are "too smart"; those who are "too thin" or "too fat"; "too dark" or "too fair"; "too poor" or "too rich"; those from the "wrong family" or "a prominent family"; someone "too removed" or "too sensitive" . . . the list goes on and on. Bullies attempt to find your greatest area of self-doubt or "hot button" and press it. They gain power by rendering others powerless through learning to doubt themselves. Don't give them the weapon. Know and own your hot buttons. Give more power to those who are compassionate, who care, and can provide you an honest mirror—not a distorted one that a bully might hold up.

Heightened sensitivity to the beliefs of peers is greater in teen years when your developing brain is focused on connecting with peers in order to prepare you to leave home. It is also a time when your emotions are more intense. Minor stress becomes huge, and major stress, like being the target of a bully, can seem overwhelming. It is a time when you are figuring out what you want in life, how you are going to fit in, a time of creating dreams and goals, and figuring out how you are going to accomplish them. It is a time when you are facing challenges in school, at home, with friends, and with your developing sexuality.

In teen years, we also haven't fully developed the parts of our brains that let us understand that what is happening now isn't going to last forever. Time passes and those things that seem most important today will not be as important tomorrow. "Remember that pair of jeans you loved once, but don't want to wear anymore? Remember that movie star you once had a crush on, but now are totally over? Remember that band whose older songs you were crazy about, but whose newer stuff you don't like at all? Our perceptions, likes and dislikes, preferences, and tastes are always evolving. That's how it is for everybody" (Patchin and Hinduja, 2014. p. 49).

Time passes and things change. The good news is that time does pass. What had seemed to be so important becomes less important, and the pain that seems so powerful today, will decrease tomorrow. The bad news is, you have to walk through today to get to tomorrow. Again, you don't have to walk through these hurtful times alone. If you're hurting, tell someone who can help; someone who empowers you by listening and caring. Someone who can assist you once again to find your voice, by helping you to sort out feelings and thoughts as well as possible approaches and decisions.

A strong and powerful woman, Eleanor Roosevelt, once said, "No one can make you feel unworthy without your consent." These are not just words, they are truth. Try not to let yourself be caught up in basing your self-worth on the belief of others. It is not always easy. It is difficult to be the target of humiliation and disrespect. Try not to join in their attempts to gain power by putting you down. It is hard enough dealing with the actions of bullies, without joining them by being even more critical of yourself. Give yourself positive feedback. Practice positive self-talk, "It is not about me. I am a good person. It is their problem, not mine." Your greatest weapon against the actions of those that bully, is being kind and compassionate to yourself, and by seeking out those who can stand with you.

Consider finding adults who can support you. It is easy to own the shame and powerlessness that others have thrown your way. The shame is not yours. Tell someone. Seek out the support of adults who care, and other teens who are kind and compassionate. While some adults in the past may have let you down, know there are those who will support you today. There are also online support groups and sites developed by and for teens that are powerful voices to stop bullying. Some are: *www.stopbullying.com*, *www.wordswound.or*g, *www.cyber-bullying.us*, *www.stompoutbullying.org*

Many musicians, poets, authors, actresses and actors, playwrights, television personalities, and sports stars have been in your shoes, and have started their own websites to support you. One such Australian musician, Faydee, wrote a song entitled "Unbreakable," whose lyrics speak to finding your power and your voice. The song speaks about the internal power a target can find, healing them to not become the victim of another, allowing them instead to be unbreakable.

To Those Who Have Bullied Because You Have Difficulty Standing Up for Your Values or May Have Acted in Anger

Many of you that have bullied didn't set out to cause harm. You may be the buddy of the primary bully and go along with the hurt he or she causes others to remain in the bully's good graces. You might laugh at jokes made at another's expense, ignore a person, or even stand by while another is being physically attacked. Maybe you join in by following your friend's lead and post cruel remarks about the person as well. Inside, where it counts, because you have a strong value system, you hate what you are doing. The price you pay for friendship is violating your value system. We have worked with so many like you in later life, who suffer from tremendous guilt and depression, due to the harm their actions caused another in their earlier years because they couldn't stand up to a friend who was bullying others. Years later, they can still see their target's faces, and the anguish and torment they helped cause. In some cases, the target changed schools and was never heard from them again. In some cases, the target made a suicide attempt or succeeded in committing suicide. If you are following a peer who bullies, whom you feel you need to impress, remember: friends don't ask friends to violate their beliefs. It is *you* who will live with the consequences. Also, realize that bullies are in the minority and not supported by the majority, even though many may remain quiet.

Or, you may be someone who has bullied after feeling hurt and powerless, as Taylor did in Chapter Four. You armed yourself with anger to make the hurt feel less painful. You just wanted to injure someone, as you had been injured.

We have met many of you who, like Taylor, have strong value systems, yet armored with anger, didn't feel the hurt they were causing another at the time. When you attack another in revenge in a way you never would want someone to do to you, the price you pay is violating your own value system. You may be spreading rumors or gossiping, calling the person cruel names, or attempting to get others to join you in excluding them so they will hurt like you are hurt. Unfortunately, this kind of revenge never works out. Diminishing another doesn't give you power, only momentary satisfaction. Hurting someone out of revenge doesn't stop your hurt. Many tell us years later that they would do anything to take back the words and actions that caused a peer pain. Years later, they are still having difficulty dealing with their guilt.

Impulsive revenge bullying is most commonly done by girls. It saddens us that lateral violence between girls often starts in elementary school, continues, and seems to grow over time. Lateral violence begins when a group of people are oppressed (African Americans, Native Americans, religious groups, gays or lesbians, women, etc.) and feel that they can't fight their oppressors. Instead, they turn the oppression on each other in the form of gossip, put downs, competition, gangs, religious wars, family feuds, etc. (Middelton-Moz, 1999). Girls fight girls when their boyfriend strays rather than confronting the boy who made the commitment to them in the first place. A girl will fight her best friend if a guy she might be interested in looks at her. This comes from a long history of women feeling powerless and turning the hurt on each other. Perhaps you, as youth, can change this hurting of one another.

Think before you act. Focus on the goals and values that are most important to you. Ask yourself if this action against another fits with your goals and values. Don't use your e-mail, text, or go to media sites when you are angry. Take a break, calm down, breathe, and think things through. Listen to yourself as you speak to friends. Are you bullying? Is it helping? What other actions could you take? What actions would actually empower you?

To Those with a History of Bullying

Many of you with a history of bullying have or are growing up in environments where you get punished no matter what you do. You feel unprotected and alone. Others are growing up in environments where you have never been given the respect of being allowed to take responsibility for your actions no matter what you've done and sometimes have gotten rewarded when you did nothing to merit the reward. What's common to all of you is that YOU haven't been seen. We need to be seen and felt ourselves in order to see and feel others. We need to be loved for who we are in order to love others fully.

When you are not SEEN as you grow, it is difficult to accurately assess the behavior of others. Sometimes you see humiliation or the intent to harm, when no such intention exists. You may believe others are out to pull one over on you, when they have accidently bumped into you in the hallway, are more popular, or score a touchdown. You believe you have to get back and get even, when there was no intention to harm you in the first place. You have been taught that aggression and rendering others powerless is the answer to life's problems by an adult that modeled the behavior or those who didn't protect you.

One thing the bullies in this book, and others we have worked with as well over the years, had in common is that they wished someone had stopped them earlier. Being allowed to hurt others without being held accountable was not supportive to their growth and well-being, and not respectful of their ability to change and do the right thing. Many remember bullying others as early as kindergarten, and continued

Make sure there is balance in your life; emotional, physical, mental and spiritual. Texting, watching television, and playing video games to the exclusion of face-to-face connection, sitting by a stream, working on a paper, dreaming, sleeping, spending time with family, working with others to create change in your world, is not balance. "The brain becomes what it does most frequently. It is shaped every day by what we do—and what we don't do. If we don't practice empathy, we can't become more empathetic. If we don't interact with people, we can't improve our connections to them. If we don't ease one another's stress through caring contact, we will all become increasingly distressed" (Szalavitz and Perry, 2010, p. 289).

Start creating a kind community in your school. Work to become the best person you can be in order to make your school a safe place where everyone belongs. Adults in your schools can create programs, lesson plans, and rules about behavior. Legislators can pass laws regarding youth cyberbullying, sexting and harassment. It is you, however, who will make the real difference by doing your part to create schools and cyber communities that are safe and kind. As many courageous teens have learned, kindness feeds and spawns more kindness. One person, like Kevin Curwick, can make a difference. In your school, that person could be you!

10

Bullies in Relationships

There are two ways of meeting difficulties.
You can alter the difficulties or you can
alter yourself meeting them.

Phyllis Bottome

William's Story

"When I bullied others I attempted to coerce them
into thinking, believing or acting in a manner that let
them know that I had control over them. For the most
part when I was in the midst of my bullying behavior,
I wasn't aware that I was bullying. My understanding was usually hindsight. I began my bullying behavior when I was about
twenty-four years old.

"My targets changed over time. In the beginning, I only had a
'golden tongue' and could be very charming and persuasive. At
that time, I had absolutely no money. As I became wealthier, the

217

targets and the tactics changed. With respect to my wife, Mary, for example, there was no way she would have been on my radar screen had I not had money. She was from a different country and didn't speak much English. It's difficult to be persuasive with someone who has no clue what I'm saying. Essentially, my money persuaded her.

"The majority of my targets were women with whom I had affairs or relationships. I have never used bullying within my work environment. I always thought that bullying was linked to the use of force or causing physical harm. In my case, depriving [someone of their] emotional, physical, or material well-being were the channels for my bullying.

"In the earlier days, I would bully by my 'silence,' until I got what I wanted. I also made sure that women I related to were aware of the conditions that would lead to the 'silence,' so that the next time they would give in faster. I took advantage of knowing their weaknesses and would manipulate them in order to coerce the outcome I was seeking. What made the particular events different than normal 'give and take' and/or compromise situations were that both sides clearly understood that it was a demand rather than request on my part and that there would be consequences. These could be like losing my company for a time or possibly even ending the relationship, if I didn't get my way.

"Later on, especially over the last ten years of my bullying, I used veiled threats of depriving financial security. I made certain that everyone knew that my lawyers were the best money could buy and that I was more eligible, as a man of wealth, than ever before.

"The feelings that I had before I would bully were primarily anger that I was not getting my way. I was afraid of losing control. The bullying was satisfying, seeing the familiar reaction of insecurity, defiance, and knowing that I still had influence and *power over my victim. As an active alcoholic my bullying behavior was loud and erratic. I would storm out of the house, for example. However, and thank God, no physical violence of any sort ever took place. After a bullying episode, I would either feel self-justification or self-hatred. I could also feel empathy for my victim, as I had known bullying based on emotional and material deprivation from my father.*

"I was an alcoholic for the last eight of my twenty years of bullying. The previous seven years, alcohol was prevalent in the relationship.

"The first five years of my bullying were my coming-out years. It was at that time that I began to recognize and fine tune my bullying characteristics. This was a very different society than the one I ran from in my country. It was the land of choices, and the only area I felt a sense of permanency in was my work. Pretty much everything else, certainly relationships, were grounds for learning, experiencing and moving on.

"Bullying became one of the tools I used to ensure change. Again, I see this only in hindsight from the work I have done in recovery. If my bullying kept working, I became bored. Consequently, I would escalate the bullying until it became intolerable, the relationship would end and my victim would leave. Then, the cycle would start once again. The bullying at that time was often quiet, subtle and 'underground.' My persona in the real world was one of quiet intelligence, love for music and entrepreneurial endeavors.

"I believe that my need to bully was linked to other issues: low self-worth, people-pleasing, fears, anxieties, fears of rejection and not being liked, and past experiences. When I was nine years old, I was at a public swimming pool in London. Three much bigger boys came up to me and told me to pull down my swim shorts in front of several girls my age. I did. It is still vivid to me today. I felt shame,

deep anger and branded myself a coward. My father also bullied me
by depriving me of his affection or praise whenever I did not achieve
his goal for my class grades, even though I had done my best.

"I remember being tormented by the fact that every relationship
was essentially turning out to be the same. I knew that there was
something very wrong with me and I needed to change if I didn't
want to be alone for the rest of my life. As soon as a new relationship
started, I felt that this one would be different. I had a tremendous
amount of confidence in my intellect and ability to problem-solve.
Until I reached my bottom, sucking on the tailpipe of my car in a
desperate attempt to die, the solution was not at hand.

"I was rarely held accountable for my bullying behavior until
the very end. Then I was faced with the possibility of a divorce
with no child custody and the loss of my impressive CEO job. My
bullying had been linked to an attempt to neutralize the ill effects
of years of people-pleasing when I was young and low self-worth.
I was an 'egomaniac with an inferiority complex.'

"I had finally bottomed out in my alcohol addiction. I was faced
with losing my family and my job, and with them the rationaliza-
tions for my bullying behavior: 'Look at how hard I work and all
the things I give my wife so that she can enjoy her life'; 'No one
really understands the pressure of my work'; 'I am really a good
person at heart and just need to have time alone.'

"Treatment helped me to change my life and stop my bullying
behavior. I was confronted on my behaviors, feelings, and beliefs. I
was taught how I had harmed others and myself with my bullying
behavior. I studied my past and was guided to learn the changes I
needed to make, rather than use it as an excuse for self-destructive
behaviors or the emotional abuse of others.

"In treatment, I was given choices, new behaviors, feelings and
beliefs. I realized that I could learn to become the healthy, happy

person I had always wanted to be. I was taught how to put balance in all areas of my life.

"As I work daily to keep balance in my life, I still find it hard at times to identify and accept my lack of control although it's becoming more manageable with each passing year. Asking for and accepting help and learning to be a healthy father are also challenging. It hasn't been nearly as difficult for me to regain a sense of faith and spirituality. I behave and think in ways that are far from instinctive, and I credit this change to my spiritual awakening."

Come Dance with Me

In earlier chapters, you have read about the internal reality and behaviors of childhood bullies. Without intervention, these feelings and beliefs become ingrained, and the behavior patterns strengthen, continuing into adulthood. The bullying behavior was originally used to defend and protect developing egos from real and perceived threats. Without confrontation and logical consequences, bullying behavior and the underlying anxiety and depression increase. Reality becomes increasingly distorted, and the world is seen as a threatening place. The intentions of people become increasingly suspect. By the time bullies enter committed relationships or marriages, they may have been bullying for years.

The bully has problems with social interactions, stemming from feelings of inadequacy, vulnerability, low self-worth, fear and loss of internal feelings of control. As so well-portrayed in William's story, bullies can learn to "protect" themselves through arrogance, controlling, sarcasm, rage, manipulation, possessiveness, silence and dishonesty. The more vulnerable they feel, the more they defend.

As bullies begin to feel attraction to another, they often feel a sense of desperation and become hypervigilant in beginning relationships—examining every interaction, motive, word or gesture in order to ensure themselves that they will not be hurt and can maintain control over the other person and ultimately themselves. They have internal feelings of inadequacy and fear normal feelings of love and need for another. Because of difficulties in attachment in their original relationships with caretakers, they are terrified of commitment, intimacy, dependency and ultimately loss of control.

When they begin to sense growing commitment, strong feelings of attachment and intimacy, bullies become frightened and vulnerable. Because their beliefs and feelings are distorted and cluttered with ghosts from their pasts, they begin to see attacks and criticisms where there are none. A dance begins between bully and victim that can sometimes last a lifetime. Bullies lead and victims wittingly or unwittingly follow:

1. The bully's feelings of developing intimacy and attachment lead to increasing fear, hypervigilance, anxiety and vulnerability. Vulnerability is frightening, and the bully begins to feel the loss of control. Distorted beliefs take hold, and the need to defend strengthens. Bullying behavior begins.

2. The bully's victim experiences feelings of confusion, fear, shame, anxiety, and vulnerability at the onslaught of verbal, mental and sometimes physical abuse. The bully's internal feelings now belong to his or her victim.

3. The victim's powerlessness and vulnerability engender feelings of power and control in the bully, and his fears, anxieties and vulnerabilities diminish.

4. The bully, feeling more in control, returns to his charming self and may even comfort the victim. The victim feels confused and emotionally shell-shocked, but pleased at the return of a normal relationship.

   The relationship continues until the dance begins again: one, two, three, four; one, two, three, four; a perfect box step.

Bullies use many behaviors in continual efforts to protect themselves from perceived threats. "Bullying" is a compulsive need to dis-
place aggression and is achieved by the expression of inadequacy
(social, personal, interpersonal, behavioral, or professional) by projection of that inadequacy onto others through control and subjugation
(criticism, exclusion, counter-accusations, pretenses of victimhood)
and perpetuated by a climate of fear, ignorance, indifference, silence,
denial, disbelief, tolerance, and evasion of accountability" (Field,
2000, p. 1–8).

Bullies come from dysfunctional environments. If adult bullies
have also experienced previous relationships of hurt, rejection, and
fear, their defenses, denial, and distortions can be more pronounced in
attempts to maintain control and avoid hurt and rejection. It becomes
a vicious cycle. Most bullies promised themselves in childhood that
they would never be the bullies their caregivers were, only to find
that their relationships and the accusations of significant others feel
all too familiar.

"Though I hated my father, I expressed that hatred eloquently by
imitating his life, by becoming more and more ineffectual daily, by
ratifying all the cheerless prophecies my mother made for both my
father and me. I thought I had succeeded in not becoming a violent
man, but even that belief collapsed. My violence was subterranean,
unbeheld. It was my silence, my long withdrawals, that I had turned
into dangerous things" (Conroy, 1968).

Fleeting moments of awareness of bullying behavior only serve to
strengthen the denial of bullies. Brief glimpses of themselves repeating their caretakers' actions produce more fear and anxiety, heighten-
ing the need for stronger defenses. Because of deep-seated feelings
of worthlessness, bullies are terrified of being proven "wrong," criti-
cized and again abandoned. These feelings increase lifelong survival
skills and the determination that "I will not let you hurt me. I will

not let you control me." As they repeat the mantra that has become the foundation of their lives, "egomaniacs with inferiority complexes," so well-portrayed by William, strengthen their grip on power and control.

Janet's Story

"My mother was a tyrant with a smooth and cutting tongue. She could calmly and rationally cut you to ribbons as she pointed out the exact nature of your faults. The attacks could go on for hours. The targets of her attacks were my father and I. We couldn't do anything right. On the other hand, my brother could do no wrong. He was the crown prince. I got straight A's and won countless awards, and he was the one that got average grades and goofed off. Yet, he was the one that made her proud. I could never match up no matter how hard I tried. I realized much later in life how hard her smothering attention and rejection of me was on my brother.

"As a child, I was always trying to prove that I was really okay. I was terrified to make a mistake. It's interesting, my mother never hit me, but I felt bruised all over. No matter what I did, I couldn't earn her praise. She would always point out what I had done wrong.

"I never could understand why my father didn't fight back, but he didn't. At least I wasn't aware enough back then to understand that his passive-aggressive behavior was his defense. She couldn't make him do what she wanted. They always fought about money, and he often 'accidentally' overdrew the account. She'd ask him to do things around the house. He'd pleasantly agree and then never quite get around to doing them. She'd rage at him and he'd just pleasantly smile and seem confused. It must have worked for them because they stayed married, still are.

"*I was never attracted to boys that were attracted to me. It was only the ones that were somehow unattainable that attracted my interest. They were a challenge. I realize now that once they were interested, I wasn't anymore. I thought I had just fallen out of love.*

"*I met David in my senior year. He was kind and quiet but also a bit aloof. It was love at first sight. He was always very nice and sometimes we'd study together, talking for hours about current events or whatever subject we were working on, but he seemed content to be buddies. He had been dating another girl in the class since our freshman year. She was always nice to me but I hated her and would gossip about her with my friends. I realize now this was another pattern that I'd had since childhood. I would gossip and spread rumors about other girls that I had conflict with or was jealous of. I'd be nice to their faces, but sometimes really mean behind their backs.*

"*David was almost an obsession with me. It became my goal to get him to be interested in me sexually. I would flirt, compliment him and make him special foods. I worked to build him up and subtly tear his girlfriend down. It worked.*

"*We got married the year after we graduated. I was so much in love and was working to be the 'perfect wife.' He was very appreciative and attentive. I don't know when it began but it was like all that love just went away. His behavior began to irritate me in small ways. I didn't tell him at first, but after a while I began to criticize him openly. He would look at me with confusion and hurt in his eyes, and it was like I couldn't stop. When he would do something differently than I would have done it, it was like he was making a personal attack on me and I'd attack him back for the way he did things. I'd accuse him of not caring and point out all the ways he had let me down. I'd withdraw affection and always*

*had a reason for it. After a lengthy attack, he'd just quietly walk
out and I would tell myself I had to stop, but I couldn't.*

*"David was from a healthy family, and I think my behavior
really shocked him. He kept trying to listen to what I was saying
and be more considerate. I really hurt him and he just kept being
nice. When he'd apologize, and he usually would, I'd feel like I'd
won. After, I would feel guilty because I knew on some level that
he hadn't done anything to apologize for, but I couldn't let him
know what I was feeling. It was like I was trying to make him feel
as insecure as I felt. When he did, I felt powerful. It was crazy. I'd
be super nice for a while, then I would start on him all over again.*

*"As time passed, David stopped apologizing. He suggested that
I go to a counselor. I was enraged and told him that if anyone
needed a counselor it was him. One day, he told me he couldn't
stand it anymore and he thought we needed to separate. I felt like
my world had ended. I was 'in love' again to the point of obsession.
I tried all the old behaviors that had once pleased him. I became
very affectionate and appreciative again, but it didn't work. He
just became more and more distant. The more distant he became,
the harder I tried. Then, I started to become really depressed.*

*"David told me that he would like to work on our marriage
but if I wasn't willing to go to counseling with him, he'd have to
leave. I agreed.*

*"It took us three attempts to find the right counselor. The first
one spent more time talking about her problems than ours. The
second seemed to focus on David as the problem. Even I knew that
was wrong, but I was good at presenting a perfect picture. There
was too much at stake. I knew I really needed to make changes.
On some level, I knew I was out of control and needed someone
to understand or I would lose my marriage. I knew David meant
what he said.*

"We found a counselor who was compassionate but also was able to be confrontive. One day in a session, I said something to David and she very pleasantly asked him if he was just going to let me knock him down. It was weird, I hadn't even known that what I said was a put-down. When she stopped me, I realized I was talking to him with my mother's voice and words. I felt enormous pain. That was just the beginning. The counselor helped me to realize that when David was distant, I became that pleasing little girl trying to get her mother's love. When he was there, all my anger came out. I became like my mother, and he would begin to feel the hurt and powerlessness I had felt as a child but repressed. My bullying behavior stopped my anxiety and I felt temporarily powerful. David acted powerless and I hated him for it, just like I had hated myself. It was like a crazy dance. I'm now glad David decided he didn't like the steps."

Victims: Learning to Dance

When individuals live with bullying behavior in their relationships, they are victims of abuse in one form or another. Sometimes the abuse is physical: shoving, hitting, kicking, etc. More often the abuse is delivered through words or actions: telling another person they are dumb, stupid, ugly, unlovable, bad, clumsy, inept, a bitch or a whore, or they are criticizing and rejecting as Janet had been to David. There are often threats of violence or threats to leave, get a divorce, commit suicide, take away the children, or withdraw financial support. There is public and/or private belittling or humiliation, unreasonable accusations like being accused of being unfaithful, impatient, or demanding, the use of silence and isolation, as well as sarcasm and insults.

After a time, victims can become prisoners in their own homes and indoctrinated into believing what the bully wants them to believe. Victims are often terrified to confront bullies, and some fear for their lives.

Many victims come from dysfunctional families as well. They have made promises to themselves, telling themselves repeatedly that they would never care about or love anyone that would bully, neglect, or abandon them as they had been in their growing-up years. Like the bully, victims can find themselves in relationships that seem dangerously close to the family systems they vowed to escape. With temporary insight that they are indeed typecast in the same role they grew up with, they build stronger denial, telling themselves, "This is not happening to me, this is not happening to me." Their fears and anxieties heighten, and their dysfunctional behaviors, beliefs and feelings become stronger. Both bullies and victims "survive" life rather than "live" life.

There are also victims, like David, who are in bullying relationships who did not grow up in painful families. Some come from healthy, loving, nurturing environments where they have observed and experienced acceptance, understanding, forgiveness, support, honesty, balance and responsibility to self and others. They are frequently embarrassed and ashamed at the first realization that they have fallen in love with individuals who bully and abuse them: "I can't believe I did this." They have no point of reference as to how to function in a bullying relationship, so they try harder to use the skills they learned in their own families.

Victims sometimes stay in painful relationships longer than is healthy because they either "can't believe this is happening" to them or believe "it surely will change soon." They begin to develop victim characteristics: hypervigilance, anxiety, depression, low self-esteem, learned helplessness, etc.

Some individuals, who have a strong sense of self-worth and have been raised in healthy families, stay in bullying relationships as they begin to believe the words and behaviors of the bullies in their lives, and learn to question their own beliefs, feelings and behaviors. They can begin to lose their identity, their self-esteem, and all they once learned about healthy relationships. Beliefs about love become distorted: "He's really a wonderful person. He just gets upset at times." They can love the bully's "good" behavior and "hate" the abusive behavior, learning to pay a high price for a few good times. We've heard the same statements again and again from victims: "But he really is a good person. I just need to learn to ignore it or stay out of the way when he is in a bad mood. He doesn't really mean it." To this we often reply, "If I walk over and kick you, even though I don't mean to, are you going to tell me to stop or move away? If I tell you I don't mean it, are you going to let me continue hurting you?" These victims often tell us that the first time the bullying occurred they were "shell-shocked," almost frozen in place. When normal behavior returns, they begin to believe that the bullying was a rare occurrence, didn't happen, they misunderstood or somehow they caused the attack. The behavior becomes normalized: "If she acted like that *all* the time, it would have been easier for me to leave, but she didn't."

The reality is that as time passes, the bully may be kind and loving 8 percent of the time and abusive 92 percent of the time. The victim learns to focus on the good behavior and begins to deny how bad the situation really is. Over time, victims can lose their self-worth, believe everything the bullies tell them and begin to take responsibility for the bully's abusive behaviors, believing that they have caused the abuse. Victims slowly begin to change their beliefs, feelings and behaviors to please bullies with the hope of stopping the abuse, still longing for the person they see 8 percent of the time. They begin to defend bullying behavior in an attempt to protect their own newly established feelings, beliefs and behaviors. Because victims are not responsible for the behavior, beliefs or feelings of others, all attempts to change the behaviors fail. When attempts repeatedly fail, victims feel like failures. At this point, they have internalized their partners' deep-seated feelings about themselves and the bullies' projections are complete.

The Relationship

Bullies need victims in order to continue their bullying and abusive behaviors. They need people who will put up with their emotional, mental and/or physical abuse. They need victims in order to continue to project their illusions of having power and control. They need to continue "the dance."

The rules that bullies demand that their partners follow are: "Put up with everything I put out. Don't tell anyone. Never confront me. I am allowed to control you and make unreasonable demands on you. I can blame you for all my dysfunctions and you must accept the blame without question. You must defend me against others who may try to make me accountable for my behaviors, feelings or beliefs. I will be powerful and in control, and you will be powerless and out of control. If you don't follow these rules, I'll hurt you, leave you or kill myself."

We have worked with bullies for over twenty-five years. In that time most have told us that they have an "instinctive" ability to know when others are good "targets" for their bullying behaviors. They select individuals as "dance partners" who present themselves as helpless, inadequate, shy, passive, fearful or needy. Bullies carefully observe the actions of the people around them, how they interact with others, how they dress and how they behave. They "read" people and develop an awareness of who can be controlled and who can't be. Those who we have worked with have reported that even people who appear strong and independent often give away their weaknesses. If there are weaknesses, bullies know how to capitalize on them and use them to their own advantage.

They also have a keen awareness of other bullies. They have reported that when they meet other bullies it has been challenging and exhilarating to find their weaknesses and use these weaknesses to control them.

In some relationships, individuals take turns being bully and victim. In these relationships, the rules continually change as to who will be victim and who will be bully. The power and control can change hands according to who has the most power in different situations. For instance, one partner may have control over the money, the other over the children. One may control when to have sex, the other may control friendships or time spent with extended family. In these relationships, "head games" are constant in an effort to wear the other down; the battle is constant until one temporarily gives up power and control.

Young Love—a More Lethal Dance

In recent years young people are dating and getting involved in relationships at much younger ages: eleven, twelve, thirteen and fourteen. Some of these young people are from dysfunctional families where there is little affection, understanding, caring or support. They feel a strong need to be cared about and get into relationships to feel a sense of belonging, affection, understanding and support.

These young people have little or no awareness of what their responsibilities are to the other person in a relationship. They do the best they can and rely on what they were taught by their parents. If their parents' relationships are dysfunctional, unhappy, abusive, etc. and they have suffered from it, they may attempt to behave in different ways than their parents modeled for them. They get ideas from television or movies and/or other couples that they have observed in their short lives. They may attempt to model that behavior and expect the other person in the relationship to behave in kind. Needless to say, this doesn't work. Because of fear and confusion, they revert to what they have known best. If their point of reference is of bullying or victimization, the pattern continues for one more generation. They don't understand healthy relationships and often don't know where to turn or who to ask for guidance when problems arise.

Bullying and/or victim behavior in teenage relationships can be similar to that of adult relationships and marriages, without the same finely honed defense mechanisms. Jealousy and possessiveness often lead to emotional and physical abuse. Sometimes the hopes and dreams of finally getting out of dysfunctional families and finding someone who loves and cares about them die quickly and serious depression follows. Feelings of rejection in first love relationships support early beliefs that they are not loved because they are, in fact, unlovable.

One of the major triggers for suicide in teenagers is the breakup of first love relationships. The breakup triggers feelings of anger, self-loathing, loneliness, hopelessness and helplessness caused by years of emotional pain and abandonment. These are overwhelming to immature defenses. The young person who has no support systems sees suicide as a way out of the pain. As one youth put it, "In hindsight, I realize I didn't really want to die, I just wanted the pain to stop. Part of me also wanted them to suffer. I thought they'd finally be sorry when I died."

Some young people may begin to drink or use drugs as early as ten or eleven to make the pain go away. Others, striving for love, affection, control and release from anxiety, may develop eating disorders.

Others will stay in a relationship and over time will be able to get out of dysfunctional families by marrying someone or having the child that they believe will finally give them the love they've never had. The relief of getting out of the family is tremendous and the hope that their lives will be better is high.

Some youths from healthy family systems also get into relationships with bullies. The bully can come across as extremely charming and fun to be with. These young people get sucked in and don't know how to get out.

Date Rape

Date rape, or *acquaintance rape,* is being forced to have unwanted sexual activity including intercourse with someone you know. Date rape occurs with teenagers in high school and on virtually all college campuses. One of the major reasons for date rape is lack of consideration for the rights and wishes of women. These young men have learned that they have the right to take what they want. Acquaintance rape is not a crime of passion or miscommunication. It is an attempt to assert power and release rage. As with any bullying behavior, young men who commit date rape are insecure and angry. Forcing a girl to have sex makes them feel strong temporarily because it makes others weak. The primary motivation is the desire to control and dominate.

Young men commit the overwhelming majority of date rape incidents with young women. As with any case of aggressive bullying behavior in relationships, there are frequently warning signs that can be seen in boys that commit the offense. Boys who ignore emotional and personal boundaries, don't listen to or completely ignore what another is saying, who are intimidating, jealous, possessive, "macho," belittling, and/or sarcastic may commit date rape.

Some tips for young women to follow are:

1. Pay attention to gut-level feelings.
2. Act quickly, don't stay in situations that don't feel safe; don't allow yourself to be conned by messages like "If you really loved me," or "Maybe I should date someone who isn't so frigid."

3. Keep yourself safe. If you drink, be sensible or date in groups with others who are not drinking and can watch out for you.
4. Be clear about what you want and don't want.
5. Act independent and in charge of yourself.
6. Avoid dates with young men who drink too much or are using drugs.

An excellent article for girls beginning to date is "Friends Raping Friends—Could It Happen to You?" by Jean O'Gorman Hughes and Bernice Sandler (1997).

Bullying in the Family

Family bullying is a crucial societal problem. Every day men and women are being bullied by their partners, children by their parents and older siblings, and elders by their adult children, nieces, nephews and grandchildren. Family bullying can include mental, emotional and sometimes physical abuse. When there is physical abuse in a family, there is usually mental and emotional abuse. Evidence of family bullying, abuse, and/or violence crowds the records in doctors' offices, emergency rooms, police departments, social services departments and courtrooms.

The bullying and abuse some family members inflict on their "loved ones" is horrendous. Consistent caring, support and safety aren't present in bullying families. Members of abusive families indicate that they love each other while at the same time inflicting pain. They defend and protect each other from consequences so that outsiders don't get involved. Bullies, like William, and their victims become experts at putting on a front. They can appear like the all-American family or perfect couple, even when feeling intense shame, embarrassment, fear, and anger. The reality of both the bully and his/her victims is usually distorted and deluded: "Everything is fine. Don't talk about it." "He really loves me, he's just having a bad day." "I shouldn't have been so pushy." Or in William's case, "Look how hard I work and all that I give my wife so that she can have a good life."

Caregivers who bully each other teach their children to abide by the rules: Don't talk, keep secrets, pretend. Children are told, "Mom doesn't mean it" or "Your dad didn't mean to hurt me. He was just tired because he works so hard." When children are the targets of bullying behavior, they are often told that the bully really "loves" them. Children develop distorted beliefs; fear is respect, love is abuse.

Many children have never seen their adult models face consequences for their bad behavior. When there are no consequences, the behavior is normalized by the victim, the children and the bully. When courageous children confront the behavior the parents or other adult caretakers may tell them they are causing problems and sometimes even blame them for the abuse ("Don't talk to Mommy like that").

Getting Help to Learn a Different Dance

The victims of bullying in a relationship need help. They need to know that they are worthy, kind, important, unique, loving and wonderful people. They need respect, kindness, understanding and support. There are many good centers for abused and battered women; there are shelters for them to stay in with their children if they have children. These shelters can provide safety, protection, education and counseling for the victims.

The bullies also need to get help. They need to face the consequences of how they have behaved and the harm they have done to themselves and others. They need to be intervened upon and given choices to change. If they have been a bully most of their lives, they need treatment to understand and acknowledge their feelings, beliefs and behaviors and then receive guidance to change their lives and become responsible people. In order to do this, they need support and understanding.

There are thousands of people in the world who are bullies and thousands who are their victims—each with their own unique circumstances of behaviors, feelings and beliefs.

In working with hundreds of bullies over the years, we found that a high percentage of them were also addicts and had used alcohol and drugs to self-medicate. In treating them, however, we found that the use of alcohol and drugs did not *cause* the bullying or abusive behavior. Drugs and alcohol may have contributed to more violent behavior, but it was not the cause of the bullying and/or abusive behavior. When not drinking or using drugs, the behaviors, beliefs, and feelings were still present.

Some bullies have attempted to use their use of alcohol and drugs and being drunk or high as an excuse for their behavior. They are still responsible for what they say, do, and feel whether drunk, high, or sober. The bullies that received help through various forms of treatment had to get clean and sober, maintain their sobriety, and then become aware of their bullying behaviors, beliefs and feelings. Once this was accomplished they had to accept responsibility and accountability, become aware of the choices necessary to make changes, and then make the changes necessary to become responsible people with balance in their lives.

Bullies in the Workplace

We are the ones we've
been waiting for.

June Jordon

B ullying can take place in any business or work environment from the largest corporation to the smallest business:
hospitals, clinics, doctors' offices, legal and accounting firms,
hair salons, spas, health fitness centers, consulting groups, colleges or
universities, police forces, fire departments, health services organizations, insurance companies, government agencies, etc. Bullying can
come from one person, a group or an entire department. Regardless
of who the bullies are, they leave behind a trail of victims.

Bullying in the workplace has been an unspoken problem for
years. Gary and Ruth Namie, authors of *The Bully at Work,* call it the
"silent epidemic" (Namie and Namie, 2000, p. 6). Bullying behavior may include blaming, criticizing, gossiping, harassing, insulting,

intimidating, pushing, shoving, racism or sexual harassment. Bully bosses can set up their targets to fail by giving them too many responsibilities, too few responsibilities, ignoring them, or ordering them to take on responsibilities that they are not qualified to perform, resulting in accusations that their job performance is inadequate. They may ultimately lose their jobs.

Bosses that bully frequently create oppressive, competitive and fear-ridden work environments, often causing workers to turn on each other. Sometimes several individuals, coworkers, subordinates and superiors gang up on a colleague, attempting to force the other to change job assignments or leave the job. This behavior has been referred to as "mobbing." "The mobbing syndrome is a malicious attempt to force a person out of the workplace through unjustified accusations, humiliation, general harassment, emotional abuse, and/or terror" (Davenport, Schwarz, Elliot, 1999, p. 40).

Bullying bosses don't provide true leadership. Instead, they intimidate, blame, distort reality, are dishonest and/or create continual chaos. Workers in bullying work environments feel confused, fearful, anxious, guilty, shameful, angry, and/or depressed.

Workplace bullies can create havoc for years, suffering few, if any, consequences for their behavior. They sometimes quit their jobs before they can be held responsible for their behavior or face the consequences of their actions. They find other jobs and start the same bullying behavior in new work environments.

Many bullies come from dysfunctional family systems. They pack distorted behaviors, beliefs and feelings in their briefcases and bring them to their work environments. Unsuspecting employees or coworkers who may or may not come from healthy family systems can enter the work environment and unknowingly become the targets of bullies.

Dan's Story

Dan worked for a corporation. He had been both a bully and a victim in his work environment.

"I communicated with my words, actions, and body language that I was better than those who worked under me. I gave the impression that others were less than me in every way and that my thoughts and feelings were more important than theirs. When I first began working, I was a pest. I wanted to learn more, faster than others. Then, as I gained both knowledge and experience, I was looked to as a problem solver and an aide to the successes of others. My enthusiasm in this role led to my advancement to new positions at higher levels. I would make people do things my 'way.' I made others feel less successful. I would bully anyone who disagreed with me or wouldn't do things exactly as I wanted them done, or would say something that I found offensive to the self-image I needed to protect.

"I bullied those whom I felt I could intimidate and get away with it. If coworkers would dare question the validity of what I said, I would immediately belittle their comments, providing evidence as to why and how I was correct and their thoughts and beliefs were without merit. I bullied others when I felt threatened. When bullying, I felt energized and high. Afterwards, I felt powerful most of the time but sometimes empty when I sensed that I didn't really 'win.' I didn't feel empathy for my victims at the time.

"At that time in my life, I felt a lot of seemingly contradictory feelings: fearful, anxious, annoyed, resentful, threatened, guilty, inadequate, righteous, empowered and entitled. I was also bullied by those in higher levels who would use the power of their position *to talk down to me, making demands based on their positions of power rather than the validity of their arguments. I would feel resentful and angry.*

"At one point, my manager confronted me, pointing out that my value as a resource was becoming greatly diminished because workers didn't want to talk with me because of the way I sometimes treated them. I was afraid that my position would be eliminated because of my behavior. My manager said that I needed help and I became willing to get help. This was the second time that my manager had confronted me with my behavior. The first time was as a part of an evaluation process that affected my income. I was defensive and arrogant the first time I was confronted but realized after the second time that I had to take responsibility. I asked for help. Today, I have changed many things about myself. I still work for the same corporation. I no longer bully others or allow others to bully me."

When there is bullying in the workplace and nothing is done about it, the cost is paid in lower productivity, costly consultants, high staff turnover, hundreds of hours of lost time due to sick leave, costly legal actions and, increasingly, loss of life. It has been estimated that in America, 500,000 workers have missed 1,751,000 working days per year due to fear of the aggressor in the workplace (Yeates, 2001).

Support in dysfunctional work environments is conditional and has little to do with competence on the job. Pleasing the boss, having "connections," physical appearance, cultural background, political party, or silence and secrecy can determine how much approval or disapproval is shown towards employees or coworkers. There may be harsh disciplinary action for making choices, confronting others or taking risks. Speaking up, acknowledging mistakes or reporting bosses for bullying or unethical behavior can lead to severe and unjust consequences.

Consultants are often brought in by management in order to find the cause of the problems that exist. Workers who are in denial of the real problem or are afraid of the consequences often give consultants inaccurate information. New strategies are formulated and changes are made and put in place that may serve as temporary solutions or placebo effects ("The consultant came in; we must be better"). The real problems are not recognized and therefore never addressed.

The dysfunction caused by allowing bullying to take place can be insidious and hard to identify in a work environment. Unfortunately few consultants have been sufficiently trained to identify bullying in the workplace and are unaware of the devastating effects on victims and organizations. Even when bullies are identified as the source of the problem, victims, not bullies, are often advised to change their behavior. "They tell us either to avoid exposure—change your work schedules as to limit contact with your boss, and take special care to work around a boss's pet peeves—or they advise us on how to live with the pain—focus on strengths, they urge, or simply meditate. This advice is nonsense" (Hornstein, 1996, p. 6).

Too often consultants, knowingly or unknowingly, become weapons used by bullying bosses against their targets. They are brought into dysfunctional work environments in order to give the appearance that problems are being addressed—then they may be directed to gather their information only from specific individuals. Bosses, and those supporting them, are more than willing to talk. Victims are repeatedly blamed for problems that exist and in many cases are not allowed to defend themselves. Many targets are left out of the process entirely, and competent workers too frequently suffer consequences without a forum to voice their concerns and points of view. Two victims we spoke with said that consultants were brought in when they were on vacation. "I read the consultant's report that repeatedly highlighted my weaknesses. I had never even met this man, let alone been allowed to give my point of view. Others that were aware of the boss's tyrannical behavior weren't interviewed either." Competent workers are often demoted, fired or put under disciplinary action.

Bullying Behaviors on the Job

Bullying in the work environment can be a one-time situation or can go on for weeks, progressing into months and even years. One person's bullying behavior can spread through an organization like a malignancy, resulting in the loss of reliable, honest and productive employees. The longer the bullying is allowed to continue, without intervention, the higher the cost to the organization. A major step in preventing bullying in the workplace is training everyone—from boards of directors to workers—to recognize the behavior.

The Many Faces of Workplace Bullies

1. Bullies may appear outgoing, funny, charming and fun-loving—individuals that everyone wants as friends. Bullies may attempt to get people to confide in them in order to gain information about the victim that is private and personal. These bullies use this information to manipulate and threaten their victims.
2. Sometimes bullies are sarcastic and put others down through negative humor. When confronted, these bullies will say, "I was only kidding. Don't you have a sense of humor?"
3. Some may appear arrogant, brag and make others aware that they are more important. They convince others that they are smarter, have more knowledge and expertise, better track records, know the "right" people and/or are close personal friends with people in authority. Bullies have a need to feel in control of everyone and everything. If they are unable to convince others of their ultimate power and control, they may further attempt to impress others by

giving false information; for example, lying about "connections," accomplishments, work history, etc.

4. Bullies are selfish and self-centered, wanting to be the focus of positive attention, and will often take credit for the ideas and accomplishments of others. This is particularly true of "bully bosses" who may take credit for the creativity and hard work of their employees for years while, at the same time, keeping them in their place by subtly discounting and undermining their ideas, personal attributes, popularity, backgrounds, work performance and/or accomplishments. They may convince their employees that they are their major supporters or that they "owe" them for their jobs.

5. Some bullies present themselves as tough, angry and defensive, consistently giving the impression that others should never cross them. They may threaten, violate physical boundaries, degrade, throw temper tantrums, and/or push and shove in an effort to intimidate others.

6. Some bullies are overt in their behavior, using public humiliation, criticism, ridicule, fear and intimidation in an effort to gain ultimate power and control. Some consistently make derogatory and demeaning comments about age, sexual orientation, race, ethnicity, and gender.

7. Some bullies are covert in their attempts to gain power and control and may spread vicious rumors, gossip, patronize, isolate their victims from others, make liberal use of the silent treatment and/or use guilt inductions. These bullies often manipulate others to turn against their victim through lies, insinuations, creating competition and/or through the use of fear tactics ("I heard that one of us is going to be laid off. I think she's gunning for you").

8. Some bullies accomplish their need for power and control by sabotaging the work performance of their targets. They may give false or incomplete information about work assignments,

apply impossible deadlines, "forget" to advise victims of important meetings or deadlines, and/or give work assignments for
which employees are not sufficiently trained, then deny training requests. Some tell their victims not to worry about any
mistakes that have been made or that they will "cover" for
them, only to keep a running list of mistakes made by their
victims to use against them in the future.

9. Bully coworkers and subordinates may give supervisors false
information on their victims, swearing them to silence regarding the origins of this negative information. "If I tell you this,
you have to promise you won't say where you got the information. I shouldn't be telling you this. I feel terrible. I just thought
you should know in the best interests of the organization."

10. Some particularly charming bullies are expert at blaming and
scapegoating targets for financial difficulties or morale problems in the workplace. They are experts at making themselves
the "heroes" and problem solvers through the use of "divide
and conquer" techniques. Consider, for instance, how the
charismatic Hitler was able to convince his followers that the
Jews were responsible for the economic decline in Germany
and thus became their unquestioned leader and hero.

Bullies may use many of the above behaviors in attempts to fulfill
their needs for power and control. They may major in one bullying
behavior and minor in another. Many bullies are inconsistent, appearing charming and helpful one day and tyrannical the next. They often
change their behavior dramatically from person to person, and sometimes minute to minute. This behavioral inconsistency adds to their
victims' confusion and may back up erroneous beliefs held by victims
that they are the cause of bullying behavior.

Effects of Workplace Bullying

The targets of bullies in the workplace often suffer in silence, terrified of losing their jobs. They are often fearful of confronting the bully or going to higher management to report abusive behavior. If the bully is the CEO, administrator, or appears to be in an alliance with these powerful people, the victim can feel helpless and hopeless, believing that nothing can be done to stop the hurtful behavior.

Those victimized by bullies in the workplace often leave their jobs. Gary Namie and Ruth Namie (2000) reported that in their survey of bullied targets, 75 percent of the victims had to leave their jobs to make the bullying stop. Many of the individuals that we have seen in therapy have suffered from severe depression, experienced panic attacks or have been referred to us after making serious suicide attempts triggered by job-related stress. Others have suffered from the effects of stress-related illnesses.

Being a target of bullying in the work environment can be debilitating to health, injuring body, mind, and spirit. The American Institute of Stress states that job stress is the leading source of stress for adult Americans and is estimated to cost billions of dollars every year (Namie and Namie, 2000). "Workplace trauma, as psychologists refer to the condition caused by employee abuse, is emerging as a more crippling and devastating problem for employees and employers alike than all other work-related stresses put together" (Wilson, 1991, p. 47). Research conducted in Sweden estimated that 15 percent of the suicides in Sweden can be attributed to bullying in the workplace (Leymann, 1998).

Victims of bullying may experience headaches, fatigue, sleep pattern disturbances, nightmares, weight loss or weight gain, inability to swallow, nausea, digestive tract problems, spastic colon, diarrhea, dizziness, constant aches and pains, anxiety, panic attacks. They may have feelings of confusion, anger, guilt, shame, fear, terror, grief, depression, hopelessness and/or helplessness, low self-worth, insecurity and isolation.

Targets of bullying in the workplace need the support of families, friends, counselors, coworkers, management and unions. They need to be reassured that they are not the cause of the bad behavior of bullies and that the physical and emotional effects they are suffering are due to cumulative trauma. They are neither "weak willed" nor "crazy," but are, rather, victims of abusive behavior. Victims need to be supported to take action on their own behalfs.

 Sarah's Story

"I look back on that time in my life and can't quite figure out if I was incredibly courageous or just stupid," Sarah laughed. "It's much easier to joke about it now. But back then, it was devastating.

"I had accepted a job as a high-level manager in a large health-care organization. When I applied for the job, I was impressed with the organization. They served a large, diverse, urban population, had a tremendous number of services, excellent benefits, a standardized salary scale, written job descriptions, a clearly written organizational chart and what appeared to be an excellent policies and procedures manual.

"I was impressed by the other people on the management team who seemed to be highly competent and compassionate professionals. I realize now though that I always had uncomfortable feelings about the executive director. He had difficulty looking me in the eye during the job interview and, as silly as it seems, I didn't like the way he shook my hand.

"After I had been working for the organization for a time, three things tipped me off that things weren't exactly as they appeared.

First, I began to hear rumors that the executive director some-times had 'temper tantrums' and many of the staff were afraid of him. When I asked one of the other managers about this, he just laughed and said, 'Well, yeah, he's like that sometimes. We just know when to avoid him when he's in a bad mood and you learn to avoid things that might set him off.' I asked why people were taking responsibility for his bad behavior and was told that the president of the board was one of the executive director's best friends.

"I soon realized that the staff's morale wasn't good and that people didn't expect to be treated fairly. One day a worker in one of my departments asked to see me. I had an open-door policy and thought that the individual just wanted to get to know me. I soon realized they had come to complain about their supervisor. I sug-gested that I would be happy to call the supervisor and we could all discuss the issue together and hopefully arrive at a satisfactory resolution for all concerned. My statement was met with shock and surprise. Despite the organizational chart, many employees were used to jumping over their supervisors and registering complaints or getting special favors from upper-level managers or the execu-tive director. I assured the employee that this type of behavior would not work in my departments.

"As time passed I realized other significant things about my boss. He wasn't always truthful in his reports to the board of direc-tors or funding authorities. He liberally rewarded programs that made a lot of money and ignored the others. He also took an inordinate amount of 'vacation time,' and his son, who lived out of town, used one of the company cars. He had already wrecked one vehicle and was now on his second.

"After a year, I found that I was becoming more discouraged about the organization. I became aware of the temper tantrums that had once only been rumors. My office was next to the executive

director's and I could hear him scream at office personnel, the other managers and their employees. He had never screamed at the workers in my unit or me, even though I seemed to disagree with him frequently. I wondered if he didn't bully me because my units were making money or because I stood up to him. I also became more aware of what I considered 'borderline' unethical behavior. He seemed to push through policies that benefited him personally. I usually voted against them, but the other managers supported them. It was clear to me that they were afraid of him, and I kept telling myself it was none of my business.

"Finally, it became my business. He had pushed through a policy requiring all unused vacation time and sick time that had accumulated over the past two years to be paid out. It was a policy of the organization that all checks other than payroll and regular operating expenses had to be cosigned by the business office and one of the managers or the executive director. Obviously, we couldn't cosign our own checks.

"The executive director strolled into my office one day and pleasantly asked me to sign a check that had been made out to him for an enormous amount of money. According to him, he had taken only two days of vacation and no sick time for the past two years. He had never asked me to sign a check in the three years that I had worked there, and now I realize that he would never have asked me to sign this one if the other managers had been in the building. For a few minutes I felt almost paralyzed. I knew I couldn't in good conscience sign the check. I finally worked up the courage to speak. I let him know firmly but kindly that I would not sign the check.

"His pleasant manner disappeared and he began screaming at me, ordering me to do as he instructed. I explained that I couldn't sign the check in good conscience because I knew that he had taken far more vacation time and sick time than the stub indicated. He *continued to scream and began calling me names. He towered over me as I sat at my desk and started poking me in the chest with his finger. I don't know where I got the courage to stand up but I did. I moved his hand away and in a firm voice told him that I would call security if he touched me again.*

"He moved away but continued to scream. He told me that I would either sign the check or he would fire me. I briefly thought of my family, my good salary, the job that I loved and replied, 'You can't buy my ethics. I will not sign the check; that is my choice. You will have to make your own choices.' He did, and fired me for failure to follow a direct order.

"After he left my office, I just sat there stunned. I felt that I had been hit by a Mack truck and briefly questioned my sanity. I had a family I needed to help support. I had been fired. I had never been fired before. When I could think clearly again, I realized that the personnel policies were very specific, you could only be fired without probation for 'failing to follow a direct order that if not followed would put the safety or well-being of patients or staff at jeopardy.' I realized that not signing the check certainly didn't put anyone in harm's way. According to policies he couldn't fire me, but he could make every day of my employment a nightmare.

"I thought how sad it was that no one had come to help me even though they must have heard his abusive behavior. Then I realized that I hadn't gone to help anyone in a similar position over the past three years. I had convinced myself that it was none of my business because it hadn't affected my staff. Of course it had, it affected everyone. The organization was like a domestically violent home with scared children hiding in their offices instead of under the bed.

"I put in a call to the chairperson of the board of directors. Joyce had been on the board for years but had only recently become the

chair. The executive director's 'friend' had stepped down because of a crisis in her family. I knew that Joyce had been handpicked for the board by the executive director as well, but I figured I had nothing to lose, only my job. I still wasn't willing to sign the check and hoped my family would understand. I couldn't live with myself if I did. We had some money in savings and I thought I could probably get another job, although probably not another one that paid as well.

"Joyce listened to me intently and set up a meeting with me outside the office. Before she hung up, she told me that my job was reinstated. She also let me know that she had had concerns about the executive director's ethics for some time. Before I left for the meeting, I realized that one of the other managers had returned. I saw the executive director leave his office and knew my coworker had signed the check. I stopped by to see him on my way out. He looked sad and guilty. I asked why he had signed it. 'I'm afraid of losing my job,' he said. 'I know it's wrong. I don't know what else to do.' I told him about my meeting with Joyce and he looked frightened when I left. He said, 'I hate conflict.'

"Joyce told me that she would conduct an investigation and that it may take some time. She also told me not to leave the site until the matter was cleared up and that if I was fired again, I was to call her immediately. She gave me various phone numbers where she could be reached.

"I was fired two or three times a week for a month and yelled at every day. The other managers called in sick often and I worked hard to keep the stress on our level of management, trying to prevent the stress from passing down to supervisors, other staff and patients. I lost weight and had trouble sleeping. I had nightmares and headaches. I was grateful for the support of my family and friends, although some of my friends thought I was nuts.

"Finally, the investigation was over and the executive director was fired for unethical behavior. It seemed that he had been doing unethical things for years as well as subjecting staff to outrageous bullying behavior. He had been in his position for over twenty-five years and somewhere along the way had confused leadership with 'owning.' He felt that he 'owned' the organization and everything in it, including the staff.

"I feel indebted to Joyce. She was everything a chair of the board should be. She was professional, ethical, compassionate, firm, responsible and committed to the organization and its mission. She told me that the board had to assume a great deal of responsibility for the abuses that had occurred within the organization. The board had never evaluated the executive director. It occurred to her that the policies and procedures manual had applied to everyone in the organization but him. Joyce said that it probably had taken him three years to turn his outrageous behavior on me because on some level he was afraid of me. I guess bullies instinctively know who they can abuse and who they can't."

Bully Prevention in the Workplace

Bullying can only happen in organizations where management and boards of directors condone it. Although bullying can happen in any workplace, bullies are often attracted to organizations that reward aggressive behavior or deny bullying behavior and its effects. As Joyce pointed out, bullies have a keen ability to read people, get what they want from them and are more likely to succeed where "winning" and financial gain are far more important than relationships. For instance, basketball coach Bobby Knight was repeatedly accused of humiliating people, throwing things, physical attacks on individuals and swearing at kids long before someone finally took action. Indeed, many of his bullying behaviors were presented to viewers on national television.

It is believed that the reason that Knight's behavior was ignored for so long was that he produced "winning teams": three NCAA titles and eleven Big Ten titles. Most people value winning above all else and actually believe that abusive treatment is part of the makeup of successful athletes, managers, business executives, and corporate leaders, just as many believe that aggressive bullying on the playground is just "boys being boys."

In order to build work environments that support "winning" and healthy working relationships equally, strong foundations need to be built. The strength of these foundations governs the manner in which people respond to each other in the workplace. Some elements necessary to consider when building strong foundations for healthy work environments are:

1. Antibullying policies which include: the description of bullying behavior, clear grievance policies and procedures that prohibit retaliation in any form against individuals filing bona fide complaints, and clearly written consequences for bullying behavior that include treatment for first-time offenders.

2. Training for all staff, management and members of board of directors and advisory boards on: bullying behavior, its effects and early warning signs in organizations; harassment; workplace violence; professional ethics; diversity; and conflict resolution provided by trainers and consultants with knowledge and expertise in each area.

3. Mission statements that include language that supports teamwork, diversity, empowerment, respectful and open communication, cooperation, and recognition for the contributions of employees.

4. Policies and procedures that include: clear anti-bullying policies, grievance policies and procedures (mentioned above); conflict resolution policies and procedures; fair and open hiring policies and

procedures that stress relationship skills, conflict resolution skills, and strengths in working successfully on teams and with diverse populations; policies and procedures for meritorious recognition; disciplinary policies that clearly spell out probationary periods with goals, objectives, and opportunities for treatment and training, as well as clearly spelled-out offenses that warrant immediate dismissal; critical incident review policies and procedures for healthcare and service organizations.

5. Selection of members for boards of directors and advisory boards should be based on knowledge, skill, diversity and teamwork abilities, rather than the strength of their current or past relationships with management or hidden agendas. Duties and responsibilities of the board of directors and advisory boards should be clearly defined and available to all staff.

6. Standardized salary scales should be developed with procedures for advancement and merit increases.

7. Clearly defined organizational charts should be created that are available for all staff.

8. Job descriptions should be created for every employee, including management, that clearly define duties and responsibilities.

9. Yearly performance appraisals or reviews for all staff, including management, that include evaluation of teamwork, professional conduct, staff relations, community relations, and management skills (when applicable). Two-way performance appraisals allow staff to evaluate themselves and offer recommendations for improvement prior to evaluation by supervisors. Recommendations should include goals and objectives that are time limited as well as specific recommendations for future training. Cross-training should be available whenever possible to strengthen teamwork and job performance in the organization as a whole. Supervisory and management evaluations

should include avenues for assessments by staff that are anonymous
and where confidentiality is ensured.

10. Supervisors and managers should be trained in effective management styles that foster open communication, open-door policies,
teamwork, decision making by consensus when appropriate, regular
staff input, empowerment, and effective conflict resolution.

11. Health insurance coverage should include mental health counseling by private practitioners. Staff should be entitled to release time
from work to attend counseling sessions provided by independent professional counselors. Workers should be allowed to keep
the nature and reason for self-referral confidential. If there is an
Employee Assistance Program (EAP) available, EAP counselors
should be trained in job-related stress and workplace bullying and
its effects.

Corporations, organizations and all work environments need to
become aware of the seriousness of bullying in their environments
and make a plan of action to intervene and confront the situation
when it occurs. Work environments need to have policies that have
zero tolerance for bullying. Bullying needs to be stopped if it is pres-
ently taking place and the message given that it will not be tolerated
in the future. Bullies are also people in need of professional help, and
workplaces need to provide them the opportunity to get help. Policies,
procedures, and financial assistance need to be put in place to allow
them to get the help they need.

Anyone can be a victim of bullying in the work environment.
Bullies have what appears to be an inner instinct about whom they
can and cannot bully. If the instinct is incorrect and the bully attempts
to control another person, he becomes quickly aware that the other
person will not be controlled. Bullies live in fear of their inadequacies and vulnerabilities. So as not to feel fearful or vulnerable, they

believe they must be in control. So they move on to another person. When the bully becomes aware that someone can be controlled, they make their move. From the bully's distorted belief system, anyone can cause them to feel threatened or vulnerable. Anyone can become a challenge or a target to get control over. Generally, the victim is not aware that he or she is a challenge to the bully. The victim feels the negative and abusive results of being bullied, and is confused and in disbelief that it is happening.

A dysfunctional work environment where bullying is taking place can become a functional workplace when the organization is aware of the problem, accepts that there is a problem and makes a plan of action for the changes necessary to become a healthy and safe place for all people to work.

There are now resources to help victims in the workplace. Businesses that don't know what to do when bullying is occurring in the workplace have options today. There are people who know and understand what bullying is and how it affects the victims and workplace production. These people will help and have solutions that will work for the benefit of all. People who are responsible for providing a safe, respectful and healthy workplace need to ask for help.

Reaching the Bully

It is never too late to be what you might have been.

George Eliot

I n a society where bullies and aggressive and controlling people are viewed as heroes, there can be serious problems. Today people in prison who have murdered, beaten, maimed, robbed, and traumatized their victims receive fan mail, are interviewed on national television, and look back at us from the covers of magazines. Violent movies gross millions of dollars. TV personalities, rappers, rock stars, sports legends and political figures who have exhibited bullying, controlling and abusive behaviors are defended and too frequently protected from suffering consequences. Often aggressive behavior seems to have more rewards than consequences; this can strengthen the distorted beliefs held by bullies that abuse is acceptable. Media "heroes" who receive rewards rather than consequences for unacceptable behavior also make an impression on children who watch, listen, and play out their fantasies on playgrounds across our nation.

Bullying seriously affects victims, causing them physical, mental, emotional, social and spiritual damage, and too frequently triggers suicide and acts of violence. What steps can concerned individuals take to prevent further victimization in a society where most have allowed bullies "free hand" and few have intervened? How do we reach individuals whose negative behaviors affect so many?

We have learned a great deal from the bullies we have treated and from those who have willingly told their stories in this book. Those who have been bullies have told us that their recoveries began when individuals were willing to present them with "honest mirrors" and hold them accountable for their behavior. They have told us that the compassionate confrontation that they feared most was also the very thing they needed to begin their recovery and ultimately lead happier and healthier lives.

Sometimes, the louder the person is, the more fearful inside. Bullies are generally fearful of being found out and confronted. They are terrified that others will see their inadequacy and loneliness and, in the seeing, offer them a mirror to see themselves. They are afraid to be responsible for their behavior and to ultimately face themselves. When confronted, they put their defenses into high gear in an attempt to make others back down. They are experts at defensive behaviors that have protected them in the past. Through years of practice and desperation, bullies have become masters at deflecting the issues and projecting their vulnerabilities, helplessness and fear on to others.

In order to stop bullying and violence in the world today, we need to stop being silent witnesses and empower first ourselves and then others to stop being victims. We need to learn to recognize bully-ing behavior and make bullies aware that we are no longer willing to accept their abuse—or to allow others in our presence to be vic-timized by them. We need to respect ourselves and the individuals that bully enough to expect that they *can* find the courage to face their pain and ultimately make the necessary choices to change their behavior. We need to develop skills in compassionate confrontation and intervention, and hold those who bully accountable for abusive behavior. If once-silent witnesses and victims are not willing to compassionately confront bullies and be their honest mirrors, the bullies will not make the choices necessary to change their behavior or improve the quality of their lives.

It is important to confront bullies with concrete facts, followed by specific consequences. Idle threats, crying, or discussions of the problem are not effective and can actually become challenges for individuals that bully. Rational discussions with irrational people don't work.

Some bullies come from abusive environments and have been bullied since childhood. Others come from environments where they are rewarded no matter what they do and therefore may act privileged on the outside while diminished on the inside. Many have been repeatedly controlled and/or abused. Through these traumatic experiences, they have come to believe that being controlled by others is dangerous and will lead to further abuse. They have learned to survive through holding on to the belief that they must be in control of everyone and everything, and must never allow themselves to become vulnerable.

Bullies live their lives in fear and anxiety. Without appropriate confrontation, guidance and support, they continue to create the fear and anxiety in others that they can't tolerate in themselves. They are in denial that they have become like bullies that they once hated.

Bullies who have received help have told us that when they were aggressive, manipulative, conning, etc., they felt powerful, in control, highly energetic and experienced a relief from their anxieties. They felt a sense of gratification when maintaining control over others. However, feelings of gratification were short-lived and they would quickly return to feelings of emptiness, inadequacy and insecurity. Therefore they needed to feel in control of someone or something most of the time in order to experience even temporary relief from their anxieties.

Some bullies reported that they experienced heightened anxiety followed by depression when they had no one or nothing to control. Bullying partners, parents and executives reported that they experience depression to the point of contemplating suicide when their relationships ended, they became estranged from their children, or they lost their jobs. Relief from anxiety and depression came through bullying and maintaining power and control over something or someone.

Recognizing the Defensive Behaviors of Bullies

Bullies fear the exposure of their inadequacies and insecurities and have learned to defend themselves by using anger, deception and distraction. When confronted, some may yell, scream or use profanity. They are anxious and fearful and have learned to defend and protect their vulnerability and powerlessness with righteousness, anger and/ or rage. Many bullies perceive anger as strength and use it to control, dominate, and deceive others in an attempt to keep others from seeing the fear and terror they live with continually. Others arm themselves with righteousness, put-downs, and sarcasm.

Some bullies use charm and deception and can be very convincing. They may portray themselves as kind, concerned, funny, caring, sympathetic, empathetic, in control and "together." The more anxious bullies become, the more they need to defend and escalate bullying behaviors. When faced with people who are willing to confront them and hold them accountable for their behavior, they may use one or more of the following defensive behaviors:

They may become . . .

Righteous	Manipulative
Unforgiving	Devious

Unpredictable	Vengeful
Scheming	Inflexible
Abusive	Impulsive
Sarcastic	Deceitful
Charming	Aggressive
Arrogant	Irritable
Judgmental	Self-Centered
Critical	Wounded
Impatient	Violent
Superficial	

Bullies live in fear and anxiety. They feel insecure, inadequate and lonely. They lack the ability to interact with others in an honest, mature and healthy manner. The more vulnerable they feel, the more they perceive the need to be in control. The perception of their own behavior and the behavior of others is distorted, which heightens their need to be well-defended. They have inappropriate emotional responses that have been learned through painful childhood experiences or as the result of lengthy victimization in adulthood.

Don't expect bullies to be honest when initially confronted. If they fully accept that there may be serious consequences for their behavior, they may slowly start getting honest with themselves and then with others.

The defenses of those who bully have been kept in place for very good reasons. Facing fears and becoming honest with themselves and others about their bullying behavior is difficult, painful and takes time. A man who was impatient about the time it was taking for personal healing asked a wise elder, "How long will it be until I stop feeling all this pain, anyway?" As wise elders do, the old man answered his question with a question, "If a man walks four miles into the center of a forest, how many miles does he have to walk out?"

Intervention and Confrontation

Bullies have powerful defenses, distorted beliefs and deficient empathy skills. They must be held accountable for what they do and what they say, and faced with the effects that their behavior has had on others, in order for them to be open to the possibilities of change. They need to be told firmly and compassionately that others are not responsible for their behaviors, beliefs, and feelings and that they alone have the power to change their lives.

Bullies have difficulty learning from past experiences. They need to be helped and guided in order to make necessary changes in their lives. When planning an intervention, be aware of the specific behaviors that you want to confront and the range of defensive behaviors that the bully may use when threatened.

Some bullies may initially be grateful that someone has cared enough to confront them. Others may begin to cry and will take minimal responsibility for their behavior, while others may be enraged at those who confronted them.

Intervening with people who exhibit bullying, controlling, and abusive behavior is the key to stopping their behaviors. Firing them, expelling them, or getting rid of them without confrontation may be a relief to their current victims but it doesn't solve the problem. They will likely move to a different job, school, or relationship and find other people to victimize.

An intervention should be organized and performed by people who are familiar with the bully's behavior and the effect the behavior has had on others. The bully is frequently in a powerful position in the victim's life: a parent or grandparent; a partner in a relationship who has financial power; a caregiver that one depends on for survival; an authority figure in government, church, school system, financial institution or place of employment; a mentor; a healing practitioner; an older sibling, etc.

Confronting bullies one-on-one and sharing your concerns can work with bullies who are not in positions of power or highly defended. Most bullies will deny or distort what is being said to them, attempt to lie or charm their way out of the confrontation, threaten their confronters, or manipulate confrontations in ways that cause those intervening to become defensive. When the person confronting the bully becomes defensive, the bully becomes the one in charge of the confrontation. Bullies are excellent cons and manipulators, especially when originally presented with consequences for their behavior. For these reasons, we favor group intervention.

Power in Numbers

Groups of people who have discussed, arranged and planned an intervention have more power than bullies. It is more difficult for the bully to effectively use defensive behaviors on an entire group. The bully may attempt to con, manipulate or threaten someone in the group who appears to be the easiest to intimidate. But stronger members of the group who cannot be intimidated will prevent the bullying behavior from continuing. Remember that the more vulnerable and threatened bullies feel, the more they need to heighten defenses.

The term *intervene* means to come between so as to prevent or alter a course of events. To *confront* an issue is to present a problem in such a way that taking responsibility for its situation is difficult to avoid. Interventions must be well planned and confrontations firm, compassionate and specific. The following are important steps to follow when planning and carrying out group interventions with individuals who bully:

1. The group needs to choose a guide. The guide will open the intervention and guide the rest of the group in its process and progress. As a group, you may decide to ask for a professional who has worked with bullies to assist you.

2. It is important for the victims of bullying behavior to be open and honest. Keeping secrets defeats the goals and purposes of interventions. Once victims have developed the courage to seek help from others, it is important that they give specific, direct, and honest information to those who have been asked to assist in the intervention. If victims don't feel that anyone close to them can help, they can choose to seek help from a professional who can support and guide them through the process. It is critical to choose helping professionals who have experience dealing with bullying behavior and have experience guiding interventions.

3. Once the group of people who have agreed to assist the victim is formed, it is important for them to meet in order to plan the intervention and discuss effective ways to confront the bully. Sometimes role-plays are effective ways to prepare for difficult defensive behavior. Be aware that if discussion goes on outside of the group, the bully or his/her supporters may become aware and attempt to undermine the group's efforts.

4. Plan the time and the day of the intervention and make the bully aware that he or she is expected to attend the meeting. The bully will only be aware that he or she must attend a meeting. It is normal for group members to feel anxiety and tension prior to the confrontation. Remember that bullies are often hypervigilant and can often instinctively feel the tension in the room and will adjust their behavior accordingly.

5. The group should formulate a plan of action for the consequences the bully will face as a result of her or his behavior. Plans of action will differ according to the specific circumstances of the victim and the

bully. The plan should be specific, direct, honest and one that can be followed. Action plans should be set in place before the intervention takes place. Leave no loopholes in your plan of action for the bully to slip through. In making your plan of action take into consideration the safety of the victims. If treatment is one of the options presented, make certain that referrals are lined up prior to the intervention. Again, we believe that group-based treatment with professionals who understand bullying behavior is the most effective. Time lines are important. Giving the bully too much time to follow through with their responsibilities can give them enough time to con or manipulate their way out of it. If the adult bully is not willing to become responsible for his behaviors, he often needs to be removed from the situation in which he was causing emotional, mental, and/or physical harm to others.

6. Group members need specific and factual information regarding the bully's behavior and the harm he has done to others in order to be effective in the confrontation. During the intervention, it is important that group members focus on specific and factual information regarding the bully's behavior. If individuals share thoughts, feelings or accusations that are not factual, it is far easier for the bully to manipulate or con group members and make them question their beliefs and/or feelings. Individuals who bully are experts at shifting the focus off of their behaviors on to the behaviors of others. In order for the intervention to be effective, the focus must remain on the bully's behavior and the effect of his behavior on others. One bully can affect many people in a number of different ways.

7. The intervention needs to be presented with awareness, concern and understanding. Anger and threats are not effective because they enable the bully to have more power. Bullies have frequently grown up in atmospheres where anger, threats and abuse were normal and they have become well defended against them. It is much harder to defend against specific information, firm limits, and compassion.

8. The intervention needs to be done in an atmosphere of awareness, concern and understanding. Group members need to look directly at the bully and keep eye contact with her when speaking to her. This gives the message that the person who is confronting is concerned and serious about the situation. It is important to set guidelines at the beginning of the intervention that make the bully fully aware that she cannot interrupt the process when specific information is being presented, but will be given time to speak after all concerns are presented. (It may be useful to review chapter 2 to familiarize yourself with effective ways to deal with intimidating behaviors.)

Many individuals who exhibit bullying behaviors are well defended and highly dysfunctional. They need help and support to stop the behaviors that are harmful to others. It is important for them to:

1. Become honest with themselves and others about specific behaviors they have used that have harmed others, and develop awareness of the consequences of their behavior.
2. Develop empathy for those they have harmed, and when appropriate make amends.
3. Become aware of the underlying dynamics of their bullying behavior, identify the triggers that lead to their abuse of others, and develop the skills necessary to learn to interrupt the cycle.
4. Develop skills in choice-making and receive support for the choices that they make that will allow them to become healthy, balanced and responsible people.
5. Develop skills in conflict resolution.
6. Develop tolerance and respect for individual differences with the awareness that making others wrong or inferior does not strengthen their own power or rightness, and that being right and powerful won't keep them warm at night.

7. Work through their own issues of past abuse and victimization while getting in touch with feelings of fear, grief, shame, vulnerability, powerlessness and normal anger that have been previously repressed and denied. During this particular phase of bullies' work, it will be important for counselors to help them remain clear that earlier abuse and pain is not an excuse for bullying behavior.

8. Develop understanding and acceptance of themselves physically, mentally, emotionally, socially and spiritually, and learn to achieve balance in their lives.

9. Undergo specific treatment plans: Some individuals may need substance abuse treatment, couple counseling, family counseling, or classes in parenting skills in addition to tasks mentioned above.

The bully needs help! Can we care about them enough as fellow human beings to let them know that we know? Will we have the courage to let them know that their behavior is unacceptable and that they are accountable for their actions? Will we let them know that there are consequences for their behavior? Will we let them know that there is help for them and that they are responsible to get that help? Will we let them know that they have choices? Will we compassionately support them to get the help that they need? Will we? How can we not!!

The people who have shared their experiences for this book—Larry, Ann, Nancy, William, Sarah, Dan and Katherine—did so with courage and a belief in the healing process. They were victims, bullies or victim/bullies and have taken the responsibility for their behaviors, feelings and beliefs and have gotten help. All have changed their lives and shared their experiences in the hope that it will help other victims, bullies or victim/bullies to get the help that they need. They have expressed the hope that others will learn from their stories that the only power anyone has is the power to change him- or herself. "There is freedom in being accountable for what I do and for what I say."

Silent No Longer

Snowflakes are a fragile thing individually, but look at
what they can do when they stick together.

Fernando Bonaventura

There are few sights as beautiful as snowflakes grace-
fully falling on an early winter night caught in the glow of a
full moon. Each is delicate and unique. Yet, when they come
together, they have the power to paralyze a city or create a wonderland
of adventure that can provide endless hours of family enjoyment.

We often see the lessons of nature mirrored in our lives. Individuals
have tremendous strength when they come together for a common
purpose. As Margaret Mead stated so well, "Never doubt that a small
group of thoughtful, committed people can change the world. Indeed,
it is the only thing that ever has."

Today we need the courage of thoughtful and committed people
willing to re-create safe and supportive communities that foster inclusion and mutual cooperation as well as sanctions against abusive
behaviors. Without strong and compassionate communities, we have
little hope of facing the problems inherent in unchecked bullying:

hostile work environments where unjustified accusations, humiliation and harassment have forced thousands of individuals to leave
their jobs; suicides among our youth who have been brutally taunted
and teased; corporations roaming the world in search of cheap labor
for their sweatshops; growing aggressiveness in preschool children;
domestic violence, workplace violence, and school shootings. The
destructive potential of sanctioned bullying is frightening.

As with most Americans, our minds have repeatedly returned to
the images of schools where children killed and were killed before
they were old enough to vote. Yet those horrific images have begun
to dim as an image of hope takes its place: Two little boys, bully and
victim, in the Cherry Creek School District in Colorado walking away
with their arms around each other. They received the honesty, help
and support of their third-grade peers following a bullying incident. It
has taken time and a strong commitment to create a climate of safety,
inclusion and accountability, where the healthy resolution of conflict
is the rule rather than the exception.

Primary Prevention:
The Wisdom of Children

Many elders in Native American and First Nations cultures have
shared the vision that there will be a time, when things will become
very bad in our society. It is said that this is the time when our children
will become our greatest teachers. In many ways, we believe that this
time has come. Some of our children are teaching us through acts of
violence and self-destruction that we have been moving too fast down
the wrong road. Others will simply offer us their wisdom if we ask.

At the beginning of the new millennium, we decided that it was
important for adults to hear the concerns of children and youth as
well as to model a way that communities could solicit communication
from youth. We decided to ask children across North America, the

United States and Canada, to write letters to us letting us know what they wanted most from the adults in their lives in the new millennium. We received hundreds of letters from children ages six through eighteen, from all races and ethnic groups, economic backgrounds and walks of life. Some of their responses were:

> Age 12: "I would like to see adults think of their communities, not just about money. I think adults should listen to children more. We just might have the answer you've been waiting for" (Middelton-Moz, 1999, p. 28).
>
> Age 14: "In the new millennium I would like to see adults teaching their children proper values and spending more time with their families. The children are the future. If they are not taught morals and values, then what kind of future are we looking forward to? I strongly believe that the teaching of their children should be a parent's first priority. I also believe the family unit is the base of every society. If the base crumbles, then so will everything else" (Middelton-Moz, 1999, p. 123).
>
> Age 14: " . . . I'm saying help some little kids work out their disagreements on the playground. It is the solving of problems that shows the younger generation that big problems can be worked out" (Middelton-Moz, 1999, p. 6).

A large number of six-year-olds just wanted someone to say hello to them when they came home from school. Others wanted adults to laugh more, stop drinking and using drugs, spend more time with their children, stop fighting with each other, model the behaviors they ask of children, stop hurting their children, respect and honor differences, take more responsibilities for their actions, spend time with their children, and begin to teach them accountability and values again.

What these children asked of us was so simple, so basic that it made us realize how far afield we've come as a society. We spend hours doing research to determine why we have increased violence and bullying in our schools, on our roads, and in our workplaces, etc., when it would perhaps be simpler and more cost effective to just ask the children.

Children are telling us through their words and actions that they are feeling alone, afraid, unprotected and in need of role models who will teach healthy values and accountability for actions, not violence.

Children search for belonging, support and values. When families and communities do not provide those very basic requirements, children frequently form their own families and communities that operate on values of aggression and/or where killing may be a rite of passage.

Sanyika Shakur aka Monster Kody Scott grew up in South Central Los Angeles. He joined a gang at the age of eleven. He is now serving time in San Quentin. He writes: "My home boys became my family, the older ones were father figures. They would congratulate me each time I shot someone, each time I recruited a combat soldier, each time I put another gun on the set. When I went home I was cursed for not emptying the trash. Trash? Didn't Mom understand who I was?" (Shakur, 1993, p. 256).

Those who have been bullies tell us that they grew up in environments that were violent, abandoning, abusive, lacking in healthy values, and without limits and consequences for their behavior. They needed people throughout their childhoods and into their adult years who were willing to offer support, compassion, provide honest mirrors, set limits, and confront and hold them accountable for their behavior.

The children in many Cherry Creek schools and the adult bullies who have been interviewed for this book have told us that creating community environments that are supportive, honest, open, caring and inclusive, where people hold each other accountable for behavior, will prevent, stop and/or reverse bullying behavior.

The bottom line is when something isn't working, it's a good idea to do something different, particularly when we know what does work. Our new values of "me" not "we," "ignore or punish," "Don't snitch," "You're not accountable if you don't get caught," and "That's his business, not mine," are not working.

Most of our behaviors are guided by the standards and beliefs that were modeled in our families and communities. The norms (i.e., unspoken rules) of our communities impact the way we parent our children and care for one another. It is often hard to face the fact that our children are mirroring what they've been taught. It is far easier to believe they are suffering from one or another biochemical imbalance outside of our control than to accept the responsibility for the lessons we are teaching them.

In our interviews with bullies and victims, we learned about the interventions that worked. In many cases, it was the caring and support of neighbors that made the difference in these people's lives.

Three Stories of Hope: Empowering Others to Empower Themselves

Tina's Story

"Until I met Rose, bullies had victimized me all my life. I grew up in a family that was mentally, emotionally and physically abusive. My dad would beat my mother and my mother would beat me. I was told that I was 'no good,' 'stupid,' and would never amount to anything.

"I was extremely shy and didn't have any friends. I was afraid and lonely and my best friend was food. I was chubby as a child, then fat in adolescence because I ate all the time. My weight only added to my problems. Other kids, from kindergarten on, teased me. I still remember their cruel words, 'Hey Fatso,' 'Whatya doing,

Blimp?' 'Hey, Blimpo, you going to the prom?' Some kids didn't call me names, but they didn't want to hang around me because the bullies were the popular kids and I guess they didn't want to 'catch' whatever I had. I was always the last one picked for a team in gym class. The teachers would just look at me with pity in their eyes but wouldn't do anything. One gym teacher even told me that I wouldn't be targeted by the bullies if I'd just lose weight and quit being so shy. It was like she thought I set out to be shy and overweight and could just stop it. No one ever intervened. The lonelier I felt, the more I ate and the lonelier I was.

"I thought about suicide a lot in my teen years. Thank God I was too big of a chicken to do it. Back then I don't remember kids killing themselves, maybe today I would have. It seems like more kids are doing it today.

"One good thing was that I was really smart. I graduated in the top of my class and went to college. I met Paul in my first class. He was a loner like I was, really shy. We just started hanging out together. He wanted sex and I thought, Why not? He was the first person that really paid any attention to me and I was grateful I guess. We got married right after graduation. I realize now that I didn't really love him. I didn't know what love was. I didn't really even know him.

"Paul was in control of everything: the money, the car and my life. When I would start to feel good about something that I did, he'd immediately put me down. I remember one day being so proud of a new promotion at work. I wanted to celebrate. Out of the blue he said, 'I don't mean to hurt your feelings but I think you should go on a diet or something. You really are kind of fat.' Yet, when I'd go on a diet, he'd bring me candy and pastries.

"I'll never forget the day I met Rose. I never knew my grand-parents, and she was like the grandma I never had. We had just moved out of an apartment and into a little house in this beautiful tree-lined neighborhood. I had taken a week's vacation at work so I could get the house in order. Rose appeared at my door the second day with a basket of fruit and some bread she had made. She was so nice. We had tea together and she complimented me on the way I was decorating the house.

"A day later, I was planting some flowers in front of the house. She was sitting on her front porch and chatted with me while I worked. I had some extras so I planted some for her in the window boxes on her porch. Then, she hugged me. It was so natural for her and I think I was 'touch starved.' I know I was really awkward the first time she hugged me, but it didn't seem to faze her. Being loving and warm was just part of her.

"Rose and I became fast friends. I'd take her soup when I made a pot and she'd bring me jam and pickles she'd made. I met her family. They were as wonderful as she was. Paul would never go to Rose's with me or sit in the kitchen when she'd come over. He spent his free time watching TV or at the computer. One evening when I came back from Rose's he said, 'Why are you hanging out with that old lady anyway? We're not her kids, let them hang out with her.' Oddly enough, that was the first time I had ever been angry with Paul.

"One Saturday I had worked in the yard all day. I was so proud of my little house and I loved keeping it beautiful. Paul's only words to me when he came out on the porch in the late afternoon were, 'Hey, when are you going to start dinner anyway? I'm tired of you fixing leftovers. I think you forgot to get the mail, too.' He went back into the house. Rose was sitting on her porch. She called over, 'Tina, I really don't know how you do it. Your yard is just a picture. It's so beautiful, just like you. Why don't you come over after supper and we'll sit on the porch and have some iced tea, relax and admire the hard work you've done?'

"*Later, while I was sitting on the porch with Rose, she commented, 'Tina, you are one of the kindest young women I have ever met. I have been wondering if it hurts you when Paul puts you down or doesn't seem to appreciate the things you do? I've heard him put you down so many times in the year I've known you. You don't deserve that.'*

"*I was shocked. I realized I didn't even hear the putdowns most of the time and didn't expect to be appreciated. I replied softly, 'He doesn't ever hit me,' thinking that said it all. Rose took my hand and when I looked at her, I saw tears in her eyes.*

"*We sat in silence for a minute then Rose said, 'Tina, you seem to expect so little. You deserve so much more. You are a kind and beautiful person. It hurts me when you don't receive basic kindness and appreciation. I have wanted to say something for a while and to let you know I'm here if you want to talk. I can't make you think more of yourself but I can let you know what I see. I know you've never had a grandma, and I'd be honored if you'd be my granddaughter.'*

"*Rose saw in me what I had never seen in myself. I began to see a different person reflected in Rose's eyes and over time I began to believe in my kindness and beauty. She cried the tears I couldn't cry and later I was able to cry my own tears. Over time I became stronger.*

"*Rose's daughter recommended a counselor and I began therapy. I wanted Paul to go to counseling with me. He wouldn't go and belittled me for going. Soon, I no longer tolerated his continual bullying and let him know that I would eventually make the choice to leave him if he wasn't willing to work on himself. I explained that it would not be a rejection of him but rather an acceptance of myself. I meant it and he knew it.*

"*In time, Paul started going to therapy. For the first time, we began to get to know each other. Paul came from a background very similar to mine and oddly enough we had never talked about it. We do now. We talk a lot. Now on a sunny day, he's working in the yard with me while our children play.*

"I don't know where I would be today if it hadn't been for Rose. I learned how much the kindness of one person affects another's entire life. In my case, Rose's willingness to intervene affected Paul, me and in many ways the children we later had. Rose had been a teacher. When I would visit her, old students would drop in from time to time. I wonder sometimes how things would have been different for me if she had been one of my teachers. I now realize that until I met Rose I had probably been depressed since childhood. When I met her it was like someone finally turned on the sun."

Luke's Story

"When I was a kid my mom was really overprotective. I was an only child and she was a single mom. She loved me a lot and did wonderful, fun things with me. The problem was, she wouldn't let me grow up. She never let me go to other kids' houses. When I played with kids at my house and we'd have normal arguments, she would always send them home. She never waited to see if I could handle it myself.

"When I started school and would tell her about a fight with one of my classmates, she would immediately blame them and would call the teachers. Needless to say, I soon became very unpopular. She changed my school three times before I was nine because the teachers weren't 'attentive enough' and didn't understand that I was a 'sensitive boy.' It took me a while, but I learned not to talk to her about things that went on in school.

"By the time I was eight and starting my third school, I was really shy and afraid. My mom didn't trust that I could handle *normal interactions myself, so I never learned to trust myself. She was anxious and I became anxious. Needless to say, I was a sitting duck for every bully in the school. They could probably see me coming a mile away. They would call me 'a fag' and 'a momma's boy.' I had very few friends. It was my mom and me against the world.*

"The teasing hurt a lot but I had no one to talk to. I didn't know how to protect myself and I didn't want my mom calling the school or the other kids' parents so I did nothing. Now I understand what was going on, but back then it was really confusing. My mom would tell me that I was really special and then I'd get bullied in school every day. I didn't want to be special; I wanted to be like the other kids.

"When I was nine, the Daniels family moved into our neighborhood. They bought a house two down from us. I will never forget them as long as I live. They had a boy, Todd, who was a year older than me, and two older girls. One day, about a week after they moved in, I was sitting in the backyard staring into space as usual. I could see Todd, his dad, his mom and two sisters playing soccer in their backyard. Todd's dad must have seen me, too, because he came over and asked if I'd like to play soccer with them. I was really embarrassed but managed to tell him I didn't know how to play. It was weird; he just took it in stride, put his hand on my shoulder and said, 'No time like the present to learn.'

"When I asked my mom if I could go, she looked really concerned and almost said no until Mr. Daniels leaned his head in the door and asked her if she would like to play, too. She didn't, but she let me go. I was really bad at it, but no one laughed. They all just helped me learn. Todd was really nice.

"It became a habit that I'd play soccer at Todd's house after his dad got home from work. I got better and better. At one point, Mr.

Daniels asked if I'd like to join the soccer team that he was coaching. Todd was on the team, too. I didn't believe my mother would ever let me join, but Mr. and Mrs. Daniels talked to her and she let me. To this day, I don't know what they said to her. I do know that she and Mrs. Daniels started to become friends.

"My first practice was difficult. Some of the kids from my school were there and immediately began to tease me. Todd heard them and talked to his dad. When his dad went over to them, I thought it was going to be like my mom all over again but it wasn't. He called me over and got us in a circle. Todd sat next to me. Mr. Daniels talked to all of us.

"He made it clear that there would be no bullying on his team. He talked to us about teamwork and about sportsmanship. He asked what kind of a team we'd have if he allowed us to bully each other. Then Todd talked about how he'd felt hearing them talk about his new friend. I couldn't believe it. He was calling me his friend. Then his dad came over and put his hand on my shoulder. He wanted me to talk about how I was feeling. I really got tongue-tied. I'd never been asked before. I had to fight not to cry. He just waited. Finally, I told them how I felt and asked them why they bullied me so much. One guy talked about how my mom was always defending me. I said that wasn't my fault.

"We talked for a while and then one by one the guys apologized. One guy even talked about how he had felt when he was bullied. Then, we just started practice. It was finished. They didn't bully me again.

"It took me a while to learn how to joke around like the other guys and stand up for myself, but I learned. Mrs. Daniels talked to my mom a lot and they became friends. She gave my mom the name of a counselor. At one point I went into a session with her and she was able to tell me a little about her own life. She had *been abused a lot. She apologized to me for not letting me grow up and for not helping me find my own way.*

"I'm a freshman in college now and all that is behind me. I owe a lot to the Daniels family. I hope to repay my debt someday by coaching a community soccer team myself. There are a lot of kids out there that need a hand on their shoulder and a little push in the right direction."

Katherine's Story

Katherine is a woman in her seventies. She lived fifty years of her life being bullied by a husband who'd go into rages seemingly out of the blue. He would yell and scream and call her demeaning names: "stupid," "dumb," "incompetent" and worse. She had wanted to leave early in her marriage but felt that he "had the power to take everything," leaving her no way to support her children or herself.

Katherine would make comments to others about the abuse and they would reply, "He is such a 'good catch,' stay with him." She stopped sharing her problems and concerns with anyone.

Katherine became more and more depressed, anxious and angry. She started to drink. She was also prescribed numerous medications for severe health problems and became hooked on these medications. She self-medicated in order not to feel the anger, hurt, self-hate, grief and guilt. In order to survive, she learned how to numb her feelings.

Katherine admitted to her addiction at the age of seventy. She asked for help and worked with people who were willing to guide her into healing. She developed a supportive network of friends in her sobriety and began to grow spiritually and emotionally. With the support of her friends and guides, she learned that she didn't have to continue to put up with abuse and was strong enough to live on her own. She used her inner strength, courage, faith and hope to overcome her fears.

In her early sobriety, she lived through the last bullying incident with her husband. After fifty years of being emotionally, mentally, and verbally abused, she left, refusing to be a victim any longer. Today Katherine continues to receive the support of friends, family and members of her community. She continues to work on making healthy changes in her life. "I feel like I have been in prison for years, and now I'm free," she says.

The victims of bullies come from all races, family systems and financial backgrounds. Some have experienced being a bully's target once, for months or sometimes years. There are some victims, like Tina, that can never remember a time in their lives when they weren't bullied and abused. Being a victim is all they know. Parents, siblings, peers, teachers, coaches, partners, neighbors, employers, coworkers, religious leaders, and/or government agencies may have bullied victims.

Most of the people we have talked to about bullies had a story to tell. One thing they all shared in common was the pain of the experience: "I will never forget it," or "I can still remember every detail like it just happened yesterday." They remembered feeling ashamed, terrified, worthless, lonely, vulnerable, hopeless, and helpless. We were surprised at the number of people who told us that they had considered killing themselves because they knew no other way out of the pain. Yet, they told no one.

For fifty years, The National Child Development Study has followed 8,000 children in England, Scotland, and Wales. In 1958 they found that 28 percent of them had been bullied. They checked in on the participants at age twenty-three, forty-five, and fifty-five, and found that those who had been bullied showed the same long-term effects as children that were abused or had been placed in public care. Some of these effects are physical and cognitive health problems, poor social functioning, and lower levels of education. (Bowerman, 2014)

When we started this study, we were surprised by the statistics. The number of people being abused in schools, workplaces, relationships, sports, hospitals, government agencies, etc., seemed unbelievable. Now, after talking with hundreds of people and listening to their stories, we believe the numbers are actually greater than the statistics indicate.

Three of our greatest concerns are:

1. Virtually all of the bullying incidents described by victims and bullies alike were witnessed by others who did nothing. This fits with research studies with children that indicated that approximately 85 percent of bullying incidents were witnessed by others (Pepler and Craig, 1995; DeRosier et al., 1994).
2. Most victims who were courageous enough to talk to others were ignored, shut down, their pain was minimized, they were blamed for the abuse and held accountable for making it stop, and/or were told bullying was just part of life and to toughen up.
3. Bullies were esteemed, ignored, or rejected, but rarely held accountable for their behavior and offered the support necessary to make choices to change and improve the quality of their lives. All of the bullies that we interviewed for this book bullied for years before someone finally intervened.

Those who have generously shared their stories for this book, and others we have worked with through the years, continue to give us tremendous hope. They have taught us that with the support of compassionate individuals willing to intervene, healing for victims and bullies is not only possible but also probable.

From "Me" to "We"

A number of years ago while traveling across the country with my family, I was saddened by three bumper stickers proudly displayed on the fenders of cars: "I'm not on earth to live up to your expectations and you are not here to live up to mine," "Tell it to someone who cares" and "You must have confused me with someone who gives a damn."

The voices and actions of our children are evidence that far too many people in our communities are focused more on "me" than on "we." "In recent decades we have been tilting too far in the direction of letting everybody do their own thing, or pursue their own interest and concerned ourselves too little with our social responsibilities and social commitments" (Etzioni, 1993, p. 38).

The civil rights movement of the sixties paved the way for a new sense of freedom for oppressed people throughout the world. The nation finally began honoring the equality of African-Americans, Native Americans, and women. We also witnessed essential changes in children's rights and the rights of employees. An oppressive society began to be challenged.

As we moved into the nineties, however, our fixation on individual rights began to damage the fabric of our communities. Far too many have substituted increased individual rights for the development of healthy values regarding others and thereby sacrificed responsibility and accountability in the process. Perhaps we began changing things in the sixties without truly accepting that it was self-serving "me-ness" that created the problems in the first place. It is important to understand and learn from history or we are doomed to repeat our mistakes. The foundations of our country were based on "religious freedom" for the few, oppression for many and the silence of the majority. Our history offers us many lessons in bullying and victimization.

Many writers have referred to those in our society today as being "soul dead." I don't think anything is further from the truth. Instead, I think many have been sleeping. The painful actions that have been taken recently by our children are beginning to wake up the sleeping. It is important to recognize the fact that things will get worse until members of all of our communities begin to take responsibility for solving the problems that we have created.

It is more important than ever before that we turn off the television, silence the phone, and place our iPads, iPods, computers, and cell phones in the off position in their docking stations, and have dinner as a family. Our children need our connection, our attention, and our modeling. They need to see us helping others, cooperating with neighbors, and serving as role models for empathy, kindness, and compassion. They need our time.

Bullies are both temporarily empowered and injured by our helplessness, apathy, and silence. We need to create communities where aggression towards others is totally unacceptable, not because of strict laws and severe punishment, but because we care about one another.

Courage does not mean that we are without fear; it means that we don't let our fears stop us from taking action. "It is not death or pain or loss that robs us of power: it is the fear of death, the fear of pain, the fear of loss that turns the manipulated into victims and the manipulators into terrorists" (Abdullah, 1995).

When we watch injustice to others without taking action, we are frozen by the memory of a few who have been hurt by taking action, rather than the majority who have enriched the quality of their lives through empowering others. People risk their lives every day to rescue children and volunteer their time to build playgrounds and reach out to those in need.

The people who we have been waiting for to make the changes necessary to live safer and more fulfilling lives are ourselves. Having hope is not passively waiting for something to happen from outside of ourselves, but believing in the possibilities that exist around us while actively participating and fully giving of ourselves to create change. As stated so well by United States Congressman Bernie Sanders, "I hope you understand that you can only have a say in how the world works if you are participating. Life is not a spectator sport" (Middelton-Moz, 1999, p. 40).

The rules that paper the walls and are held in the hearts of students and teachers in some Cherry Creek schools need to be the norms in our workplaces and in our communities:

Zero tolerance for bullying;
Active aid, compassion and support for victims;
Accountability, concern, choice-making skills for bullies;
Inclusion, caring and support for all members of the community.

We need to rebuild communities where the voices and actions of the "caring majority" replace the apathy and fear of the "silent majority."

As Marilyn Grey said, "We know not where our dreams will take us, but we can probably see quite clearly where we'll go without them" (Audra and Carlson, p. 8).

"It is time to recognize the damaging consequences bullying brings to our world. We, as individuals, need to begin to address our aggressiveness, victimization and silence, and have the courage to take responsibility for our choices in order to make changes. We need to have a vision of a world without fear. We hope this book has helped you take steps to realize that vision.

References

BOOKS

Abdullah, Sharif M. *The Power of One: Authentic Leadership in Turbulent Times*. Philadelphia: New Society Publishers, 1995.

Adams, A. *Bullying at Work*. London: Virago, 1992.

Aftab, Parry. *The Parent's Guide to Protecting Your Children in Cyberspace*, New York: McGraw-Hill, 2000.

Bocij, Paul. *Cyberstalking: Harassment in the Internet Age and How to Protect Your Family*. Greenwood Publishing Group, 2014, p.14.

Bryce, Darrin W. *Hazing 101*. Intention Publishing, 2010.

Campbell, A. C. "Friendship as a Factor in Male and Female Delinquency." In H. C. Foot, A. J. Chapman and J. R. Smith (eds.). *Friendship and Social Relations in Children*. New Brunswick, N.J.: Transaction Publishers, 1995.

Carter, Jay. *Nasty People: How to Stop Being Hurt by Them Without Becoming One of Them*. Lincolnwood, Ill.: Contemporary Books, 1989.

Ciccheti, D., E. M. Cummings, M. Greenberg, and R. Marvin, "An Organizational Perspective on Attachment Beyond Infancy: Implications for Theory Measurement and Research." In M. Cummings (ed.). *Attachment in the Preschool Years*. Chicago: University of Chicago Press, 1990.

Conroy, Pat. *The Prince of Tides*. New York: Bantam Books, 1968.

Davenport, Noa, Ruth Distler Schwartz, and Gail Pursell Elliott. *Mobbing: Emotional Abuse in the American Workplace*. Ames, Iowa: Civil Society Publishing, 1999.

Derber, Charles. *The Wilding of America: How Greed and Violence Are Eroding Our Nation's Character*. New York: St. Martin's Press, 1996.

Dozier, John W. Jr.and Sue Scheff. *Google Bomb, the Untold Story of the $11.3M Verdict That Changed the Internet*. Deerfield Beach, Fla: Health Communications, Inc., 2010.

Etzioni, Amitai. *The Spirit of Community: Rights, Responsibilities and the Communitarian Agenda*. New York: Crown Publishers, Inc., 1993.

286

Farmer, Sam. "For Cam Cleeland, Hazing Incident Altered His NFL Career and Life, *Los Angeles Times*, November 7, 2013. http://articles.latimes.com/print/2013/nov/07/sports/la-sp-farmer

Field, Tim. *Bully in Sight: How to Predict, Resist, Challenge and Combat Workplace Bullying: Overcoming the Silence and Denial by Which Abuse Thrives.* Oxfordshire: Success Unlimited, 1996.

Fraiberg, Selma. *The Magic Years.* New York: Charles Scribner's Sons, 1959.

Frankl, Viktor E., *Man's Search For Meaning, An Introduction to Logotherapy.* New York: Simon and Schuster, 1959.

Fried, Suellen and Paula Fried. *Bullies and Victims: Helping Your Child Through the Schoolyard Battlefield.* New York: M. Evans and Company, Inc., 1996.

Garrity, C., K. Jens, W. Porter, N. Sager, and C. Short-Camilli, *Bully Proofing Your School.* Longmont, Colo.: Sopris West, 1994.

Gallagher, R.P. and W.W. Graham. *National Survey of Counseling Center Directors*, 2005. http://iacsine.org/2005%20National%20Survey.pdf

Gilligan, James. *Violence: Reflections on a National Epidemic.* New York: Vintage Books, 1997.

Grossman, Dave. *On Killing: The Psychological Cost of Learning to Kill in War and Society.* Boston: Little, Brown and Company, 1995.

Hillebrand, Friedhelm, ed., *The Creation of Global Mobile Communications,* GSM&UMTS. John Wiley and Sons, 2002.

Holmes, Ronald W., Ph.D. *How to Eradicate Hazing, The Holmes Education Post. LLC, 2010.*

Hornstein, Harvey A. *Brutal Bosses and Their Prey: How to Identify and Overcome Abuse in the Workplace.* New York: Riverhead Books, 1996.

Hoover, Nadine, Ph.D. and Normand J. Pollard, Ed.D., Principal Investigators, *Initiation Rites in American High Schools: A National Survey,* Alfred University, 2000. *www.alfred.edu/news/html/hazing.study.html*

Hoover, Nadine, Ph.D., Principal Investigator, *National Survey: Initiation Rites and Athletics for NCAA Sports Teams,* Alfred University, 1999. *www.alfred.edu/news/html/initiationrite-sandathletics/study.html*

Jaffe, P. G., D. A. Wolf, and S. K. Wilson, *Children of Battered Women.* Newbury Park, Calif.: Sage Publications, 1990.

Karr-Morse, Robin and Meredith S. Wiley *Ghosts from the Nursery: Tracing the Roots of Violence.* New York: The Atlantic Monthly Press, 1997.

Kaufmann, H. *Aggression and Altruism.* New York: Holt, 1970.

Kolker, Robert. "OutofBounds," *NewYorkMagazine,* 2010. http://nymag.com/nymetro/news/features/n_9391/

L'Bate, Luciano. *Family Psychopathology: The Relational Roots of Dysfunctional Behavior.* New York: The Guilford Press, 1998.

Lefkowitz, Bernard. *Our Guys.* New York: Random House, 1997.

Loffreda, Beth. *Losing Matt Shepard: Life and Politics in the Aftermath of Anti-Gay Murder.* New York: Columbia University Press, 2000.

Lorenz, Konrad, Das Sogennante Boese. Wein: Dr. G. Borotha-Schoeler Verlag, 1963.

Lorenz, Konrad. *Here Am I—Where Are You? The Behavior of the Greylag Goose.* New York: Harcourt Brace Jovanovich, 1991.

Lundeen, Richard. *Hazing, Rituals of Bondage.* Charleston, South Carolina, Create Space. Revised and updated 2013.

Mate, Gabor, M.D. *In the Realm of Hungry Ghosts; Close Encounters with Addictions.* North Atlantic Books, Berkley, California, 2008.

Middelton-Moz, Jane. *Children of Trauma: Rediscovering Your Discarded Self.* Deerfield Beach, Fla.: Health Communications, Inc., 1989.

———. *Shame and Guilt: Masters of Disguise.* Deerfield Beach, Fla.: Health Communications, Inc., 1990.

———. *Boiling Point: The High Cost of Unhealthy Anger to Individuals and Society.* Deerfield Beach, Fla.: Health Communications, Inc., 1999.

———. *Welcoming Our Children to a New Millennium.* Deerfield Beach, Fla.: Health Communications, Inc., 1999.

———. *Values from the Front Porch, Remembering the Wisdom of Our Grandmothers.* Health Communications, Inc., Deerfield Beach, Florida, 2005.

Miller, Alice. *The Drama of the Gifted Child.* New York: Basic Books, 1981.

McClure, Vimala, *Infant Massage; A Handbook for Loving Parents, 3rd Edition.* Bantam Books, New York, 2000.

Namie, Gary and Ruth Namie. *The Bully at Work: What You Can Do to Stop the Hurt and Reclaim Your Dignity on the Job.* Naperville, Ill.: Sourcebooks, Inc., 2000.

Newer, H. *Broken Pledges.* Marietta, Georgia, Longstreet Press, Inc. 1990.

Newer, H. *Wrongs of Passages: Fraternities, Sororities, Hazing and Binge Drinking.* Bloomingdale, Indiana, University Press, 1999.

Olweus, D. *Aggression in the Schools: Bullies and Whipping Boys.* Washington, D.C.: Hemisphere Publishing, 1978.

———. *Bullying at School: What We Know and What We Can Do.* Oxford: Blackwell, 1993.

Parke, R. D. and R. G. Slaby. "The Development of Aggression." In P. H. Maissen (ed.). *Handbook of Child Psychology,* 4th ed., vol. 4. New York: Wiley, 1983.

Patterson, G. R. "Maternal Rejection: Determinant or Product of Deviant Clutch Behavior." In W. Hartup and Z. Rubin (eds.). *Relationships and Development.* Hithdale, N.Y.: McGruner Hill, 1986.

Pearl, P., L. Bouthilet and J. Lazar (eds.). *Television and Behavior, Vol. 2: Technical Reviews.* Washington, D.C.: U.S. Government Printing Office, 1982.

Perry, Bruce D., M.D. and Maia Szalavitz. *The Boy Who Was Raised As A Dog, And Other Stories From a Child Psychiatrist's Notebook.* New York: Basis Books, 2006.

Peurifoy, Reneauz Z. *Anger: Taming the Beast.* New York: Kodansha America, Inc., 1999.

Pollack, William S. with Todd Shuster. *Real Boys' Voices.* New York: Penguin Books, 2000.

Randall, P. E. *A Community Approach to Bullying.* Stoke-on-Trent: Trentham Books, 1996.

Randall, Peter. *Adult Bullying: Perpetrators and Victims.* London: Routledge, 1997.

Rigby K. and P. Slee. *Manual for the Peer Relations Questionnaire* (PARG). Adelaide: University of Southern Australia, 1995.

Rigby, K. *Bullying in Schools and What to Do About It.* Melbourne: Acer, 1996.

Scalavitz, Maia and Bruce D. Perry, M.D., Ph.D. *Born for Love; Why Empathy is Essential and Endangered.* William Morrow/Harper, New York, 2010.

Siegal, Daniel J. M.D. *Brainstorm: The Power and Purpose of the Teenage Brain,* New York: Jeremy P. Tarcher/Penguin, 2013.

———. *Parenting From the Inside Out; How a Deeper Understanding Can Help You Raise Children that Thrieve.* New York: Jeremy P. Tarcher/Penguin, 2003.

Sullivan, Keith. *The Anti-Bullying Handbook.* Oxford: Oxford University Press, 2000, pp.21–22.

Tattum, D. P. and D. A. Lane (eds). *Bullying in Schools.* Stoke-on-Trent: Trentham, 1989.

Walker, Scott. *The Graywolf Annual Ten: Changing Communities.* St. Paul, Minn.: Graywolf Press, 1993.

Wilson, K. J. *When Violence Begins at Home: A Comprehensive Guide to Understanding and Ending Domestic Abuse.* Alameda, Calif.: Hunter House Inc., 1997.

Zadra, Dan. *Together We Can: Celebrating the Power of a Team and a Dream.* Lynnwood, Wash.: Compendium Inc., 2001.

Zadra, Dan and Susan Carlson. *Brilliance: Uncommon Voices from Uncommon Women.* Edmonds, Wash.: Compendium, Inc., 2001.

Periodicals/Articles

Adams, A. "Bullying at Work." *Journal of Community and Applied Social Psychology,* 7 (3): 177–180, 1997.

Advertisement in the *New York Times* for *Newsweek,* special edition on Birth to Age Three, April 22, 1997.

Aftab, Perry. "The Federal Stalking Law." *http://www.aftab.com*

Aftab, Perry. "Cyberbullying…Wired Safety, Cyberbullying/Stalking and Harassment" *http://www.aftab.com*

"Life Sentence in Belluardo Case." *Atlanta News,* Sept. 5, 1999, p. 89.

Baldry, Anna C. and Farrington, David P. "Parenting Influence on Bullying and Victimization." *Legal and Criminological Psychology,* 3(2): 237–254, 1998.

Block, J. H., J. Block and A. Morrison. "Parental Agreement-Disagreement on Child-Personality Correlates in Children." *Child Development,* 52: 965–974, 1981.

Bowers, L., P. K. Smith and V. Binney. "Perceived Family Relationships of Bullies, Victims and Bully/Victims in Middle Childhood." *Journal of Social and Personal Relationships,* 11: 215–232, 1994.

Bowerman, Mary. "Childhood Bullying Can Cause Problems Decades Later," *USA Today,* April 17, 2014. http://usatoday.com

"The Brief History of Social Media." University of North Carolina at Penbrook. Sources, W3C, CERN, NCSA, DAR PA, *New Media Today, Time Magazine, Newsweek Magazine*, 1-3.

Brown, Robbie. "Criminal Charges for 13 in Florida A&M Hazing Death." *New York Times*, May 2, 2012. http://nytimes.com/2012/05/03/us/13-charged-in-hazing-d…

Carlson, V., D. Cicchetti, D. Barnett and K. Braunwald, "Disorganized/Disoriented Attachment Relationships in Maltreated Infants." *Developmental Psychology*, 25 (4): 525–531, 1989.

Chaudhuri, A. "Deadlier than the Male." *Guardian*, October 1994, 6.

Chu, Judy, "Military Hazing Has Got to Stop," *New York Times*, August 3, 2012. *http://www. nytimes.com/2012/08/04/opinion/military-hazing-ha*

Cooke, Harriet, December 2012. *www.dailymail.co.uk/news/article-221743/text-messages-mark-20-year-anniversary*

Curtis, Anthony, 2013. The Brief History of Social Media. http://www2.uncp.edu/home/acurtis/ NewMedia/SocialMedia/SocialMediaHistory.html

Dawson, G., D. Hessel and K. Frey. "Social Influences on Early Developing Biological and Behavioral Systems Related to Risk for Affective Disorder." *Development and Psychopathology*, 6: 759–799, 1994.

Day, N. and G. Richardson. "Comparative Teratogenicity of Alcohol and Other Drugs." *Alcohol Health and Research World*, National Institute of Alcohol Abuse and Alcoholism, 18 (1): 42–48, 1994.

DeKok, David, "Father Blames Son's Suicide on Fraternity Hazing at Penn State," Reuters.com March 20,2014. *http://www.reuters.com/assets/print?aid=USBREA2J28520140320*

DeRosier, M. E., A. H. N. Gillessen, J. Coie and K. A. Dodge, "Group Social Content and Children's Aggressive Behaviors." *Child Development*, 65: 1068–1079, 1994.

Dodge, K. A. and N. R. Crick. "Social Information-Processing Bases of Aggressive Behavior in Children." Special issue: Illustrating the Value of Basic Research, *Personality and Social Psychology Bulletin*, 16: 8–22, 1990.

Faydee Lyrics. "Unbreakable", http://azlyrics.com/lyrics/faydee/unbreakable.html

Field, T. "Infants of Depressed Mothers." *Infant Behavior and Development*, 18: 1–13, 1995.

Field, Tim. "Abuse," Those Who Can Do—Those Who Can't Bully, Web site: Bully On Line, 1–8, Oct. 19, 2000. *www.successunlimited.co.uk*

Fishel, Anne, Ph.D., *The Family Dinner Project; The Importance of Eating Together*, http://the familydinnerproject.org/resources/faq/ retrieved March 14, 2014.

Gilbert, Susan. "Bully or Victim? Studies Show They're Much Alike." *New York Times* archives on the Web, Aug. 10, 1999.

Greenberger, Scott S. "State Issues $1M in Grants to Help Schools Battle Bullies." *Boston Globe*, June 24, 2000, pp. B1–B4.

Harp, Justin. "Patricia Arquette quits Facebook After Alledged "Cyberstalking, "*Digital Spy.* 10/11.

Hart, C. H., G. W. Ladd and B. R. Burleson. "Children's Expectations of the Outcomes of Social Strategies: Relations with Sociometric Status and Maternal Disciplinary Styles." *Child Development*, 61: 127–137, 1990.

Hughes, Jean O'Gorman and Bernie R. Sandler. Project on the Status of Women, Association of American Colleges. "Friends Raping Friends—Could It Happen to You?" April 1987. *www. cs.utk.edu/~bartley/acquaintrape.html.*

Jacobson, N. S. "Behavioral Couple Therapy: A New Beginning." *Behavior Therapy,* 23: 493–506, 1992.

Keltner, Dacher. "The Compassionate Instinct: Think Human's are Born Selfish? Think Again." *Greater Good*(April, 2004) 6-9.

Kleinrock Ph.D., Leonard. "History of the Internet. UCLA, 1.

LaBier Ph.D., Douglas. "Are You Suffering from Empathy Deficit Disorder?" *Psychology Today.*

Ladd, G. W. "Having Friends, Keeping Friends, Making Friends, and Being Liked by Peers in the Classroom: Predictions of Children's Early School Adjustment." *Child Development,* 61: 1081–1100, 1990.

Lamborn, D. D., M. S. Mounts, L. Steinberg and S. M. Dornbusch. "Patterns of Competence and Adjustment among Adolescents from Authoritative Authoritarian, Indulgent and Neglectful Families." *Child Development,* 62: 1049–1065, 1991.

Lampert, Joan Buttrick. "Voices and Visions: Adolescent Girls' Experiences as Bullies, Targets and Bystanders." *Disser Abstracts International,* Section A: Humanities and Social Sciences, 58 (8–A): 2986, Feb. 1998.

Leo, John. "Community and Personal Duty." *The Graywolf Annual: Ten Changing Communities,* Scott Walker (ed.), 29–32, 1993.

Lewin, Tamar, "If Your Kids are Awake, They're Probably Online," *New York Times, www. nytimescom/2010/01/20/education/20wired.html?_r=0*

Leymann, Heinz. *The Mobbing Encyclopedia.* Internet Resource *www.leymann.se/.*

Leymann, Heinz and Annelie Gustafsson. "Suicides Due to Mobbing/Bullying—About Nurses' High Risks in the Labour Market." Geneva: WHO (World Health Organization) Internal Report, 1998.

Lovett, Ian. "After Students' Hazing-Related Deaths, Fraternity Eliminates Tradition of Pledging," *New York Times,* March 10, 2014. *http://www.nytimes.com/2014/03/11/education/after-learners-h...*

Newport, Frank. "U.S.Young Adults Admit Too Much Time on Cell Phones, Web." *www.gallup. com/poll/153863/young-adults-time-cell-phones-web.aspx*

Martin, Roland. "Only Students Can Truly End Hazing" *CNN Opinion,* December 20, 2011. *http:///www.cnn.com/2011/12/16/opinion/roland-martin-hazing/...*

Medina,AntonioChacon,2003. http://www.acosomoral.org/pdf/Art_NUEVA_CARA_INTERNET_ACOSO_ETIC@NET_2003.pdf

McClure, Vimala, *Tues Tip: Show a Little Respect to Babies Communicative Cries,* November 13, 2012, blogging4baby.wordpress.com/tag/vimala-mclure/ retrieved March 1, 2014.

McCutcheon, L.E., Lange, R. and Houran, J. "Conceptualization and Measurement of Celebrity Worship," *British Journal of Psychiatry,* 2002 pg. 67, 87, 93.

Moharib, Nadia. "Bullied to Death/Harassed B.C. Teen Wanted Lessons Learned from His Suicide." *The Calgary Sun,* April 16, 2000, 10.

Muller, Judy. "Next Wave of Discrimination." *www.NPR.org/news/specials/americatransformed.* 2001.

Mulrine, Anna. "Once Bullied, Now Bullies with Guns." *U.S. News and World Report,* May 3, 1999 p. 24.

Natterson-Horowitz, M.D and Bowers, Kathryn. *Zoobiquity; The Astonishing Connection Between Human and Animal Health,* Vintage Books, New York, 2013.

Nelson, Richard E, Ph.D. and Judith C. Galas. *The Power to Prevent Suicde; A Guide for Teens Helping Teens.* Free Spirit Publishing, Minneapolis, Minnisota, 2006.

Nissen, Beth, Ann Pleshette Murphy, Diane Sawyer and Charles Gibson. "American Family." *ABC Good Morning America,* Jan. 19, 1999.

Olweus, D. "Familial and Temperamental Determinants of Aggressive Behavior in Adolescent Boys: A Causal Analysis." *Developmental Psychology* 16: 644–660, 1980.

Olsen,Ted."Youth in a Haze,"*ChristianityToday,*July1,2003. *http://www.christianitytoday.com/ct/2003/july/25.13.html*

Patchin, Justin W, Ph.D. "Advice for Adult Victims of Cyberbullying" Posted blog. Co-Director of the Cyberbullying Research Center.

Peoples Law Guide, "Hazing Within the Workplace," *Broward Bar.* May 26, 2013. *http://www.browardbar.org/articles/florida-employee-hazing.html*

Pepler, D. J. and W. M. Craig. "A Peek Behind the Fence: Naturalistic Observations of Aggressive Children." *Developmental Psychology,* 31: 548–553, 1995.

Peterson, Karen S. "Bullies, Victims Grow into Roles That Can Last a Lifetime." *USA Today,* Sept. 8, 1999, p O7D.

———. "When School Hurts: Continued Violence Has Schools, States Taking a Hard Look at Bullying." *USA Today,* April 10, 2001, p O6D.

Purcell, B.A., M. Psych., Michelle Pathe M.B.B.S., F.R.A.N.Z.C.P. and Paul E. Mullen, M.B.B.S., D.Sc., F.R.C.Psych, "A Study of Women Who Stalk," *American Journal of Psychiatry,* Vol. 158. No.12 12/01.

Quine, Lyn. "Workplace Bullying in Nurses." *Journal of Health Psychology,* 6 (1): 73–84, 2001.

Reese, Mark. "Pee Wee's Legacy." *www.NPR.webmaster@npr.org.* 2001.

Rican, Pavet. "Family Values May Be Responsible for Bullying." *Studia Psychologica,* 37 (1): 31–36, 1995.

Rideout, Victoria J., MA, Vila G. Foehr, Ph.D. and Donald Roberts, Ph.D. "Generation M2: Media in the Lives of 8-18 year-olds," *Kaiser Family Foundation Study,* January 2010. Kaiserfamilyfoundation.files.wordpress.com/2013/04/8010.pdf

Salmivalli, Christina, Kirsh Lagerspetz, K. Bjoerkquist, and Karin Oesterman, et al. "Bullying as a Group Process." *Aggressive Behavior,* 22 (1): 1–15, 1996.

Schultz, Vicki. "Sex Is the Least of It: Let's Focus Harassment Law on Work, Not Sex." *The Nation,* May 25, 1998, 11–15.

Shakur, Sanyika. "Can't Stop, Won't Stop." *The Graywolf Annual: Ten Changing Communities,* Scott Walker (ed.), 239–260, 1993.

Sherer, Jill L. "Sexually Harassed Health Care Industry." *Hospitals and Health Networks,* 69: 54.

Shpiegel, Ben. "A Classic Case of Bullying, Miami Dolphins," *New York Times,* February 2014.

Shore, Eliezer. "The Soul of the Community." *The Graywolf Annual: Ten Changing Communities,* Scott Walker (ed.), 3–7, 1993.

Siris, Elizabeth. "The Bully Battle: Are Nasty, Mean Kids Making Your Life Miserable? Take Action!" *Time for Kids,* Oct. 27, 2000.

Smith, Bryan. "Trial Jury Does Rich Doc $1 Million." *The Oregonian,* March 12, 1997, pg A1 and A14.

Smith, Peter K. and Rowan Myron-Wilson. "Parenting and School Bullying." *Clinical and Child Psychology and Psychiatry,* 3 (3): 405–417, 1998.

Suckling, Lee. "Here Be the Trolls: Hunting Down On-Line Haters." Fairfax NZ News, 2013, 1.

Walker, K. B. and D. D. Morley. "Attitudes and Parental Factors as Intervening Variables in the Television Violence-Aggression Relation." *Communication Research Reports,* 8: 41–47, 1991.

Wilson, Brady, C. "U.S. Businesses Suffer from Workplace Trauma," *Personnel Journal,* July, p. 47-50, 1991.

Wilson, Simone. "LaPuente High Horrors: Soccer Players Claim to Have Been Hazed, Sodomized with Poles, *LA Weekly,* Sports, September 24, 2014.

Winton, Richard. "Three Teens Charged With Sexually Hazing Soccer Players," *Los Angeles Times,* November 6, 2012. http://articles.latimes.com/print/2012/nov/06/local/la-me-hazing

Wright, Brad. Producer Contributor. "Hazing Is Pervasive in High School Sports, Study Finds. *CNNfyi.com.* September 21, 2000. edition.cnn.com/2000/fyiteachers.ednews/09/20/school.h

Yeates, Nigel. "Bullying in the Workplace: A Study of Victimization," *www.sufpolfed.co.uk/articles/bullyingarticle.htm.* 2001.

About the Authors

Jane Middelton-Moz is the director of The Middelton-Moz Institute for Consultation, Intervention, and Training in Montpelier, Vermont, and Liberty Lake, Washington. She speaks internationally on the issues of multigenerational trauma, delayed grief, and the importance of safe and trauma-informed schools. Middelton-Moz has appeared on national radio and television including *Oprah, Montel Williams* and *Maury Povich*. She is the author of ten books including *Shame and Guilt, Children of Trauma, Boiling Point, Welcoming Our Children to a New Millennium, Values from the Front Porch: Remembering the Wisdom of Our Grandmothers.* She is the co-author of *After the Tears; Helping Adult Children of Alcoholics Heal Their Childhood Trauma,* and *The Ultimate Guide to Transforming Anger.*

Mary Lee Zawadski has worked in the field of addiction and dependency since 1976. She is an international lecturer and consultant who teaches at colleges and universities, treatment centers, and other public and private facilities. She authored *The Magic Within* and has been seen on local and national television including *Good Morning America*.